PRAISE FOR
AMBER K & AZRAEL ARYNN K

Candlemas

"An excellent read, fun and informative. It is a pleasure to add this book to my collection."—*PanGaia*

"An excellent resource to help deepen your Imbolc celebrations."—*Circle Magazine*

True Magick

"This well-crafted book is invaluable and insightful reading."—*Ghostvillage.com*

RitualCraft

* *Winner of the COVR Awards for Book of the Year and Best Wiccan/Pagan Book*

"This is a wonderful book, and highly recommended for anyone doing ritual."—*Lisa McSherry, FacingNorth.com*

CovenCraft

"An essential part of any coven library. Most highly recommended."—*Elizabeth Barrette*

"All the information a coven member could ask for is here…."—*NAPRA Review*

How To Become A
WITCH

About the Authors

Amber K was born just outside New York City. She was not trained in the Craft at her grandmother's knee and does not come from a long line of hereditary Witches.

In 1978, she joined the Temple of the Pagan Way in Chicago, and received her initiation and ordination there. She has worked with Circle, New Earth Circle, the Pool of Bast, and the Coven of Our Lady of the Woods, and she was a co-founder of the Ladywood Tradition of Wicca. She has served three terms as National First Officer of the Covenant of the Goddess, the world's largest network of Witches. She taught in the Cella (priestess) training program of Re-formed Congregation of the Goddess, a national Dianic network. She has a son, Starfire, who resides in New Mexico and is part of the Pagan Spirit Gathering.

Azrael Arynn K was born in New Mexico. She brings to the Craft her experience as a police officer, race car driver, stockbroker, and architectural designer, as well as a degree in law. She is a talented costume designer and ritualist, and she is also a certified NLP practitioner.

Both Amber and Azrael are third-degree priestesses in the Ladywood Tradition of Wicca. They met in 1991 at a Wicca 101 class sponsored by Our Lady of the Woods and were handfasted in 1994. They have taught many workshops at Pagan festivals and conferences, including PantheaCon, Heartland, United Earth Assembly, Dragonfest, Florida Samhain Pagan Gathering, Starwood, and others.

Amber and Azrael are part of Ardantane Pagan Learning Center in northern New Mexico, an hour northwest of Albuquerque in the Red Rocks area of the Jemez Mountains. Amber serves as executive director, Azrael is dean of the School of Sacred Living, and they both reside at the growing Ardantane campus. (For information, see the website at ardantane.org or write to Ardantane, P.O. Box 307, Jemez Springs, NM 87025.)

Azrael likes to read mysteries, shop for antiques, drive good cars, and study nutrition and healing. Amber enjoys hiking, photography, the Native American flute, science fiction, collecting ancient keys, and the Peanuts gang, especially Snoopy. They share interests in travel, pink transferware china, Chinese checkers, art, and all things magickal, including their lovely hybrid dog, Kyoshi.

How To Become A
WITCH

The Path of
Nature, Spirit & Magick

AMBER K &
AZRAEL ARYNN K

Llewellyn Publications
WOODBURY, MINNESOTA

FIRST EDITION
First Printing, 2010

Book design by Rebecca Zins

Cover design by Lisa Novak

Cover illustration by Melissa Findley

Interior illustrations by Wen Hsu

Leaf image from *Ready-to-Use Old-Fashioned Floral Illustrations* (Dover Publications, Inc., 1990)

Llewellyn is a registered trademark of Llewellyn Worldwide Ltd.

Library of Congress Cataloging-in-Publication Data
K, Amber, 1947–
 How to become a witch : the path of nature, spirit & magick / Amber K
& Azrael Arynn K.—1st ed.
  p. cm.
 Includes bibliographical references (p.   ) and index.
 ISBN 978-0-7387-1965-8
 1. Wicca. 2. Witchcraft. I. K, Azrael Arynn, 1955– II. Title.
 BP605.W53K3 2010
 299'.94—dc22

2010033539

Llewellyn Worldwide Ltd. does not participate in, endorse, or have any authority or responsibility concerning private business transactions between our authors and the public.
 All mail addressed to the author is forwarded, but the publisher cannot, unless specifically instructed by the author, give out an address or phone number.
 Any Internet references contained in this work are current at publication time, but the publisher cannot guarantee that a specific location will continue to be maintained. Please refer to the publisher's website for links to authors' websites and other sources.

Llewellyn Publications
A Division of Llewellyn Worldwide Ltd.
2143 Wooddale Drive
Woodbury, MN 55125-2989
www.llewellyn.com

Printed in the United States of America

More Books by Amber K

Moonrise: Welcome to Dianic Wicca
   (Re-formed Congregation of the Goddess, 1992)

The Pagan Kids' Activity Book
   (Horned Owl Publishing, 1992; out of print
   but will return in 2010 from Amber K)

True Magick: A Beginner's Guide
   (fifteenth anniversary edition, revised and expanded, Llewellyn, 2005;
   also available in Spanish, Portuguese, Hebrew, and Russian)

CovenCraft: Witchcraft for Three or More
   (Llewellyn, 1998)

More Books by Amber K and Azrael Arynn K

Heart of Tarot: An Intuitive Approach
   (Llewellyn, 2003)

Candlemas: Feast of Flames
   (Llewellyn, 2003)

RitualCraft: Creating Rites for Transformation and Celebration
   (Llewellyn, 2006: winner of the COVR award for
   Best Wiccan/Pagan Book of 2006 and Book of the Year 2006)

Amber and Azrael also contributed chapters to *Exploring the Pagan Path:
   Wisdom from the Elders* (New Page Books, 2005)

*We dedicate this book to all those ancestors
and teachers, both those known to us and those
whose names and stories are lost, who passed
down to us the traditions and their wisdom,
the love of the Goddess and the Old Gods, the
ways of magick, and the understanding that
the earth and all of nature are sacred.*

Contents

I AM A WITCH[1]

Some find their home in the Witches' Craft,
Touching magick, wielding power,
But each must seek and find their path,
Is this your way, is this your hour?

Sing to Goddess, moon times three,
Touching magick, wielding power,
Drink to God, stag-hornéd he,
I am a Witch at every hour.

Celebrate as the Wheel turns,
Touching magick, wielding power,
Dance and leap as the balefire burns,
I am a Witch at every hour.

Water, fire, earth, and air,
Touching magick, wielding power,
Ruled by spirit, all is there,
I am a Witch at every hour.

---

1 "I Am a Witch" by Amber K, 1998; revised and expanded by Amber K and Azrael Arynn K, 2009.

Based on knowledge, filled with love,
Touching magick, wielding power,
As below, so above,
I am a Witch at every hour.

In darkest night, in forest deep,
Touching magick, wielding power,
In broad daylight, awake, asleep,
I am a Witch at every hour.

At your altar, seek the way,
Touching magick, wielding power,
With Spirit start and end each day,
I am a Witch at every hour.

An ye harm none, do as ye will,
Touching magick, wielding power,
Heal always, never kill,
I am a Witch at every hour.

I cast the circle, raise the cone,
Touching magick, wielding power,
And pour the wine when magick's flown,
I am a Witch at every hour.

Work your will, but earth revere,
Touching magick, wielding power,
And every creature living here,
I am a Witch at every hour.

Soar upon the astral planes,
Touching magick, wielding power,
Visit woodland faery fanes,
I am a Witch at every hour.

Dance the round with Pagan folk,
Touching magick, wielding power,
'Neath the stars, beside the oak,
I am a Witch at every hour.

I am Goddess, neverborn,
Touching magick, wielding power,
I wear the crescent, wear the horn,
I am a Witch at every hour.

We may forgive, but we can't forget,
Touching magick, wielding power,
We'll claim our place in sunlight yet,
I am a Witch at every hour.

Many seek, a few may find,
Touching magick, wielding power,
That Witchcraft feeds the heart and mind,
I am a Witch at every hour.

Why Do You Want to Become a Witch?

Some find their home in the Witches' Craft,
Touching magick, wielding power,
But each must seek and find their path,
Is this your way, is this your hour?

Merry meet! That's a traditional greeting among Witches. We're glad you decided to look at this book, and we will be even happier if it helps you begin your journey into the world of Witchcraft and Wicca.

Perhaps you heard about the Craft, became interested, and are exploring it alone. This book is a good introduction. Or perhaps you've found a coven, and they have recommended this book (or handed it to you and said, "Read it!"). Most exercises/activities are designed for someone working alone, but they can easily be adapted for anyone working in a coven.

Almost everything you have seen and heard about Witches in popular comics, cartoons, role-playing games, songs, books, television shows, and movies is wrong. Those are fairy tales—fantasies—entertainment.

There are real Witches, and we are two of them. Amber has been an initiated priestess for over thirty years, and Azrael entered the Craft about twenty years ago. Both of us have traveled and taught the Craft throughout the United States; Amber has served as first officer of the largest Witch network in existence, and we both help run an institution of higher learning for Witches and other Pagans—Ardantane Pagan Learning Center. We know something about the modern Craft.

But Witchcraft is incredibly diverse from place to place, coven to coven, individual to individual. There is no One True Way to be a Witch—and that is one of the glories of the Craft. There is room for individuality and freedom and different points of view, which are the bedrocks of Witchcraft. It is no place for dogmatics, followers, or sheep. If you want to be told what to believe and how your spiritual life should be, look elsewhere.

Start with this fact: Witchcraft is partly craft (the arts and skills of magick) and partly spiritual path. Some Witches focus on the first part, some on the second. Many of the spiritually oriented people, including us, call ourselves Wiccan Witches, or priestesses (or priests) of Wicca.

Our heritage as Witches is in the ancient, nature-loving religions and folkways of Europe. Our formal spiritual path, Wicca, as a modern Neopagan religion, got its start in the 1950s in England. Our future is unlimited.

Witches abhor dogma, creeds, ironclad rules, authority, and anything that stifles the human spirit or treats people as subjects, market segments, or mere consumers. Witches prize individuality, spontaneity, creativity, and freedom. We seek wisdom, love, and power to be used for individual freedom and the common good.

Witches are explorers. We believe in the value of science and technology when carefully and ethically used. But we know that science has barely touched the mysteries of life and death, and so we are also mystics and adventurers in the realms of mythology, magick, meaning, and the realms of Spirit. We know that there are realities beyond the material world and consensus reality, and we intend to explore them. We move among goddesses and gods, animal allies and plant devas, faeries and legends, sylphs and salamanders, speaking stones and talking trees, and our world is deeper and richer, more colorful and harmonious, than most people will ever know.

You will need courage to follow this path. Dwellers in the ordinary world will call you crazy, or foolish, or possibly evil. Yet there is something harder than facing their condescension or ignorance: facing the changes that will happen within you. Of the Goddess, we say, "Everything she touches changes," and if you wholeheartedly enter our world, you will be changed forever. Some of the changes will be exhilarating and wonderful, empowering and intellectually expanding. Others will make it harder for you to relate to the "muggle world"—less content with convention and habit and mindless labor. Your spirit will be Goddess-touched, and you may become a little wild, a little fey, and a little weird. Accept that or seek another path.

This world is not for everyone. Most people would do better to choose a different spiritual path with more rules and guidance and fewer challenges. But if you are heart-drawn to the Craft, then you are welcome—whether you are female or male; white, black, brown, yellow, or red; straight, gay, bisexual, or transgender. Most Witches know that the outer package matters very little; what matters is your courageous heart, your open mind, and your questing spirit.

TO BE OR NOT TO BE

If you stop and think about it, it's pretty strange that anyone would want to be a Witch. After all, most of us have been raised to think "Witch: green skin, pointy nose, warts, scraggly hair, nasty, old, with a shrill cackle…." Of course you know better, but that image is still there under the surface. What could possibly be attractive about that?

Let's look at some of the reasons, good and bad, that you might be reading this book.

Some Really Good Reasons for Choosing Witchcraft

There are several very solid reasons for becoming a Witch, and yes, one of them is a desire to affirm your worth. Becoming a Witch doesn't make you better than other people…but it may help you understand that all people, including you, are part of the divine energy that creates and sustains the universe. Thou art Goddess. Thou art God. You are not the Creator, but you are part of the Creator's essence. Knowing that places a great responsibility on you to act wisely, lovingly, and thoughtfully; Witchcraft can train you to handle that responsibility with grace and honor.

You may feel a deep need to connect with your heritage: with the people of field and forest, the healers, farmers, hunters, warriors, and explorers of the past. If you have been a Witch in past incarnations, or simply a proud Pagan, the old ways may call to you. If the modern world and mainstream faiths seem alien to you, maybe exploring a faith rooted in nature will feel like coming home.

If you are female and have grown up in a culture that still belittles you, then you might need to affirm the power and beauty of being a woman. As a Witch and priestess in service to the Goddess, there will be honor and strength and self-acceptance in a way you have never experienced before. Wiccan women have the whole range of goddesses to inspire us—not only pretty and gentle ones but warriors, scholars, leaders, and wild ones.

If you are male but feel disgusted at the macho posturing and power games that society expects of you, and if you are looking for other models for being a man, Wicca might be the spiritual home for you. As a male Witch, you can be courageous and strong without being a tyrant; gentle and loving without being effeminate; and sexual and lusty without being an exploiter or game player. (In fact, the strong women of Wicca won't stand for games, and it takes a strong man to enjoy the company of powerful women.)

You may be called to Wicca or the other Pagan paths because you love nature far more than you could ever love a "holy book" or the inside of a church. For you, perhaps, the wind flowing through tall pines is sacred; a stone warming in the sunlight is sacred; wolves and hawks and silvery fish are sacred. If you are inspired and empowered and healed and free when you are in the wilderness, Witchcraft is one path that is a natural fit.

Or you may have an abiding curiosity about the deep energies and mysteries of the universe. You may or may not be drawn to science as a career, but you know in your heart that there is more to the cosmos than science has yet discovered. You are called to be a magician, a mystic, or perhaps an artist or poet. Through inner journeys, using the very personal and subjective tools of mind and spirit, you want to explore the metaphysical heart of reality.

You may have come to the Craft with a powerful need to explore the shadow side of reality. By this, we do not mean that you want to steep yourself in evil. But you do understand how a worldview that is all rainbows and sunshine cannot equip us to handle the darker side of life. There is pain and anger and fear in the world and in ourselves, and if we do not face these powers and come to terms with them, they will control us. Some religions conveniently divide the whole world into good and evil, and simply tell their followers to embrace what they define as "good" and reject what they have labeled "evil." If only it were that simple! Wiser heads know that we must face and understand and heal what is hurting and hurtful inside us before we can face evil out in the world. Wicca has the tools and the will to encourage this inner journey.

Another reason for the appeal of Wicca is that we understand and accept the inner child, or younger self, within each person. We may be adults on the outside, but that childlike, playful, curious, and adventurous part never really goes away, although many people try to squash it into submission or at least hide it. Witches don't. That inner child is what keeps our minds and hearts youthful. Its laughter heals us, its delight gives us joy, its curiosity makes us creative. So Witches dance and sing, light bonfires and make love, play music and put on costumes, feast and drink mead. When no one is harmed, why not?

Pause now, and think. Which of these aspects of the Craft, if any, call to you? Which ones feel like a cool drink to one who has wandered too long in the desert?

Some Really Lame Reasons for Choosing Witchcraft

If this path calls to you, you must weed out any motivations that are shallow, ignorant, or fleeting.

Being a Witch can be a great way to get attention; often the wrong kind, but some people crave attention so badly that they'll do anything to get it. Being honest with yourself, is that what you want? People staring at you, whispering comments, gossiping about you?

One might become a Witch because of low self-esteem. "I'm a bad person. Everyone must know I'm bad. Okay, then; I'll show them how bad I can be. I'll be the worst thing they can imagine—a Witch!" Then, when "they" scold you or avoid you, it's a self-fulfilling prophecy.

Some young people choose things, including a religion, to show that they are more liberated and adventurous than their boring old families. They may even want to deliberately shock their parents. Of course, whether you copy your parents' lifestyle or choose one that's the exact opposite, it's still letting them control who you are. It's still all about them, not you. It's far more empowering to choose your religion according to what is exactly right for you, regardless of how it compares to your family.

Some are drawn to the Craft just because they want to be interesting, special, and unique. Well, you are that already! It might be hidden from others or even yourself;

it may be that you've never expressed the authentic person you are. But there is absolutely someone unique and fascinating in there. Don't cover it up with Witch trappings unless **THAT** is exactly who you are.

Some people come to the Craft because, frankly, they're lazy. They assume that they can have whatever they want with the flick of a wand or a muttered spell. They've been reading and taking Harry Potter too seriously, or they've seen too many fantasy movies. They don't realize that magick is work, sometimes more work than getting stuff the old-fashioned way.

Another uglier reason that some are attracted to the Craft is that they want power. Not just self-empowerment (which is certainly a virtue in the Craft) but power **OVER** others, as in control and manipulation. As in "I can make you do my will, serve me, love me. I can use the robes and dramatic props—and maybe even magick itself—and be the master!" Not only is that selfish and unethical, it's just stupid. Why? Because whatever energy you send out to the world comes back to you. If you send out nasty, arrogant stuff, you have just attacked yourself. It will come back.

CHOICE VS. BLUNDER

Have you explored other paths? If you choose Wicca, let it be an informed choice.

Almost every religion has within it great truths and wonderful people. All can be paths to the Divine if followed wisely, lovingly, and diligently. But any religion can also be misused, as an instrument of prejudice, hate, fear, and violence. Look at the Crusades, the Inquisition, the Holocaust, and the religious wars between Catholics and Protestants, Sunni and Shiite Muslims, and so on.

The challenge is not only to find a spiritual path, but to find the heart of that religion and let it guide all your actions.

Why not explore other paths? Your cultural heritage gives you a place to start. Are your ancestors from Ireland, Lithuania, Japan, Polynesia, Spain, or Brazil? All had, and have, their own ancient religious traditions.

Have you ever looked at Shinto, Druidry, Taoism, Candomblé, Unitarianism, Sufism, Asatru, the Mayan faith, liberal Catholicism, the Society of Friends, Church of Antioch, or Zen Buddhism? How can you choose a spiritual path if you know nothing about all the choices that are out there?

Most of you have the privilege of living in a land with religious freedom. In some nations, it is actually illegal to practice certain faiths. You are lucky. So use your freedom to learn and explore!

Religion is all about reconnecting with the divine source of all things, and you can either find your path by trusting yourself or by trusting someone else. The world is full of people who claim to have the truth; it is revealed in a holy book, spoken by a prophet, or channeled through a preacher. Of course, all these spokespeople for God disagree with one another about the truth, but each declares that there is only ONE path to God—and that religion is a one-size-fits-all garment that can be obtained only through that particular person.

Wiccans believe differently. We say that we cannot know the whole truth about God, the universe, and everything. Religions are only maps to help us get closer to Deity, and it's okay to choose your own route. There is not one true path; there are many paths to the same goal.

Even Jesus said, "In my father's house are many mansions." So perhaps the Baptists, Lutherans, and Catholics share the Christian fraternity house in the next life, but you can bet there's a temple for the Buddhists, a mosque for the Muslims, and a cozy little cottage in the forest nearby for us Witches.

You may decide that no single religion holds everything you need in your spiritual journey. You may discover you love parts of Judaism, Taoism, Christianity, Zen Buddhism, and six other things. That's fine, as long as your blended path helps you to play well with others, become a better person, and connect with Deity.

The only difficulty is that you may not be able to find a spiritual community that precisely reflects your beliefs. But that's okay. Find an open-minded religious community that is accepting of your core beliefs, and hang out with them. Not every church is hung up on dogma—for instance, the Unitarians, Unity Church, Quakers, and most Pagan circles.

As you create your own spiritual path and practices, listen to your inner bell, "the inner sense of truth, the inner reality, the inner knowing which exists deep within all of us."[2] You are the only one who can hear that bell; you are the only person who knows what spiritual path is right for you.

---

2   Marion Weinstein, *Positive Magic: Occult Self-Help*, rev. ed. (Phoenix, 1978), 11.

CHALLENGES
The Risks

Let's say for the moment that you feel irresistibly drawn to Wicca, and you are determined to become part of it. You have a right to know what risks are involved. (More on this in chapter 13, "The Witch in the World.")

God may be loving and open-minded, but of course that doesn't mean human beings are. Probably the greatest real risk is that somebody is going to find out you're a Witch, take offense, and try to do something nasty to you. This could include:

- Spreading lies about you

- Firing you from your job

- Trying to get your children taken away from you

- Vandalizing your home or property

- Evicting you from your apartment

- Driving you out of town

- Assaulting or murdering you

These are worst-case scenarios, and they are becoming less and less likely as we educate people about Wicca and the Pagan faiths. But they're still possible. People get hurt or even killed for being different. Of course, people also get hurt or killed for being American, or female, or Methodist, or gay, or whatever, but that won't be much consolation if you get dead for being a Witch.

You're the only one who can estimate the risk, because it will be different everywhere. Some people choose to avoid the W word entirely, except in their own heads, and present a very ordinary mask to the world. Others find a church that's pretty open-minded and make do. A few go to the opposite extreme and play "Public Witch" to the hilt, with black robes and TV talk-show interviews and enough mascara for six opera stars.

There are other risks, less dire but still serious. There is always a risk of joining the wrong coven. Now, "wrong" can be as simple as realizing "I don't like their classes, this is boring," or possibly "I don't really click with these people," or even "That person is a real jerk, and I just don't want to be in the same group with him."

"Wrong" can also mean that the "coven" and leaders are a scam to part you from your money, get you into someone's bed, or feed the giant ego of a tyrant looking for minions. There is no simple way for genuine Witches to eradicate bad apples who use the glamor of the Craft for their own unsavory purposes. However, there are warning signs you can watch for, and we'll cover these in chapter 11.

More common than the nasty ones are coven leaders who are just immature or inept. Anyone can start a coven, and they don't all have training from wise and experienced elders. Someone can read half a book and declare themselves "Grand High Witch Empress of the Totallyclueless Tradition." So before you join a coven, it's a good idea to chat with the leaders about their teachers, lineage, and number of years in the Craft.

Finally, there is the possibility that you'll get involved and discover that Wicca just isn't working for you. We have known people who thought they wanted to be Witches, and tried it, and finally realized their heart wasn't in it. They thought it would be a good path for them, the principles made sense to them, but there was no heart connection.

Well, that's okay. You don't sign any blood oaths to stay a Witch forever, and any Witch of good will and common sense would want you to find whatever religion is best for you. So reflect on what you've learned, thank your teachers for their efforts, and go find what you need.

BLESSINGS
The Rewards

Now that we've been brutally frank about the potential risks, let's cover some of the good stuff.

First, there is a great deal of intellectual and spiritual freedom in the Craft. Generally, Wiccans are averse to dogma, creeds, and must-believes or must-dos, and very open to different experiences and ways of thinking. If you go into a mainstream church and say that rocks talk to you or that you tried being Aphrodite in a ritual last night, you will get funny looks—or worse. Among Witches, you're more likely to get, "Oh, yeah? I did that last week. How did it go for you?"

Second, we live in a rootless society, where ancestors, traditions, and connections with the past don't seem to count for much. But some of us miss those roots, that sense of being grounded and part of something that has endured over time. Witchcraft provides one way to have that. Our roots and our inspiration go way back, and when we dance around the bonfire or call the Hornéd God or perform a healing spell, we know that our ancestors are smiling because they did the same.

Wicca offers the chance to learn subjects that are not part of your average college curriculum. You can develop skills in magick, divination, ritual, healing, shamanic drumming, animal communication, and more, with others who are lifelong learners. These skills may come through a coven's training classes, workshops at festivals or metaphysical stores, Pagan schools, or online programs.

Community is important to most of us; even Solitary Witches like to come out and socialize or do rituals from time to time. What kind of people will you be meeting and befriending in the Craft? The only thing that holds true 99 percent of the time is that Witches are very individualistic. Fitting into the crowd is just not on a Witch's radar, unless they live or work someplace that's dangerously intolerant.

In general, Witches are intelligent and more highly self-educated than average. They're scrupulously honest: at festivals, some merchants will walk away and leave a sign: "Take what you need, leave money in cashbox." Their goods are safe. A high proportion of Witches have some kind of skill in healing, music, or computers. Most have animal companions: dogs, cats, snakes, whatever. They wear what they please, and some go skyclad whenever they can.

Many of them are the friendliest, kindest people you'd ever want to meet. And some are cantankerous, opinionated, prickly, or just very strange.

Witchcraft will quickly introduce you to a more colorful reality than you've ever known. Most people know the customs and worldview of the place they live, and not much more. Witches are interested in how other cultures view the world, think, and do things, and want to learn about the religions and mythologies of other nations and other times. They also do past-life regressions, visiting incarnations in distant times. They mindshift into other species to learn what it's like to be a wolf, hawk, or frog. They interact with spirit beings, devas, power animals, and faery folk. They work with chakras and energy fields and earth currents.

If you feel claustrophobic in the standard Western fast-food-slow-think-one-size-fits-all consensus reality, you may like the much bigger universe that Witches live in.

Wicca gives you tools for improving your life. Magick, ritual, and spells. Holistic, natural, and alternative healing techniques. Methods for controlling, releasing, channeling, and enhancing your thoughts, emotions, and energies. Ways to relax, tune in, connect, ground, and center yourself. These are not superpowers, just a toolkit of skills that you can use to improve everything you do. They make you more competent at life.

Wicca is spirituality for the whole person. Some religions are big on doctrine and scripture and rules, and they appeal mainly to the head. Other churches offer an emotional hallelujah-chorus-rock-'em-sock-'em ecstasy of the spirit. Still others try to quiet the soul with meditation and contemplation. Witches aim to satisfy every level and aspect of ourselves: body, head, heart, and energy field; playful younger self, responsible middle self, spiritual higher self; the feminine side and masculine side of each individual; and so on. We are complex and multilayered beings; our spirituality needs to be rich enough to work on all levels.

THE CHOICE

We've explained a lot here, and hopefully it's made you think and do some self-exploration. Though it's good to understand what draws you to the Craft, in the end it will not be a choice made by weighing the pros and cons. Like most crucial decisions we make in our lives, the real choice is going to come from your gut, your need, and your true will. In your heart, you probably already are—or are not—a Witch.

You can just try it on. Say to yourself, "I am a Witch." How do you feel saying that? Neutral and blank? Afraid? Excited, empowered, eager? Your heart and body will tell you if it is true. All the rest—who you tell, what training you find, how you express yourself in the Craft—is just follow-up, and the reason for the rest of this book.

May the blessings of the Triple Goddess of the Moon and the Hornéd God of the Wilds be with you on your journey.

Blessed be,

Amber K & Azrael Arynn K

CHAPTER 1

What Is Witchcraft?

Sing to Goddess, moon times three,
Touching magick, wielding power,
Drink to God, stag-hornéd he,
I am a Witch at every hour.

In deep woods on a late summer evening, nine men and women stand in a circle. The youngest is twenty-three, the eldest seventy-one. Candles on a stone altar flicker in the light breeze, and together they drum as the full moon lifts into the darkening sky through a gap in the Minnesota forest. They chant to the moon goddess in time with the rhythmic drumbeat and send the growing power to a coven sister who is giving birth to her long-awaited child. As the moon crests the trees, they imagine they hear a newborn's cry—and a cell phone rings. The high priestess answers the call, grins, and announces that baby Selena has just been born, and mother and child are doing fine. The coven cheers and claps, and begins an impromptu dance thanking the gods. Witches have performed magick.

Willowleaf walks in the woods at noon in the early fall, talking to the trees and plants and listening for their answers. Every so often, she harvests a third of a plant with a small knife and puts it in the basket over her arm, gathering ingredients for some personal healing work. Later, she sits quietly in a clearing, her mind open to the land around her—the gnarled oaks and dogwood; the small, scurrying life; the stream to the north; the living soil. She frowns—something is not right; she picks up a dead twig and whispers, "Be thou wand, and show me." Sweeping it slowly around her, she pauses, the stick pointing north. Soon she has found the trash some careless camper left by the stream, and she takes it with her. At home, she makes a warm herbal compress with the plants she gathered and places it on a red, irritated spot on her arm, saying, "May this potion soothe my skin, and let the healing now begin." In the morning, the skin is smooth and clear, and another Witch has done her healing magick.

Diana is a fifteen-year old whose altar is in the lowest drawer of her dresser. On this night, she locks the door to her room, pulls out the drawer, and sits on the floor in front of it with her sick kitten in her lap. She mimes lighting the two pink candles, whispering, "Rose-colored for healing," then puts a small carved cat in the center of the drawer. Calling on Bast, the Egyptian cat goddess, she repeats over and over, "May my kitten healthy be, as I will, so mote it be!" After nine repetitions, she lifts the kitten and surrounds its tiny body with healing energy. She thanks Bast, "blows out" the candles, and closes the drawer. A young Witch has performed magick.

Becky sits with her husband and two small children at the kitchen table and passes around muffins fresh from the oven. "Mmm, they smell great," says George. "What's in them this time?" "Oh, blueberries, pecans, local honey, a few special herbs and spices…" "Mommy puts in lots of love," says the five-year-old. "And magick!" adds the seven-year-old. Soon Becky and George are tucking the children into bed, with a story about a wonderful dragon who lives in a cave. Becky silently senses the children's energy fields, then draws some soothing energy from the earth and gently pours it into their auras; they sleep. Their mother, a Witch, has done her own magick.

Zephyr sits absolutely still in the dark room of his apartment high above the city streets. He has no robes, candles, or ritual tools. Within him is a rich tapestry wrought by his imagination, an alternative world that could come to be. When the picture in his head is complete, the colors vivid, and all the details present, he traces a path in his mind from the present reality to what he envisions, and he draws upon the power of his spirit allies to help make it real. His breathing changes as he begins to pour energy into the mental image, certain that what he imagines and wills must come to pass. Yet another Witch is working magick in his own way.

Witches, and the ways in which they practice their craft, are as diverse as the myriad leaves of a great forest. So, what *is* Witchcraft?

Witchcraft, sometimes simply called "the Craft," consists of the arts, skills, and knowledge of the Witch, usually blended with a spiritual path guided by the Goddess and the Old Gods of nature. Some Witches prefer to call themselves Wiccan—it doesn't have as much green-skin-and-evil-potions baggage as the word *Witch*. In many people's minds, Wicca is a gentler form of the Craft, with a strong ethical and spiritual component that Witchcraft alone may not have.

We tend to use the term Witch and Wiccan interchangeably, because a Witch without ethics won't last very long (see chapter 7), and most of the Witches we know *do* follow a spiritual path as well as practice the arts and skills of the Craft.

The word *witch* derives from the Old English nouns *wicca* and *wicce*, the masculine and feminine, respectively, meaning "sorcerer/sorceress." The plural of both is *wiccan*, and *wiccecræft* was Witchcraft. In a turnaround in the mid-twentieth century, Gerald Gardner (sometimes called the father of modern Witchcraft) called the people practicing the tradition "the Wicca" and the religion "Witchcraft." The more common usage today is to call the skill and art part "Witchcraft" and the religion part "Wicca," but the boundary between them is not always clear.

The Meaning of *Warlock*

In popular movies, women are Witches and men of the Craft are—warlocks? Not actually. The term *warlock* is used by most Witches only to mean a traitor or oathbreaker—especially one who has betrayed the coven to those who intend harm against it. Never call a man a warlock unless you mean it to be a dire insult. A man in the Craft is called a Witch.

Witchcraft, as used in this book, is a combination of magick and a spiritual practice based on the sacredness of nature. We can work magick to make changes in ourselves and the world around us, but because everything is sacred, we must use our skills wisely and avoid harming ourselves or others.

The Roots of Witchcraft and Wicca

Witchcraft is derived from three primary sources: folk religion, shamanism, and ceremonial magick. It is not a "revealed religion" like Judaism, Christianity, or Islam. It has no founder, prophet, or holy scripture, and no single date when it originated.

It just grew. It is a mixture of tradition, revival, re-creation, inspiration, and imagination. It is sometimes called the Old Religion, and though some of its customs are probably very close to what our ancestors practiced, no one believes that it is the same as it was in ancient times. We are different from our forebears, children of an age of science and technology, and could not duplicate the original faith if we wanted to. Modern Witchcraft has deep roots, but they support and feed living branches that grow and change.

The folk-religion aspect is based in the pre-Christian religions, mostly those of Old Europe, although some Wiccans work with the deities and mythology of other cultures. In ancient times, religion wasn't something you did on Sundays. Religion was how life was lived, in harmony with the natural world of which people were an integral part. At least that's what we modern Wiccans tell ourselves, and it is the ideal to which we aspire. This is the part of Wicca in which the earth and all life is sacred.

This is a genuine religion, from the Latin *re-ligio*, meaning "to reconnect." All things are connected, and we can influence the world because we are connected to it. In this way, the religion part and the practice part are interwoven and inseparable in our shamanic roots.

As we dance the cycle of the seasons and the phases of the moon, we are practicing the ancient shamanic roots of Wicca. As we heal with herbs, drumming, and energy work, we are practicing the ancient shamanic roots of Wicca. When we recognize a young person's transition into adulthood, or any other rite of passage, we are practicing the ancient shamanic roots of Wicca. Calling on the energies of the four directions is an ancient practice, as are drum circles, ritual work in circles, and making decisions in a kind of tribal council. All echo our shamanic roots.

Shamanic correspondences are very direct and relate to the physical world—wearing the paw of a lion would grant the wearer the courage and power of the animal. The timing of ritual is organic—it's time to do ritual when the moon appears full or when the buds begin to show on the trees.

THE NON-MAGICKAL FOLKS

Just as the Witches and wizards of Harry Potter's world had a name for non-magickal folk, so do real Witches. Harry and his friends call them "muggles"; we also call them "cowans." The word is not an insult or put-down; it's just a term for non-Witches or non-Pagans. Many modern Witches, though, think that the Potter books by J. K. Rowling are great fun, and many have adopted the word *muggle* as their new word for the people who don't dance in the moonlight.

The other part of Wiccan practice is based on ceremonial magick as practiced in the Middle Ages and Renaissance, in which the forms and ceremonial trappings were important in reaching one's magickal goal, and belief in what you were doing was often more important than belief in any faith or religion. Magick was largely practiced outside of religion, just as some Witches today practice the Craft but do not subscribe to the spiritual part of Wicca.

So when we call the elements, archangels, or watchtowers that correspond to the four directions, we are using ceremonial magick. When we make long or ornate robes for ritual or wear ritually symbolic jewelry, we are practicing ceremonial magick. Correspondences are usually very cerebral—colors have meaning, complicated sigils have meanings beyond their form, and all correspondences must be congruent. Any time we focus on the intellect in magick, we are touching our ceremonial roots. When we consult the ephemeris or star chart to determine the precise timing for our ritual, we are practicing ceremonial magick.

The spiritual part of Wicca stems mostly from the core beliefs of ancient nature religions, and the practice of magick has its origins in both shamanic practice and the ceremonial magick of the Middle Ages. Together, they weave the rich tapestry that is modern Wicca. However, this blending was not simple, and our history is complicated.

THE MISTY HISTORY OF WITCHCRAFT

Many thousands of years ago, our ancestors were hunters and gatherers living a precarious existence in close connection with the weather, the seasons, the land, the sea, and the other animals.

They worshiped the earth and, we believe, the great Mother Goddess embodied in the earth. Later, they began to worship as well the male principle, personified in the gods. Because they were hunters and relied on wild animals for food, they created beautiful images of bison, antelope, and wild horses, both to honor the prey and to ensure success in the hunt.

Yet when we look at the religious life of Paleolithic humans, what emerges is the vast scope of our ignorance. We have no written accounts of their lives and beliefs. We have oral traditions from surviving indigenous tribes, which might or might not bear any resemblance to our ancient ancestors' traditions. We have cave paintings and no way to see into the minds of the artists, who have been dust for a thousand generations. We have a few stone tools and bone carvings, a few caves and graves.

Let's look at one type of Paleolithic artifact: the so-called "Venus figures," little carved statues of busty, round women that were scattered around Europe twenty or thirty thousand years ago. We don't know what they meant to the makers: dolls for children, fertility talismans, Paleolithic pin-up girls for lusty adolescent males, or images of a great Mother Goddess? We don't know.

All we can know for certain is what they mean to us. And to us, they are perfect personifications of Gaia, Mother Earth, our fertile and abundant planet, source of

THE DORSET OOSER

A few relics of the Old Religion still exist in Europe, such as the horns of the morris dancers. One artifact was called the "Dorset Ooser." It was a wooden mask of the Hornéd God, complete with bull horns, passed down for generations within the Cave family of Dorset. Apparently, it was worn by a dancer dressed in animal skins, in village celebrations around the Winter Solstice. Such a relic would be priceless to any museum today. Unfortunately, a mysterious stranger bought it from a family servant in about 1897, and it hasn't been seen since.

---

life and sustenance. We *intuit* that they were the same for our ancient ancestors…but that's not scientific evidence.

We do know that over the millennia more gods and goddesses were added, and each tribe personified Deity in their own way. By the time of the Roman Empire, many Pagan religions coexisted; all had numerous gods, both female and male, who held sway over the many aspects of the natural world: deities of earth, sea, and sky, of the sun and moon and stars.

All the Pagan faiths overlapped. The gods and goddesses of different lands traveled with merchants and migrations, met and mixed and intermarried. As far as we can tell, religious differences were not usually considered a reason for war. Men might go to battle for grazing land, for cattle, or for access to fresh water—but not because their gods had different names and images. Before Egypt and Sumer and the art of writing, nothing is documented, so we can't be certain of much.

The Norse Eddas give us a glimpse of the northern Pagan faiths. Druidry, a totally oral tradition, has only the descriptions left by Julius Caesar and a few other Romans, who were not only from a different faith but the ones who annihilated them. (In the year 60 CE, a final attack by the Roman legions broke the power of the Druids at the island of Mona in Wales, though they may have lingered in Ireland for a few more centuries.)

And what about Witches, or our spiritual forebears, by whatever name they called themselves? They also had a non-literate, oral tradition—the folkway of the common people. We have bits and pieces passed down through family tradition, or "famtrad," Witches. We have legends and tales gathered by folklorists. We have masks and carvings and artifacts with no colorful pamphlets to explain them.

In 325 CE, Emperor Constantine declared Christianity to be the official faith of the Roman Empire. The new faith began to spread over Europe, the Middle East, and parts of Africa.

There is evidence that early Christianity and Paganism co-existed in some places. The Culdee Church in Ireland was a happy blend of Jesus lore and traditional folk religion until Rome put an end to it. Early Christian churches in Britain had stone phalluses on the altars, Green Men and sheela-na-gig goddesses on the walls, and special doors in the north walls for the Pagans to join in the services (north was a holy direction for Pagans).

This friendly interlude did not last. The Roman Church gained political power and went to war against the Pagans, overthrowing the Old Gods and setting up their own altars on the ancient sacred sites. The Old Norse faiths fought a rearguard action for a thousand years, but they too gradually succumbed.

In the countryside, many folks still quietly followed the old ways. They honored the Lady of the Moon and the Hornéd God of the wilds, and they celebrated the turning Wheel of the Year at sabbat gatherings on the hilltops, where great bonfires lit the night sky. And when necessary, they also attended mass on Sundays and pretended to be orthodox Christians.

In time, the Roman Church became intolerant of anyone it considered threatening to its power. Jews, surviving Pagans, homosexuals, and Christians with differing viewpoints—heretics—were tortured and often executed. Women, sometimes widows who had inherited wealth, were frequent targets. In 1320, Pope John XXII declared Witchcraft a heresy and authorized the Inquisition to act against it.

Thus began the Burning Times in Europe, which lasted almost four centuries. Tens of thousands of people, at the very least, were murdered as accused Witches or heretics all over Europe. In the New World, the persecutions were mostly limited to Salem, Massachusetts, in 1692 and 1693.

The Burning Times ended any live-and-let-live attitudes among the different faiths. When people were being imprisoned, tortured, hung, drowned, and burned as accused Witches, few actual Witches were about to assert their right to religious freedom.

A HAMMER—FORGED?

In 1487, two Dominican monks named Kramer and Sprenger wrote a book, the *Malleus Maleficarum* ("hammer against witches" in Latin), explaining in great detail how to capture and torture "witches." Included were prewritten "confessions" that victims, usually women, could be forced to sign, admitting to devil worship and worse. The book included a purported papal bull (message from the Pope) and an endorsement from the Theological Faculty at the University of Cologne; some scholars believe these were forged. After it was published and spread around Europe, the persecution of "witches" intensified. It was reprinted twenty-nine times between 1487 and 1669, and you can still get a copy today.

Did the worship of the Old Gods die in those days, or did it survive underground, as our stories declare? Or did mere fragments of the elder religion survive as folktales and rural customs, while any organization, leadership, theology, and teachings were lost?

Legend has it that the Old Religion survived but went underground. Secret covens and certain families kept alive the old ways. They celebrated the sabbats in wild places. They made turnip jack-o'-lanterns to frighten the Christian folk into staying indoors at night. They disguised their phallic ceremonial staffs as besoms (brooms) and pretended to be "good Christian folk."

But after centuries of persecution, there were no visible Pagan faiths left in Europe. The Roman Catholic Church's new rivals were the Protestant reformers.

The educated folk of the Age of Reason, or Age of Enlightenment, believed there were no such thing as Witches. Surely, they said, the Inquisition was all about religious power and social conflict, or perhaps mass hysteria—Witches were straight out of fairy tales! But some people believe that surviving covens of Witches anonymously encouraged this belief and waited.

The "Witchfinder General"

During the "Burning Times," Matthew Hopkins made his living by hunting and torturing "witches"—though most of them never practiced the Craft at all. For a price, Hopkins would hire out to any town council or other organization and receive a fat fee for each "witch" discovered. He would torture the accused and look for "witchmarks," which might be a mole or birthmark thought to be the sign of the devil. When a village was empty of "witches"— or seemed to be running low on money for his fees—he would travel to the next "witch-infested" town and begin again.

In the rational, busy period from 1700 to 1900 or so, there were revivals or re-creations of both Druidry and ceremonial magick. From Witchcraft, there is mostly silence—but not total silence. We hear of Old George Pickingill (1816–c. 1909), from Canewdon in England, reputed "master" of nine covens. Occasionally a Book of Shadows will surface, purporting to describe a centuries-old Craft tradition. Stories are whispered of isolated English villages where the Old Religion was still practiced secretly well into the twentieth century.

In 1921, a distinguished British archaeologist named Margaret Murray published *The Witch Cult in Western Europe*, in which she theorized that the Witchcraft of the Middle Ages was actually the survival of an ancient Pagan religion. She followed this with *The God of the Witches* in 1931, explaining that Witches had worshiped a hornéd god of wildlife and hunting, who Christians immediately confused with their Satan figure. Though Murray was highly respected in her original field of Egyptology, conservative scholars and historians quickly dismissed her Witch theories.

Time passed.

The year was 1939. The National Baseball Hall of Fame opened, and CBS began broadcasting. Elvis Presley was four years old. General Motors introduced the automatic transmission, the first World Science Fiction Convention opened in New York, and Batman appeared in his first comic book. Meanwhile, a British civil servant named Gerald Gardner was secretly initiated into a surviving coven of Witches hidden in the New Forest of England. He would become known as the father of modern Witchcraft.

By 1949, Gardner was writing about the Craft, and in one of his later books he revealed himself to be an initiate. His two best-known works were *Witchcraft Today* (1954) and *The Meaning of Witchcraft* (1959). There has been dispute ever since as to whether the "New Forest coven" that initiated him really existed, and how much of the Craft that he passed on (the Gardnerian Tradition) was authentic and ancient, and how much was borrowed from ceremonial magick or invented by Gardner himself.

The 1950s arrived, with big red convertibles and rock 'n' roll heroes. To the public, Witches were fantasy figures from fairy tales, as unreal as giants and trolls and unicorns. In 1951, one of the last surviving laws against Witches, the Witchcraft Act of 1735, was repealed in Great Britain. And Witchcraft, led by the Gardnerian Tradition, quietly spread throughout Western Europe, North America, Australia, and New Zealand.

The ancient traditions that inspired Wicca are dimmed by the mists of time, but the modern history is clear: a vital and creative spiritual tradition continues to grow and re-create itself. In the end, it may not matter whether Wicca is a survival, revival, or renaissance of ancient religious paths. Mere age is no good measure of a religion's value, and to the extent that parts of Wicca are new—well, all religions were new at some time. The real questions are: "Does it work for the people who practice it?" and "Does it serve the communities where it is practiced and the planet we all share?"

THE CRAFT AS ART, SKILL, KNOWLEDGE & PRACTICE

So, what is this "practice" of Witchcraft? In traditional terms, the arts of the Witch include divination, magick or spellcrafting, and healing, which was sometimes indistinguishable from magick to our ancestors. Along the way, many Witches gain skills in planning and leading rituals, teaching, group leadership, creating beautiful art in service to Deity, and more. We will explore these further in chapter 12, because each of these skills can become a spiritual vocation.

Divination is the art of foreseeing trends and discovering hidden knowledge using tools such as tarot cards, runestones, a pendulum, or a scrying mirror. With such tools

AFTER SALEM

Many people have heard of the Salem Witch Trials that disrupted Salem Village and other towns in colonial Massachusetts in 1692 and 1693. Over 150 people were arrested, some after accusations by hysterical girls. Twenty people were hanged or, in one case, crushed with heavy stones.

No one knows exactly what prompted the whole crazy episode. Some say that economic rivals were using the girls' nonsense as an excuse to destroy their enemies. Others say that ergot, a natural hallucinogen, got into the food supply and drove the people mad. We may never know.

Not many people know that within a few years, many of those involved—judges, jurymen, and clergy—began to repent their actions and ask forgiveness. Soon some of the convictions were reversed and monetary damages paid to survivors and relatives. But it was not until October 31, 2001, that the governor of Massachusetts signed a resolution by the House of Representatives declaring all the victims to be innocent.

and sufficient training and practice, we can learn more about ourselves and the future than is apparent on a mundane level. We will discuss this in greater depth in chapter 10.

Magick itself has many definitions, which will be described in chapter 8. For now, it is enough to say that magick is a powerful tool for changing yourself and the world, and it is usually nothing like the fantasy magick we see on television or in movies.

Not every Witch considers herself or himself to be a healer, though all of us do healing magick occasionally. In the past, the village wisewoman was often the midwife and herbalist too, and the local "cunning man" could usually mix a healing potion or set a broken bone. Today many, many Witches have healing specialties within the mainstream (doctors, nurses, medical technicians) or outside it (herbalists, reiki practitioners, crystal energy workers).

A skill is a set of practices that almost anyone can develop, given time and instruction. An art is a set of skills with an added component of creativity. Most of what Witches do is a combination of skill and art; while anyone can learn the uses of herbs and first aid, we all know those who add something extra, the creativity and inspiration that turns an herbalist into a true healer. It is the same with divination or magick; anyone can learn the basics, but some have a natural gift for it.

Part of becoming a Witch is discovering your aptitudes and developing your particular esoteric skills, whether as healer, weather worker, spellworker, dowser, shapeshifter, or any of dozens of other special disciplines (see chapters 10 and 12).

THE CRAFT AS SPIRITUAL PATH

Witchcraft as a spiritual path is often called Wicca, although not all those who follow this path call themselves Wiccan—some just call themselves Witches.

Wicca is a religion, and like almost all faiths, it includes deities. Now, if you grew up in a family that had one god, and he was an old guy with a long white beard who was "out there" somewhere, then you're in for a surprise.

Here are the basic things you need to know about Wicca and Deity:

First, Deity is immanent in Wicca. It's not out there somewhere, above and beyond the world we live in; Deity is actively involved in the world, because it permeates all people and all things. In Wicca, God is not pure Spirit but Spirit embodied and expressed through matter—through us, among other things (and we mean all other things). Think Eywa and the Na'vi in the movie *Avatar*.

WORKING WITH DEITY

We've mentioned several times that Wiccans "work with" Deity—what's that all about? Witches tend not to worship Deity—as in veneration and adulation—so much as honor them or partner with deities in whatever magickal working the Witch undertakes. For now, it's enough to say that we view the deities as powerful partners in this magickal life. When we need something that is within the realm of one or more deities—for example, healing, for which Isis and Brigit are famous—we will do a ritual and invite them to join us, to lend their energies to our work. This is rather like asking your Uncle Charles, who is very good at woodworking, to join you when you decide to make a chair. On the spiritual level, we ask deities to join us as we work magick. And as we call them with love and respect, they lend their powers to the work at hand.

A common saying in Wicca is "Thou art Goddess" or "Thou art God." When a Witch says this, they don't mean that you are the Creator and Source of all things, but that you are an integral part of the Creator…maybe one neuron in God's brain, for example. You are not just created by Deity, you are part of Deity; you are sacred.

Second, Deity can be understood as either masculine or feminine, or both—Goddess as well as God. To say that God is only male would be as wrong as saying that only daylight hours count as real, never nighttime hours. All things are part of the Divine, and that includes all sexes.

Third, all gods and goddesses of all religions are real in the sense that they reflect some true aspect, or part of, divinity. Do you want a glimpse of the Divine? Well, you can look at Jehovah/Yahweh and read the Bible, but you can also read the stories and myths of Isis, Apollo, Diana, Changing Woman, Thor…or any of the thousands of other deities worshiped by anybody anywhen.

No single one of these can give you a full understanding of the original Creator and Source—that would be a lot to ask. But any one of them can teach you something about divinity. Is God love? If so, then you need to spend some quality time with Aphrodite, the Greek goddess who knows a whole lot about love. Is God justice? Talk to Themis. Is God power? Meditate on Zeus. Is God truth? The Egyptian goddess Ma'at can tell you a thing or two. And so on, and on....

So are there really many gods and goddesses? Yes. Or just one? Yes. There is a saying that sums it up: "All gods are one God, all goddesses are one Goddess; God and Goddess are One."

One way of looking at this is to imagine a disco ball[3]—a sphere made up of many small mirrors, each of which reflects a little bit of reality. In this analogy, each little mirror or facet is one named aspect of Deity—Diana, Apollo, Isis, Baba Yaga, etc.— and together they compose the whole, the One. What makes this really reflect (pardon the pun) the Wiccan worldview is that if you look at a disco ball, one of the facets is reflecting your image—as it should, since thou art God, thou art Goddess, you are a sacred being in your own right. And, given a large enough disco ball, it will reflect the whole universe, too.

Now, not all Wiccans agree with this all-in-one, one-in-all view. Some are monotheistic, working with one aspect of Deity exclusively; some work only with one pantheon of gods—Egyptian, Celtic, Norse, or other—and some work with whatever individual deity seems appropriate for the task at hand. The two favorite deities in Wicca are the Lady of the Moon (Maiden, Mother, and Crone) and the Hornéd God of the Wild. But it's okay for any Wiccan to work with as many or as few aspects of Deity as they wish—each individual must come to terms with Deity in whatever way makes sense to them.

So are deities really symbols or archetypes, or do they have an independent existence? Can they hear our prayers and intervene in our lives? Are they sentient, individual beings? Again, the answer is yes; if you ask ten Witches, you will get at least thirteen viewpoints.

Some Witches believe that the deities have evolved to be independent, living entities. Some think they were always that way. Some see them as powerful symbols. Some prefer the broader "Goddess" and "God" and work very little with more specialized deities. Some work with Mother Earth and Father Sun, and so on. Since we cannot ever fully

---

3   Thank you, Rowan, for this analogy.

understand Deity, it seems right that each person should work with the divine power in whatever way, by whatever name or names, are effective for that individual.

Wicca is very diverse, with no set dogma or set of beliefs standard to all. Sometimes even the members of one coven will work with different deities. In our coven, for instance, one member can be counted on to invoke the Norse pantheon anytime it's her turn to do ritual, another usually calls on the gods of the Celts, and most of the rest of us are eclectic, calling whoever is appropriate for the purpose of the particular ritual. On the other hand, some traditions, or branches, within Wicca work with a single pantheon.

Every religion has some central theme or goal, and Wicca is no exception. A Buddhist might say her goal is to release attachment and end suffering for herself and all other beings. Christians might want to achieve salvation, witness for their faith, and spend eternity in heaven after they die. A follower of Asatru might say his goal is to live and die with honor and then feast with his fathers in the Halls of Helgafjell, Valhalla, or Fólkvangr.

Most Witches would probably say that their aim is to live in harmony with nature and to become more like the Goddess and the God—that is, to grow in wisdom, love, and power through life after life, resting between lives in the Summerland. And the ultimate goal, if there is one? That's for the Goddess to know. It's our job simply to follow the spiral with all the skill, honor, and compassion we can manage.

HECATE AND HER BLACK HOUNDS

Hecate is an ancient goddess, old before the Olympian pantheon came to Greece. Her origins may lie in Turkey, Thrace, or even Egypt. She came to be known as Queen of the Witches—the goddess of wisdom, magick, night, and the crossroads.

Black hounds were sacred to her, and folklore has tales of giant black dogs with glowing eyes appearing to travelers on dark, lonely roads. Sometimes these hounds were fierce and threatening, but just as often, they seemed friendly and might even guide the lost to safety.

THE MEANING OF THE PENTAGRAM

The pentagram is a five-pointed star drawn with a single line, sometimes within and touching a circle (see page 61). It has been used for millennia as a symbol of protection, balance, and the Goddess. The points represent earth, air, fire, and water, under the guidance of spirit.

Its possible origin: if you carefully watch the apparent motion of the planet Venus in the sky, it produces a pentagram over eight years' time. Venus is named for the goddess of love and life.

Today the pentagram, usually crafted in silver, is revered and worn by many Pagan folk, especially Witches.

THE UNIVERSE ACCORDING TO WICCA
Common Beliefs

Witches live in a complex, beautiful, and multilayered universe—a very big universe. Not only is it billions of years old, with a hundred billion galaxies or more, but it has levels of reality superimposed and co-existing—different worlds, planes, or parallel universes. These other worlds have names such as the astral plane or the shamanic Underworld. Each has its own rules and its own inhabitants: elementals; discarnate humans; faery folk; guides, allies, and guardians; animal spirits; plant devas; and others who are even less familiar. Many Witches visit these places and meet the entities who dwell there. (We will explore this more in chapter 10.)

If this seems like pure imagination or fantasy to you because you haven't seen it, then we would ask: when was the last time you saw a quark, or gamma radiation, or, for that matter, love or justice? Just because you cannot sense something with your standard senses doesn't mean it's not real.

We also model the universe as formed of five basic elements: earth, air, fire, water, and spirit. Everything we know can be categorized as one of the first four, and spirit pervades them all. (We will explore this more in chapter 3.)

Everything is energy in different forms or flavors, and everything is connected to everything else. Magick works by manipulating this energy to change things.

As we've seen, Wiccans tend to see the universe as entirely sacred—even the bad parts are there for us to learn from, so that we can avoid repeated pitfalls in our own spiritual growth.

Where did it all come from? Witches don't care very much about creation myths; we care more about how the world works now. So in that respect, we have no quarrel with the scientific view that the universe is billions of years old and humans only developed into our modern form a few thousand years ago. The innumerable creation myths found around the world are all equally inventive attempts to understand something fundamentally beyond our comprehension. Central to all these stories is the basic truth of magick: that an idea, with will behind it and focused energy to make it happen, can create anything. That's how the universe was created, and that's how Witches do magick today.

Witchcraft, or Wicca, has no single sacred text, no Bible or Koran, but there is one text that most Witches cherish, called the "Charge of the Goddess." The Charge has become the closest thing to "gospel" that Witches have. A version first appeared in Charles Leland's book *The Gospel of Aradia*, which explored the history of Strega, or Italian Witchcraft. Gardnerian priestess Doreen Valiente expanded it, and Starhawk has published a modernized version. We have blended all three and added a few touches of our own, resulting in this version:

THE CHARGE OF THE GODDESS[4]

Listen to the words of the Great Mother, who of old was called Danu, Freya, Gaia, Inanna, Isis, Quan Yin, Pachamama, Tara, and by many other names:

Though I am known by a thousand names, the whole round world honors me. I am the Queen of Heaven and Earth, Mistress of the World Ocean, and Ruler of the Realms Beyond Death, and I say to you:

Whenever you have need of anything, and at least once each month, and best it be under the open sky when the moon is full, you shall gather and

---

4   Revised by Amber K and Azrael Arynn K, Samhain, 2010.

adore the spirit of me, the Queen of all the Wise. You shall be free from slavery, and as a sign that you are truly free you may be naked in your rites. Let my worship be in the heart that rejoices: sing, feast, dance, make music and love, all in my presence, for all acts of love and pleasure are my rituals and my gift of joy on earth. Nor do I demand any sacrifice, for I am the mother of all the living; my law is love unto all beings, and my love is poured out upon the earth.

My body encircles the universe: I am the beauty of the living earth, the radiant moon among the stars, the mystery of the waters, and the divine fire within your heart. I am the soul of nature who gives life to the universe, and I call to you, for thou art goddess and thou art god. Unleash the coiled splendor within you, spread wide your wings, and come unto me. Let there be beauty and strength, power and compassion, honor and humility, laughter and reverence within you. Keep pure your highest ideals, and harm none. Seek your true will; strive ever to fulfill it, let nothing stop you or turn you aside. And you who would learn all magick, yet have not won its deepest secrets, to you will I teach all things as yet unknown. To you I will teach the great mystery: what you seek you must find within yourself, for you will never find it without.

I am a gracious goddess, the cup of the wine of life, the cauldron of woman's womb; and mine is the holy gift of rebirth. In life, I give the delight of my constant presence and knowledge of the spirit eternal. And beyond death, I give peace and freedom and reunion with your beloved who have gone before. From me all things are born and to me they must return; for I have been with you from the beginning, and I am that which is attained at the end of desire.

NAMES:

EGYPTIAN *Isis* CELTIC *Danu* NORSE *Freya*
CHINESE *Quan Yin* SOUTH AMERICAN *Pachamama*
MIDDLE EASTERN *Inanna* GREEK *Gaia* DRUID *Tara*

Most key Wiccan ideals are there: how to worship, how to live, the promise of life after death, freedom, the equality of all people, the sacredness of **ALL** expressions of love and pleasure, the joy of this life, the love of the Goddess and the God, and more.

What are the other principles of Witchcraft? The Council of American Witches was a short-lived group—only active in the mid-1970s—but their 1974 statement still holds true today. The Principles of Wiccan Belief are a good summary of most Witches' beliefs and practices.

COUNCIL OF AMERICAN WITCHES
Principles of Wiccan Belief

1. We practice rites to attune ourselves with the natural rhythm of life forces marked by the phases of the moon and the seasonal quarters and cross quarters.

2. We recognize that our intelligence gives us a unique responsibility toward our environment. We seek to live in harmony with nature, in ecological balance offering fulfillment to life and consciousness within an evolutionary concept.

3. We acknowledge a depth of power far greater than that apparent to the average person. Because it is far greater than ordinary, it is sometimes called "supernatural," but we see it as lying within that which is naturally potential to all.

4. We conceive of the Creative Power in the universe as manifesting through polarity—as masculine and feminine—and that this same Creative Power lies in all people and functions through the interaction of the masculine and feminine. We value neither above the other, knowing each to be supportive of the other. We value sex as pleasure, as the symbol and embodiment of life, and as one of the sources of energies used in magickal practice and religious worship.

5. We recognize both outer and inner, or psychological, worlds—sometimes known as the Spiritual World, the Collective Unconscious, Inner Planes, etc.— and we see in the interaction of these two dimensions the basis for paranor-

mal phenomena and magickal exercises. We neglect neither dimension for the other, seeing both as necessary for our fulfillment.

6. We do not recognize any authoritarian hierarchy, but do honor those who teach, respect those who share their greater knowledge and wisdom, and acknowledge those who have courageously given of themselves in leadership.

7. We see religion, magick, and wisdom-in-living as being united in the way one views the world and lives within it—a worldview and philosophy of life that we identify as Witchcraft, the Wiccan Way.

8. Calling oneself "Witch" does not make a Witch—but neither does heredity itself, nor the collecting of titles, degrees, and initiations. A Witch seeks to control the forces within her/himself that make life possible in order to live wisely and well without harm to others and in harmony with nature.

9. We believe in the affirmation and fulfillment of life in a continuation of evolution and development of consciousness that gives meaning to the universe we know and our personal role within it.

10. Our only animosity toward Christianity or toward any other religion or philosophy of life is to the extent that its institutions have claimed to be "the only way" and have sought to deny freedom to others and to suppress other ways of religious practice and belief.

11. As American Witches, we are not threatened by debates on the history of the Craft, the origins of various terms, the origins of various aspects of different traditions. We are concerned with our present and our future.

12. We do not accept the concept of absolute evil, nor do we worship any entity known as "Satan" or "the Devil," as defined by Christian tradition. We do not seek power through the suffering of others, nor do we accept that personal benefit can be derived only by denial to another.

13. We believe that we should seek within nature that which is contributory to our health and well-being.[5]

---

5 From the Council of American Witches, 1974. Due to the efforts of the council's chairman, Carl Weschcke, these principles were later incorporated into the chaplain's handbook for use in the U.S. Army.

THE WITCH'S VALUES

What qualities of character do Witches cherish? You may have a pretty good idea from what has been said so far, but let's sum it up.

First, there is **HARMLESSNESS**. One of our core principles says "harm none"—no one, including yourself. (So much for the stories about Witches flinging curses at anyone they dislike!)

RESPECT for all nature and every being is essential. If Spirit is embodied in all—if we look at someone and think "Thou art God, Thou art Goddess"—then disrespect becomes unthinkable. Most Witches celebrate diversity; matters like race, sexual orientation, lifestyle, etc., interest us but don't divide us.

Our desire for **HARMONY WITH NATURE** and its cycles logically follows. We are part of nature; we cannot transcend or control it, but we seek ways to live in balance and sustainably.

We cherish **WILL**: our true will, our destiny, our highest purpose, what we are on this planet to accomplish.

We need and demand **FREEDOM**. Call it autonomy—the right to manage our own lives as long as we don't harm others. Witches are an independent bunch and don't tolerate control by others. "You shall be free from slavery," says the Charge.

Another goal is to give and receive **LOVE**. As the Goddess "pours out her love upon the earth," we hope to do the same. "My law is love unto all beings."

We seek **WISDOM**. After all, we are called the Craft of the Wise, and we try to live up to that name. Wisdom is a combination of understanding, clarity, insight, experience, and judgment.

You cannot have too much **KNOWLEDGE**. Witches are lifelong learners, and it's a rare Witch who doesn't have a stack of books next to the bed. Of course, knowledge also comes from other people, experience, experimentation, and, perhaps most of all, from nature.

Then there is **POWER**. Witches are neither power-mad nor allergic to it. We don't seek power over others, but we do aim to develop our own inner strength and power, and to empower others.

HONESTY is treasured by Witches. To lie is to weaken our power; our deep minds must know that every word from our mouths is always true, so that when we say "So mote it be!" ("So it must be"), there will be no doubt.

SELF-RESPONSIBILITY is vital to Witches. You can't be a victim and a magician, or in charge of your own life while you blame others for what you bring on yourself. You are responsible for every thought, word, and action that you send out into the world.

Though we don't talk about it much, we value SILENCE. This can mean being discreet, or meditating quietly, or seeking that still place at your center.

We open ourselves to JOY, celebrate life, and share pleasure with others. The Goddess says, "Let my worship be in the heart that rejoices: sing, feast, dance, make music and love, all in my presence, for all acts of love and pleasure are my rituals and my gift of joy on earth."

WHAT WITCHES DO
Common Practices

Witches could probably argue endlessly about theology and values, but mostly we don't bother. In many ways, we are united by what we do—our practices—rather than by our beliefs.

For instance, we celebrate the changing of the seasons in the holy days we call sabbats, and the cycles of the moon in celebrations called esbats. These are covered in more depth in chapter 2, so we will give just a brief overview here.

There are eight sabbats, not counting any we might invent for fun. Collectively, they are known as the Wheel of the Year. Witches think in circles and spirals whenever possible, rather than straight lines. For instance, we see time as both circular and a spiral, rather than as linear. The Wheel of the Year is a circle because it keeps turning, coming back to the same point each year, and yet it's also a spiral, because we are not the same people we were last year, and the world is not the same place. Autumn is always autumn, yet no two autumns are the same.

Some Witches begin their year at Samhain (pronounced either *sow'-wen* or *sov-veen'*), others see Yule as the beginning of the year. It's rather like starting the day at midnight or at dawn—there are good arguments to be made for both. The eight sabbats occur approximately every six and a half weeks around the Wheel.

Witches also celebrate the phases of the moon; almost all do ritual at the full moon, and many celebrate other lunar phases too. We will talk more about ritual in chapter 8.

We also do divination and spellwork frequently, and keep animal friends close by, and talk to plants, and much more that will be covered in later chapters.

WITCHES BY THE NUMBERS

So, how many Witches are there? No one can do a complete census, because many Witches are deep in the broom closet and will never reveal their path to any pollster.

Even the American Religious Identification Survey (ARIS), done in 2008 by Trinity College in Hartford, Connecticut, lumps Pagans of all stripes (Witches, Generic Pagans, Druids, whatever) with Unitarian-Universalists, New Agers, Scientologists, Santerians, and others in a category called "New Religious Movements and Other Religions." Even with all that company, we "New Religious" types only make up about 1.2 percent of the U.S. population, or fewer than 3 million folks—if the survey is accurate.

Granted, Witchcraft/Wicca seems to be growing rapidly. But at some fraction of 1.2 percent, we're not exactly taking over the world—which is all right, because that's never been our goal, anyway. We have no desire to convert the world to our path, because we believe that Witchcraft is not for everyone.

We have mentioned the American Witch population but should make it clear that Wiccans/Witches live in many countries. Great Britain is the birthplace of modern Witchcraft, but our Craft brethren also can be found throughout Western Europe and in Canada, Australia, and New Zealand. Smaller numbers are scattered around the world, including those serving in the military who are stationed overseas.

So what are Witches? We are people who follow a spiritual path and way of living that is inspired by the practices and worldview of our ancient ancestors. We keep close to nature. We celebrate the cycles of life and the seasons. We connect with Spirit in many forms. We perform divination and magick. And we learn, grow, and heal ourselves and others. This is the heart of Witchcraft.

THE FEMALE FACTOR

Roughly two out of three Witches are female. Perhaps women are drawn to the Craft because, hey, the Goddess is here, and it's great to have a divine female role model—or, actually, many of them! Perhaps we like the idea that we can be priestesses, with as much respect as the men get in the male-dominated religions. On the other side, maybe some guys aren't sure what to do with the male deities in the Craft: all that Hornéd-God, Sun-God, Warrior-God energy. It's quite a change from Jesus. Nobody knows why there are more female Witches, but the male Witches are happy, and we women are glad that we have as many really great Craft brothers as we do.

CHAPTER 2

Seasons of the Sun, Cycles of the Moon
The Wheel of the Year

Celebrate as the Wheel turns,
Touching magick, wielding power,
Dance and leap as the balefire burns,
I am a Witch at every hour.

Nature moves in cycles, in circles and spirals. Earth orbits the sun, and the seasons flow from one to the next and repeat the cycle through the millennia. We call it the Wheel of the Year, and for modern Witches, it governs the rhythm of our lives. The Wheel is a circle, coming back to the same seasons and sabbats again and again, but it is also a spiral, because it moves through time. At each year's spring, we are in an equivalent place—but not the same place. Also, when we reincarnate, we come back to Earth, but it is not the same world we left the time before.

Likewise, the moon orbits, waxes, and wanes in her changing phases, and the tides rise and ebb. The lunar cycle is also part of our lives and our magick. And when we celebrate, we do it in circles, not lined up in rows, watching someone else have all the fun. Everyone in the circle participates. We live and plan and think in circles and cycles rather than lines.

Most Witches celebrate eight major holy days, or sabbats, through the year, spaced roughly six and a half weeks apart. Four are called the lesser sabbats, one every three

The Wheel of the Year

months at the solstices and equinoxes. The other four are the greater sabbats, and they are in between the lesser sabbats. See how they are placed on the illustration.

These are very ancient holy days; not everyone in those days celebrated all eight, but most modern Pagans do. The names are taken from the Irish language, but most have been around so long that they have more than one name. The dates of the greater sabbats (Beltane, Lughnassad, Samhain, and Imbolc) are approximate; they vary a little in different traditions. The lesser sabbats are determined by the astronomical calculations of the solstices and equinoxes, and these vary from year to year. Here's the list, with approximate dates:

Yule (or Midwinter, Winter Solstice): December 20–23

Imbolc (or Oimelc, Brigit's Eve, Candlemas): February 2

Ostara (or Eostre, Spring Equinox): March 20–23

Beltane (or May Eve, Mayday, Walpurgis): April 30

Litha (or Midsummer, Summer Solstice): June 20–23

Lughnassad (or Lunasa, Lughnasadh, or Lammas, August Eve): August 1

Mabon (or Harvest Home, Fall Equinox): September 20–23

Samhain (or Hallows Eve, November Eve): October 31

In practice, many covens hold their celebrations on the weekend nearest the traditional date so that members with weekday work schedules can attend. Samhain poses an interesting challenge, because most modern Witches celebrate it on the same date as Halloween, no matter what day of the week it falls on. Many non-Pagans confuse the two, but Halloween has evolved into a modern, secular children's holiday and is very different from the Witches' sabbat.

THE MYTHOLOGIES BEHIND THE WHEEL OF THE YEAR

Witches and other Pagans have various mythological cycles that follow the Wheel of the Year; no single one is the "official" mythology, and often they intertwine in happy confusion. It's not logical or consistent, but few Witches care.

Myth Cycle #1: The Oak King and the Holly King. The Oak King rules half of the year, from the Winter Solstice (Yule) to the Summer Solstice (Litha). Then he is challenged by the Holly King; they battle fiercely, the Oak King is overthrown, and the Holly King rules until Yule. The resurrected Oak King battles him in turn, and takes the crown until Litha…and so on.

Myth Cycle #2: Birth, life, and death of the Sun God. The Sun God is born of the Mother Goddess at Yule, grows to young manhood and takes the Maiden Goddess as his lover at Beltane, reaches his greatest strength at Litha, and becomes the Grain God and sacrifices himself to the harvest at Lughnassad. Then he is reborn at Yule.

Myth Cycle #3: Maiden, Mother, and Crone phases of the Goddess. The Goddess is the Mother at Yule, transforms to the Maiden in the spring, grows into her power as the Mother once more by Litha, and ages to become the Crone in the autumn, and then the Mother again at Yule.

Scottish Variant: The Winter Hag pursues the Spring Maiden, but the Hag's power dwindles as the spring advances. The Spring Maiden matures into the Mother through the summer, and then gradually transforms to the Hag again through autumn, and the Hag chases the Maiden again as spring begins.

Myth Cycle #4: The Hornéd God and the Goddess divide the year. The Hornéd God rules during the fall and winter, the cold season of hunting, darkness, and death. The Goddess reigns during the spring and summer, the warm season of fertility, growth, and life.

All these are mythological models for the reality of the changing seasons. As with all myths, there are perspectives on truth within each—even though no one of them is literally true. Because Witches don't need to believe literally in our myths and legends, we can embrace the discoveries of science without worrying whether some ancient tale "given by God" is contradicted. Myths are insights into the human condition, and you are free to explore the ones that seem meaningful to you and use them in your rituals.

Getting back to the sabbats, they are a celebration of life and nature and change. Our ancestors worked hard between the holidays and then played hard when it was time for a break. Let's look at how they understood each sabbat and what the sabbats might mean for us today.

Eight Sabbats Around the Wheel

We'll start our discussion with Yule, looking at the significance of each from both an external and an internal viewpoint.

Yule

Yule is the celebration of the Winter Solstice—the shortest day and longest night of the year. It happens around December 21, at the end of what some Witches call "the dark time"—that six-week period beginning at Samhain, moving into the darkest time of the year. At the solstice, we celebrate the rebirth of the sun, which will grow in strength until Litha. In British mythology, the Oak King and the Holly King battle it out, and the Oak King wins.

What It Means to You: In the old days, winter evenings might be spent mending a harness or fixing farm tools. Now, you can work on your own indoor projects—making herbal oils, researching a school paper, or learning new software for your computer.

Giving and receiving are issues at Yule. What can you give to your family, friends, and community? What do they need (never mind the glut of gadgets that the corporations want you to buy)? Also, what is being offered to you that might enrich your life and that you could graciously receive?

Rebirth is a primary theme at this time. Every year offers a fresh beginning. What kind of person will you be "reborn" as? Meditate on your lifestyle, habits, character, and persona, and decide what the "new you" will be like.

As the days lengthen, begin your year with mindfulness and intention. As life and light increase, how will you use their energy? Look ahead and make plans for the new year—even a formal list of New Year's resolutions. Begin to gather resources.

Activities for Yule: Bring in and decorate a Yule log. Decorate a living Yule tree, and plant it later. Sing Yule carols. Enjoy a visit from Mother Berchta (a Pagan winter deity). Exchange gifts. Tell stories about the exploits of sun gods and goddesses (look them up in books of mythology or online).

Deities for the Season

Mother Goddesses: Gaia, Demeter, Inanna, Ishtar, Pachamama, Aditi

Sun Gods: Ra, Horus, Helios, Apollo, Bel, Shamash, Oak King, Sol Invictus

Imbolc

Imbolc (or Oimelc or Candlemas) is celebrated on or about February 2 and is a festival of the returning light; we really can tell that the sun is getting stronger, and the days are getting noticeably longer. Spring is just around the corner, and signs of new plant life begin to emerge.

The Celtic names Imbolc and Oimelc mean, respectively, "in the belly" and "ewe's milk," for this is the time that the sheep are giving birth.

It is a time sacred to Brigit, the triple Irish goddess of healing, inspiration, and smithcraft. She is a fire goddess and has aspects that embody sovereignty and the skills of warriors. Sacred springs and wells all over the Emerald Isle are dedicated to her.

What It Means to You: Traditionally, Imbolc is a time of cleansing and purification—perhaps the origin of spring cleaning. It's a good time to clean out your house and your life—to refresh, renew, and rededicate yourself.

Many Pagans take this opportunity to clean and reconsecrate their ritual tools (that is, rededicate them to the gods and their special purposes; see chapter 3 for details). Include the candles you use for magickal work. And why not rededicate yourself to the great purposes that lie before you: your important projects, your life's work, your dreams, the legacy you will leave to the world?

Also, if you want a garden, now is the time to plan your garden, order seeds, and plant them in flats.

Activities for Imbolc: Make and decorate candles. Decorate a little indoor fountain with red ribbons and red flowers as Brigit's holy well. Tell "wonder tales" about Brigit. Consecrate or reconsecrate your tools. Take a luxurious ritual bath. (Brigit's bathwater turned to beer—will yours?)

Deities for the Season: Here are some goddesses and gods you may want to research—in addition to Brigit, of course. They are related to her three major aspects.

Smiths: Hephaestus, Vulcan, Wayland

Healers: Isis, Hygeia, Aesclepius, Apollo, Bai Zu Zhen, Unkatahe, Diancecht

Inspiration: Sarasvati, Gwydion

Ostara

Ostara, named for the Norse goddess Eostre, celebrates the Spring Equinox, usually around March 21. Spring has sprung, and the days are getting warmer—rejoice! Fertility, birth, and new beginnings are the themes, with eggs and bunnies representing the tremendous fecundity of the earth at this time. This is a time for planting not only physical seeds, but also seeds of those projects you want to accomplish during the year.

One symbol of spring is the hare, alert and quick. The hare is connected with the moon goddess as well, and this is the sabbat most closely connected with moon energy.

What It Means to You: Action has replaced planning and the gathering of energy. Your projects now begin to manifest in a tangible, physical way. It's a long way to the harvest, but you are in motion.

Think about the moon as well; her phases can represent the Maiden/Mother/Crone aspects of womanhood or a man's Youth/Father/Elder within. What face are you showing the world; what's your main role in life right now? And can you access the others—if you are a maiden, can you act as the nurturing mother or wise crone when you need to?

For men, it's a good season to get in touch with your nurturing, compassionate feminine side, what psychologist C. G. Jung called your *anima.* When you accept all parts of your nature—when you are a whole spiritual being—then your power will be complete.

Activities for Ostara: Decorate hard-boiled eggs with magickal symbols, then hide and hunt them. Make or give out stuffed bunnies. Drum up the sun. Plant things with your family or friends. Tell stories about lunar deities and the moon hare.

Deities for the Season: Some springtime and lunar deities that you may want to meet:

Maiden Goddesses of Spring: Eostre, Kore, Persephone

Moon Deities: Selene, Diana, Hecate, Luna, Sin (Mt. Sinai is named for him), Khonsu

Beltane

Beltane arrives around May 1; hence, it is sometimes called May Day. It is the celebration of love, lust, sexuality, sensuality, and the burgeoning life force. All the plants are growing, the animals have given birth and their young are kicking up their heels, and only brief snows are expected (we participated in one festival appropriately nicknamed *Snowtaine*).

The springtime work continues, but we pause to celebrate and enjoy. The May King and May Queen are crowned, the maypole is danced, and some couples slip away to a woodland bower for more private festivities. Centuries ago, babies born of a May Day union were considered specially blessed, and they were often named Robin.

What It Means to You: It is a time to rejoice in the warm new season! Enjoy your body—in sexual intimacy if you have a partner or lover, or by indulging in solitary sensual experiences. You can enjoy a foamy hot bath, a wild dance to your favorite music, good chocolate, or a simple cuddle. What will bring you pleasure? Also, how do you give and receive love in general? Do you show a face of loving kindness to every sacred soul you meet? Do you accept love and say thank you when someone shows you love?

Activities for Beltane: Dance the maypole. Make "May gads" (wands decorated with bells, flowers, and ribbons). Have a procession with a fool, a hobbyhorse, a Green Man, and everyone with their May gads. Dip strawberries in melted chocolate. Play active games that require a kiss to set "prisoners" free. Tell romantic stories about famous lovers.

Deities for the Season: Get acquainted with the gods and goddesses of romance, passion, and life:

Love Gods: Eros, Cupid, Kamadeva

Love Goddesses: Aphrodite, Venus, Freya, Erzulie, Astarte

A Divine Loving Couple: Krishna and Radha

The Merrymount Maypole Scandal

One of the early maypoles in the New World was set up by Thomas
Morton in 1626, at the colony of Merrymount in Massachusetts. It
was 80 feet tall, and the dances and feasting brought settlers and
native people from miles around. Unfortunately, the local Puritan
elders had no patience with such heathen goings-on, and in 1628
they sent Miles Standish to arrest Morton and burn the great maypole.
Morton was exiled to Maine, where he spent the rest of his life. We
have no record as to whether he erected any maypoles in Maine.

Litha

Litha is the Summer Solstice, around June 21, and marks the longest day and
shortest night of the year. The Oak King and the Holly King battle it out again, but
this time the Holly King wins to reign until Yule, when we decorate with his shiny
dark leaves and bright red berries. Litha celebrates the full height of the summer sun
and the Sun God in his glory, his warmth and energy pouring down on the crops as
they ripen.

It also brings the Sun God's transition to Grain God, as sun and earth together
bring forth the grains, vegetables, and fruits.

What It Means to You: This is the ideal time to focus your power where it will bring
you the greatest harvest. What are your priorities? These are the longest days of the
year, so you have more hours to work—and play! Call upon your favorite solar deity
to help.

Ask yourself: What are my sources of power? What are my strengths? Am I using
them to my best advantage? What new sources of energy can I cultivate in myself
now, while the sun is high? Remember your own radiance; like Aten in the ancient
Egyptian Hymn to Ra, you can "Rise in splendor, fill every land with your beauty."

For women, it's a good season to get in touch with your active, accomplishing
masculine side, what C. G. Jung called your *animus.* Cherish all parts of your nature;
when you are a whole spiritual being, your power will be complete.

Activities for Litha: Use sun tea and summer wines to toast the solar gods and goddesses. Bask in the heat of the sun. Set off fireworks. Honor the sun. Tell stories long into the evening light.

Deities for the Season

Sun Gods: Ra, Horus, Helios, Apollo, Bel, Shamash, Sol Invictus, Holly King

Sun Goddesses: Amaterasu, Bast, Sekhmet, Hathor, Arinna, Sol, Sunna, Saule

BONFIRES ON THE HILLTOPS

In olden days, people would often celebrate Beltane and Litha by building bonfires on hilltops. The word *Beltane* means "Bel's fire," Bel being a sun god worshiped in many lands.

Bonfire may have come from "boon-fire," a fire made from wood asked as a boon, or gift, or "good fire" (French *bon* or Scots *bonny*), or "bone fire," since bones burn hot and long.

Bonfires brought warmth and light, and they were wonderful for dancing around, or for cooking food for the feast to encourage the sun, or for magickally burning away illness. A bonfire is a staple at many Pagan festivals today.

Lughnassad

Lughnassad, or Lammas, is the first of the three harvest festivals, celebrated around August 1. This is the harvest where the god of the grain gives his life so that we may live through the winter. The themes are self-sacrifice for the community or individual initiation to a higher level of spiritual existence.

Other themes are abundance and how we allocate, store, and use resources. The wise management of wealth becomes an issue at harvest time, when we once again have material prosperity.

This is also the special day of Lugh, a Celtic sun god who was also High King of Ireland and the Tuatha De Danaan, "the people of the goddess Danu." He is a master of all skills: warrior, bard, healer, blacksmith, and more. According to legend, he started Olympic-style games in honor of his mother, Tailltu.

What It Means to You: Celebrate your projects that have come to fruition. Finally, you are reaping tangible results from all your work—or if not, why is your personal harvest delayed? Or are you harvesting something you didn't plan for?

Once your harvest is on track, you can think about preparing for the winter ahead, whether that means storing food, getting a new furnace, or weatherproofing your house.

Think about self-sacrifice. What sacrifices will you make for your family and community? What sacrifices will you make in order to learn, grow, and stretch yourself?

Remember that Lugh mastered many skills; maybe it's time for you to add to yours. Have confidence, be willing to sacrifice time and effort, and you can master the new skills you wish.

Activities for Lughnassad: Bake special breads to share. Hold your own "Taillteann Games" with contests and prizes. Make corn dollies out of wheat stalks or corn husks. Make a corn man with whole ears of corn, "sacrifice" him in the bonfire, and eat buttered corn on the cob. Find stories about Lugh's adventures and tell them around the fire.

Deities for the Season: In addition to Lugh, you may want to meet:

Dying and Resurrected Gods: Baal, Adonis, Melqart, Osiris, Mithras, Dumuzi or Tammuz

Deities of Many Skills: Mercury, Hermes, Minerva (Goddess of a Thousand Works), the Walawag Sisters

Earth and Grain Goddesses: Gaia, Mahimata, Pachamama, Changing Woman, Ceres, Demeter, Taillte

Mabon

Mabon, the Fall Equinox, is the second harvest festival, about September 21. The gardens and orchards are giving up their ripening bounty. The days are growing noticeably shorter—the days and nights are of equal length, and there is an autumn crispness in the air.

It is a time to share our abundance and be grateful—the "Pagan Thanksgiving." We are moving toward completion of our goals, tying up loose ends. But we'll make time to eat, drink, and be merry.

The holiday is named for Mabon ap Modron, who appeared in *The Mabinogion*, a collection of Welsh myths. He is a divine son. According to legend, King Arthur needs Mabon's hunting skills to track a great boar, but the young man is missing. After many trials, the king and his men rescue Mabon from his prison, and he aids them in their hunt and the fulfillment of their quest.

What It Means to You: You are reaping the rewards of your efforts. It is time to "count your blessings" and show your gratitude to all your family, friends, and coworkers who have helped you on the year's journey. This thankfulness could infuse your whole perspective on life if you can take joy in what you have received and experienced instead of focusing on your losses and disappointments.

It's also time to finish up this year's projects. The Chinese philosopher Lao Tzu, in the *Tao Te Ching*, said: "The wise are as careful in the completion as in the beginning of a task; thus, they do not fail." Make your priority the careful completion of your work before Samhain.

Remember that Mabon is best known as the son of the goddess Modron, or Dea Matrona. Consider the experience of being a son or daughter—what does that mean to you? If being the child of your parents or guardian was a good time in your life, take joy in that and show your appreciation. If growing up was difficult, then ponder how you can learn from that and do better for the next generation. For your sake, if not for those who raised you, work to forgive and release.

Activities for Mabon: Cook special dishes for the thanksgiving feast. Decorate the hall with cornucopias and harvest colors. Talk about your year and your harvest. Tell stories about Mabon and other Celtic heroes.

Deities for the Season: There's not a lot of information about the god Mabon, but of course most deities are sons or daughters of divine parents.

Gods Who Are Especially Known as Sons: Horus, Jesus

Goddesses Who Are Especially Known as Daughters: Persephone, Athena, Ushas, Vishnumaya

Samhain

Samhain (*sow'-wen*) is the most solemn of the sabbats and almost always celebrated on October 31. It is the third harvest—the animal harvest, when domesticated animals not likely to make it through the winter were killed and their meat preserved for the winter. This was also a time for hunting, to cull the old and infirm from the wild herds.

At Samhain, the veil between the worlds is thin, so that it becomes easier to communicate with the spirits of the dead. Therefore, it is a time for remembering our ancestors and those who have died in the last year. In some traditions, a "dumb (silent) supper" is held to honor the departed, or shrines are set up for loved ones who have passed on.

It is the beginning of the dark time, when a Witch may turn inward for quiet contemplation and do divination for the coming year (see chapter 10). Being quiet can be difficult during the muggle holiday madness, but this period of near-hibernation can restore your spirit.

What It Means to You: Think about your family lineage, your ancestry. Learn what lessons you can from your family history. Honor your elders. Remember your beloved dead.

Meditate on death, transition, the afterlife, the spirit world, and reincarnation.

Think about yourself, someday, as someone's ancestor—what will be your legacy to your descendents? Will they have reason to remember and admire you, and to take you as a role model?

Your personal harvest is done for the year, so you can spend some time in rest and reflection. In some Pagan traditions, Samhain is the New Year. For others, it is the beginning of the dark time, and Yule is the New Year. Take a deep breath. Hibernate. Spend time at home with your family. Use this time wisely.

Review the past year. What new understanding has the past year brought to you? With that perspective, what do you hope to do in the New Year that is a continuation—or different?

Activities for Samhain: Make shrines to your honored dead. Invite them to attend a dumb supper with their favorite foods. Bring out a scrying mirror, tarot cards, or runestones, and do some divination about the year to come (see chapter 10). Share stories about your ancestors, friends, and family who have passed on.

Deities for the Season: Get to know something about your deities of the dead now, so you won't be shy when you meet them later.

Underworld Gods: Hades, Osiris, Thoth, Anubis, Manannán mac Lir

Underworld Goddesses: Ereshkigal, Hel, Persephone, Ceridwen, Hecate, Selket, Ma'at, Kali, the Morrigan

Hollow Turnips?

Legend says that on All Hallows Eve, the glowing faces of goblins could be seen bobbing through the darkness. Best for good Christian folk to stay inside for safety! The "goblins," however, were large, hollowed turnips with faces carved in them and candle stubs inside. The followers of the Old Religion preferred not to have their Samhain celebrations interrupted, so they gave the Christian folk a little scare so that they'd leave the sabbat dances in peace. Many years later, in America, people found that pumpkins also made wonderful jack-o'-lanterns.

So those are the eight primary celebrations, or sabbats, that Witches observe as the Wheel of the Year turns around and around and around again.

SABBAT EXERCISES

- Research a deity appropriate to the coming sabbat.

- Find songs, chants, or instrumental music appropriate to the sabbat theme.

- If you are part of a coven, take charge of one part of the sabbat celebration: decorations and altar, the feast, the music, reading a myth or legend aloud, or the games.

- Draw your own Wheel of the Year; decorate and color it. Display it near your altar.

- Decorate your personal altar (see chapter 3) appropriately to the season.

- What ideas, impressions, or feelings does this season bring to mind? Is it connected to vividly important events in your memories? How do these color your feelings about this time of year?

- Brainstorm what you like about this season, what's difficult, and what you can do to make it easier or more joyful.

- What are your favorite and least favorite seasons, and why?

- Do you have friends or relatives who have been more closely involved with the land and the seasons than you have? Farmers, ranchers, fishermen, park rangers? Talk with them about their experiences.

- What sabbat most intrigues or attracts you? Why? Do some research on it— start with Llewellyn's sabbat series of books, listed in appendix A.

THE CYCLES OF THE MOON

To our distant ancestors, the prey of fearsome creatures that stalked by night, the moon and fire were sources of illumination and safety. To poets much later, the moon was a symbol of romance and adventure: Alfred Noyes proclaimed that "the moon was a ghostly galleon tossed upon cloudy seas." To modern society, the moon may be a handy waystation to the exploration of outer space.

For Witches, the moon is the symbol and embodiment of the Goddess as Maiden, Mother, and Crone, and it's usually the feminine counterpart to the masculine Sun God. In addition to the sabbats, Witches also celebrate some phases of the moon, at esbats (from the French word for "frolic," so clearly they are meant to be joyous events). In one version of "The Charge of the Goddess," the Lady commands: "Once in the month, and better it be when the moon is full, you shall gather in some secret place and adore Me...."

Almost all Witches do ritual at the full moon, drawing on her power for any magick needed. Some also gather at "Diana's bow," three days after the new moon, when she becomes visible as a slender crescent reminiscent of the bow of the virgin huntress Diana. This is a good time to work magick for beginning new projects. Occasionally some Witches also do ritual at the last quarter of the moon, when the slender waning crescent is called "Hecate's sickle," in reference to the goddess of night and magick. This is a time to do magick to release or banish bad habits or anything you no longer need. Many Witches also do ritual at the dark of the moon—an effective time for divination.

The phases (or apparent shapes of the lighted portion of the moon visible from Earth) are as follows:

Waxing Crescent (Diana's Bow)	◐
First Quarter or Half Moon	◑
Waxing Gibbous	◑
Full Moon	○
Waning Gibbous	◑
Third or Last Quarter	◑
Waning Crescent (Hecate's Sickle)	◑
New Moon or Dark of the Moon	●

It is wise to pay attention to when the moon is void-of-course, when the moon has left its last planetary aspect in any zodiac sign but not yet entered the next sign. This is a bad time to start anything new or make important decisions; better to relax and catch up on your reading, do housework, or finish projects already started. Voids-of-course come every two and a half days and may last from a few minutes to more than two days; they are noted in astrological calendars (such as *Llewellyn's Astrological Calendar, Pocket Planner,* or *Magical Almanac*) with the symbols V/C or VOC.

Because women have monthly menstrual periods related to lunar cycles, the moon seems particularly feminine to many people. The moon's phases can be associated with the major stages of women's lives: the waxing moon stands for the Maiden, the full moon is the Mother, and the waning moon is the Crone.

Several goddesses are associated with the moon, such as Selene, the Titan goddess of the Greeks; Artemis, the Greek huntress; Luna, the Roman moon goddess; Diana, the Roman woodland goddess who took on lunar aspects; and Hecate, a very ancient goddess who has come to be associated with the night and the waning moon.

Many cultures have moon gods, such as the Egyptian Khonsu and the Babylonian Sin. But for most Wiccans, most of the time, the moon is a Goddess aspect and the sun is a God aspect.

Each full moon has a name (or several) related to the month in which it occurs. Here is one such list, from *The Farmer's Almanac*, but there are many others from different cultures.

JANUARY: Wolf Moon

FEBRUARY: Snow Moon

MARCH: Worm Moon

APRIL: Pink Moon

MAY: Flower Moon

JUNE: Strawberry Moon

JULY: Buck Moon

AUGUST: Sturgeon Moon

SEPTEMBER: Harvest Moon

OCTOBER: Hunter's Moon

NOVEMBER: Beaver Moon

DECEMBER: Cold Moon

As the moon moves through the twelve signs of the zodiac, it has different energies in each sign. The magick you perform at a full moon esbat may be affected by the sign the moon is in. The zodiac traditionally begins with Aries, and the signs follow in order; here are the energies one can expect as the moon moves through each:

Moon in Aries (the Ram, a fire sign ruled by Mars): Spontaneity, energy, enthusiasm, action, openness, independence, passion; also temper, defensiveness.

Moon in Taurus (the Bull, an earth sign ruled by Venus): Calmness, strength, health, stability, endurance, security, conservatism, nature and environmental issues; also stubbornness, slowness.

Moon in Gemini (the Twins, an air sign ruled by Mercury): Thought, words, ideas, knowledge, communication, analysis, intelligence, social skills; also being out of touch with emotions, recklessness.

Moon in Cancer (the Crab, a water sign ruled by the moon): Home, roots, attachment, motherhood, intuition, caring, receptivity, emotions, sensitivity, memory; also moodiness, stubbornness, a narrow outlook, and oversensitivity.

Moon in Leo (the Lion, a fire sign ruled by the sun): Light, sun, warmth, love, passion, drama, expressiveness, charisma, pride, generosity, confidence; also self-absorption, craving for attention, egotism.

Moon in Virgo (the Virgin, an earth sign ruled by Mercury): Task orientation, organization, competence, effectiveness, facts and data, perfection, cleanliness, low visibility, simplicity, personal relations, young people; also self-abasement, moralism, perfectionism, fanaticism.

Moon in Libra (the Scales, an air sign ruled by Venus): Awareness, diplomacy, partnership, peace and harmony, intellect, wisdom, understanding; also instability, oversensitivity, manipulation, and fear of solitude or conflict.

Moon in Scorpio (the Scorpion, a water sign ruled by Mars and Pluto): Emotional intensity, passion, devotion, wholeheartedness, intuition, transformation; also introversion, selfishness, and addiction to drama.

Moon in Sagittarius (the Archer, a fire sign ruled by Jupiter): Idealism, enthusiasm, vision, passion, friendliness, dislike of convention, need for freedom; also fanaticism, impracticality, lack of commitment.

Moon in Capricorn (the Sea-Goat, an earth sign ruled by Saturn): Responsibility, solidity, reliability, self-control, family bonds, security, conservatism, tradition; also lack of spontaneity, distancing from others, lack of flexibility and openness.

Moon in Aquarius (the Water Carrier, an air sign ruled by Saturn and Uranus): Intellect, community, collective effort without intimacy, observation, perception; also emotional detachment, isolation, lack of self-knowledge, erratic behavior.

Moon in Pisces (the Fish, a water sign ruled by Jupiter and Neptune): Sensitivity, empathy, connection, kindness, understanding, imagination, solitude; also daydreaming, impracticality, emotional parasitism, oversensitivity.

Witches have long been associated with the night and the moon, perhaps because of the mystery and magick we feel in the moonlight. We have a reputation as "night owls," though obviously not all Witches are. Some love the dawn and the sunlight.

The world is both smaller and larger by moonlight—the known world is smaller, the unknown world is larger. Sight recedes; sound and smell and touch become more acute. The few things we can sense are more important, more intimate. Things we never notice by day—the sound of a dead leaf wind-scraped along a pavement—loom larger and more significant by night. Moonlight washes out color and leaves all in shades of gray. There is a paradox: we may be afraid in the dark because of what we can't see, and at the same time we can feel protected by darkness and there can be a sense of freedom because others can't see us.

Moonlight is a time for dream and fantasy, shapeshifting and transformation, mystery and the occult; all is fluid, hidden, unknown. The moon can help you make friends with the night, be at ease in darkness, and find the special beauty of the nocturnal realms.

The moon gives us opportunities to do pieces of large projects, short cycles of sowing and reaping within the greater Wheel of the Year. This lunar month, what can you accomplish on your way to achieving the larger goal? We get the gift of a new beginning every 29.53 days, twelve or thirteen times a year.

The lunar cycle, like the Wheel of the Year, is also a reminder of the wheel of life, the Wheel of Fortune in the tarot cards. What goes around comes around. What is low shall be raised, what is dark shall be light. As one variation of a common Pagan chant says, "All that dies shall be reborn…All that falls shall rise again."[6]

---

6 "Hoof and Horn" by Ian Corrigan, http://www.bornpagan.com/upca/song_cycle/05%20-%20Hoof_and_Horn.mp3 (this version has *All that's cut shall rise again*).

ESBAT EXERCISES

- Walk outside. Is the moon visible? What phase is she in? (If you can't see her, check the Internet.) Do this nightly; begin to get a sense of her rhythm and phase until you notice it automatically and always know what phase she is in. Watch for her waning crescent in the daytime, too.

- What is your relationship to the moon? What do you feel when you are outside at night in the moonlight? Try to sum up your feelings in a poem, and write it down. Later you may wish to put it in your magickal journal, often called a Book of Shadows (see chapter 3).

- Find more names from various cultures for the monthly full moons on the Internet.

- Think of the magick or divination work you could do that would help meet your needs at four different phases of the moon:

  DIANA'S BOW (EARLY WAXING CRESCENT)

  FULL MOON

  HECATE'S SICKLE (LATE WANING MOON)

  NEW MOON / DARK OF THE MOON

The Wheel of the Year and the lunar cycles are just two patterns that can help define and guide our lives. We can fit our projects and goals into them—whether earning a degree or building a house or doing spiritual work—and we can both blend with their energies and rhythms and use them to help achieve our hearts' desires.

There are other cycles; watch for those that are special to your life—they may involve your career, your kids and school, your hobbies or sports, and so on. Just by being aware of these and planning for them, you can "go with the flow" more easily.

Beyond these are the recurring dance of day and night, the astrological cycles of the planets, and the reincarnation cycle of your lives, deaths, and rebirths. The mysteries and powers of all these are open to the Witch.

CHAPTER 3
Power of the Pentagram
The Witches' Paradigm

Water, fire, earth, and air,
Touching magick, wielding power,
Ruled by spirit, all is there,
I am a Witch at every hour.

In our model of reality, the universe is formed of earth, air, fire, water, and spirit. On one level, they represent solid matter, gases, energy, liquids, and spirit. On another level, they are our physical bodies, minds, energy fields, emotions, and souls. All of the first four elements are connected and harmonized in spirit. The elements—and all the correspondences, or subsets of them—make up the symbolic language of Wiccan magick.

In chapter 1, we talked about the shamanic and ceremonial magick roots of Witchcraft. Of the four elemental components of being, the shamanic roots are physical (earth) and emotional (water), and the ceremonial is practically all mental (air)—but both work with energy and will, the fire element. The shaman might raise energy through drumming, chanting, dance, or song (physical and emotional expressions), while the ceremonial magician would be more likely to raise power by pure mind alone (focused and concentrated thought). So working with and directing energy is where the shaman and the ceremonial magician come together, and this is the synthesis that Wiccans use in magick.

The box below contains the most commonly used system of correspondences in modern Witchcraft. (Some traditions assign other correspondences to the four directions, and that is okay; there is no One True Way.)

BASIC CORRESPONDENCES, COMMONLY USED				
Direction	Element	Physical	Human Component	Ritual Tool*
East	Air	Gas	Mental	Sword (or wand**)
South	Fire	Energy	Energetic	Wand (or sword**)
West	Water	Liquid	Emotional	Chalice
North	Earth	Solid	Physical	Pentacle
Center	Spirit	Spirit	Spiritual	Candles, deity statues
*See chapter 4 **Varies by tradition				

At this time, you may want to make or purchase your first tool: the Book of Shadows that every Witch should keep. (We'll cover more of the tools in chapter 4.) A Book of Shadows is a blank book in which you record your journey as a Witch. Every spell, every ritual you perform or participate in, as well as notes taken in classes, should be recorded in your book. Ideally, you might make the book yourself, but you can buy your Book of Shadows ready-made. A search on the Internet will find dozens of sources for fancy blank books. Your local metaphysical bookstore will have them, or a blank book from your local stationery shop will work. Some books will be simple, usually black; some will be embossed with a pentagram, the Tree of Life, or another symbol on the cover. You may want to buy a really nice pen for writing in your Book of Shadows, a special one for that purpose alone.

Before you use your new book and pen, you may consecrate them to the service of the Goddess and the God. Pass them through incense smoke or over a candle flame, and sprinkle a few drops of saltwater on them while saying, "I cleanse and purify this Book of Shadows and Pen of Art to the service of you, the Lady and the

Lord, that I may write in your honor during my studies and in my practice of the Craft of the Wise. So mote it be!" ("So mote it be" is a witchy way of saying, "Make it so!") The smoke, candle flame, salt, and water bring the energies of the four elements to witness your words and imbue the whole spell with their power.

Although it is traditional to keep a physical, paper-pages Book of Shadows, many modern Witches keep a virtual Book of Shadows on their computers. As long as you write in it faithfully, you can use either. But we suggest that you start with a physical book, since there may be part of you that really enjoys the feel of an actual book; you can always switch to the computer if you find you aren't using the book.

Back to the pentagram.

The pentagram is a five-pointed star with the lines of the star overlapping. It is the symbol for everything—the five elements bound together, often drawn within a circle that connects them all. It has been used as a symbol of protection from ancient times: the pentagram was found stamped on the sides of grain jars in Sumer, and it was used by the Egyptians, Celts, Kabbalists, Christians, and Gypsies. Used upright, it stands for spirit ruling the world of matter—also life, health, protection, and the human being as a microcosm of the universe. Inverted, it can stand for the Hornéd God, or for Spirit hidden in matter or subject to it.

The five points can represent the limbs of our bodies with the head above, the five senses, the five stages of life (infancy, youth, maturity, elderhood, and old age), or the states of consciousness (deep sleep, light sleep, trance or meditation, ordinary waking consciousness, and ecstasy). The top point is spirit—our connection to Deity.

Different Witchcraft traditions place the elements at different points on the pentagram. In ours, the right upper point is water—emotion and intuition. Below it is fire (think an underwater volcano)—our will and vitality, energy and passion. The left upper point is air—our intellect and imagination; below it is earth (think the earth beneath the sky)—our bodies, health, prosperity, Earth herself. Let's tour the pentagram, point by point.

EARTH

Earth corresponds to the physical earth, with its mountains and valleys, fields and meadows, trees, rocks, and plants; to our physical bodies; and to all solid and material things. It also corresponds to the health of this planet and our bodies, and the abundance of the universe in all forms, including food, money, and possessions.

Why get your Earth-plane stuff together first? Because that's the world we live in most of the time. We may spend some time in our thoughts or embroiled in emotion, but we always need food, shelter, and clothing. So, some pertinent topics to write about in your Book of Shadows would be: What would your life be like if you had all the shelter, food, health, income, and possessions you need? What could you then turn your attention to? And what steps can you take to bring physical well-being and abundance?

Exercise in Grounding and Centering: Go to a place outdoors in nature—your back yard, a nearby park, or out into the countryside—and find a quiet place to sit. If it's winter, make sure you dress warmly so you can stay outside for several minutes. (If you can't get outside, do this exercise in your mind today, and make a date with yourself to do it later for real.) Simply sit and let the sights, sounds, smells, and energies of nature flow around you and through you. Breathe the air, trace the outline of a nearby leaf with your fingertip, and feel the ground beneath your feet. Just *be*. Then reach out to the rocks, plants, and animals of this place, and listen for any messages they may have for you.

For the next few minutes, feel your connection to all of nature, then picture and feel a golden cord extending from the end of your spine down into the ground, down and down until you reach the heat at the earth's core. Wrap the golden cord around that core to anchor you, and bring your consciousness back up the cord to where you are sitting. This is grounding, the first magick a Witch should learn, for you will use it in every magickal act you perform, every spell you set, and frequently in everyday life when you simply need to calm yourself.

When you can feel the serenity that comes with grounding, send your consciousness into your body, into that part of you that feels like your center. For some people it is the solar plexus, for others it's a couple of inches below the belly button—you'll know where it is for you. Feel the stillness there—that deep knowing that you ARE, and you are okay. Feel the peace of your center radiating out until it envelops you and meets the serenity of nature around you. This is called centering, and it is the second half of "grounding and centering" that you will do before every ritual and all magick. So, sit in nature, grounded and centered, for about five minutes. Then pick up your Book of Shadows and record your experience. What did you see? What did you feel, outside and in? Hear, taste, touch? How do you feel now that is different from the way you usually feel? What do you notice around you that you didn't notice before?

Spend as long as you want in this place, recording your feelings and observations, so that you can come back as often as you want in your mind, even when you are physically many miles away. When it is time to go, thank the spirits of this place for letting you be here, then return home.

In the comfort of your home, ground and center again. Think about these questions: What does Earth mean to you? What do health, strength, and abundance mean to you, and how can you enhance them in your life? Write your answers in your Book of Shadows.

Living as a Witch in the World: Find a good book about the geology of your region, and start to familiarize yourself with that face of Gaia. Go back outside at least once a week, and get to know nature at this time of year. How is she different from the last time you enjoyed her presence?

Think about how you live on the earth—gently or not so gently? Consider joining Green America (GreenAmericaToday.org) and getting connected with the best of green living. When you join, they send you the National Green Pages, which has green vendors for everything from advertising to wine and beer. Check it out, and plan the steps you can take to live more gently on this stressed planet. Write about your thoughts in your Book of Shadows.

Exercise for Abundance: Inventory your wealth according to the pentagram. How are you wealthy in terms of intellect and imagination? In terms of energy and vitality? In terms of love and intuition? In material terms? In terms of your relationship with Deity? Make a prosperity treasure map based on your greatest need or desire. A treasure map is a collage of pictures on a sheet of poster board, with a few words thrown in, to remind you of your goal in a visible way. Hang it in a prominent place in your home, and meditate on what you can do today to manifest your goals and how it will feel when you have achieved them. Make up an affirmation, such as "My life is filled with good things and good friends, and all good things come to me easily and with joy!" Repeat at least twice a day. Write down the practical steps you can take to make it real—and do them.

AIR

Air is the wind, from soft breezes to hurricane gales, the air that we breathe to survive, and the carbon-dioxide-to-oxygen cycle of the plants around us. Air also corresponds to our thoughts, intellect, and imagination. Without these three, we would not be able to appreciate our world or create magick.

Exercise: Go to a place with clean air (or get a picture of a wide-open sky above a meadow, forest, or mountains, and place it before you while you meditate). Take a deep breath and let it out, ground and center, then take another deep breath and let it out slowly. Focus on the breath moving in and out of your body, the breeze that comes in your window, the gale that brings the thunderstorm. What do thought, intellect, and imagination mean to you, and how can you enhance them in your life? When you have finished meditating, write your thoughts in your Book of Shadows.

Living as a Witch in the World: Think about the air you breathe—are you lucky enough to live in a rural area where the air is usually clean and safe, or do you live in a city with air pollution warning days? How do you contribute to air pollution (driving your car) and how can you cut back (riding a bike sometimes)? If you live in a polluted place, consider buying an air filter for your home, especially your bedroom, where you spend a third of your life. Also consider joining the Nature Conservancy, the National Resources Defense Council, the World Wildlife Federation, or some other conservation organization (contact points are in appendix C). Many of them are in the business of saving habitats, which includes the air we breathe. Or join the Arbor Day Foundation, whose mission is to plant trees (which produce oxygen). Or go to TerraPass.com or NativeEnergy.com to purchase carbon offsets.

Exercise for Imagination: Pick a tarot card at random, or a picture from a magazine of a person doing something, and imagine it in great detail. Make up a story about the character in the picture. What are they doing, how did they get there, where are they going, and why? If you draw a blank, ask yourself, "If I did know, what would it be?" You'll be surprised how that can loosen up your thoughts!

FIRE

Fire is the smallest candle flame, the hearth fire, the deep heat at the earth's core, and the fire of the sun. Fire corresponds to our desires and passions, our will, purpose, and goals. It is the energy that animates us and all living things, and that we bring to our magick to make it work.

Exercise: If you don't have a desert or volcano handy, build a small fire outdoors or light a candle in a darkened room. (Take appropriate safety precautions.) Take a deep breath and let it out, ground and center, take another deep breath and let it out slowly, then focus on fire: will, passion, and purpose. Do you want more of them in your life? What is your passion, anyway? You may have already addressed this back in the earth exercise, when we asked what you would do if your physical needs were taken care of. That may give you a glimpse of your true will—that voice inside that says, "This is my contribution to the world!" How can you make your passion a larger part of your life? Write the answers to these questions in your Book of Shadows.

Living as a Witch in the World: Think about how you use energy—sparingly or wastefully? Have you replaced your light bulbs with compact fluorescents? Again, how could you have a smaller carbon footprint? Go to the Internet and search for carbon footprint, use a calculator at one of those sites to figure your carbon offset, and choose one of their green partners to support, like Native Energy.

To Light a Fire

Sacred fires such as sabbat bonfires are sometimes made with the traditional *nied-fyr,* Anglo-Saxon for "forced fire"—that is, fire made by friction, such as the bow-and-drill method used by our ancestors, or ignited with flint and steel, or by focusing the sun's rays through a lens. Modern Witches don't always follow the old ways, though; wooden matches are very handy, and on a cold night it's not uncommon for the fire builder to "flick the sacred Bic."

Exercise for Purpose: Think about the toughest goal that you ever set for yourself—and achieved. Remember how you felt when you said, "I did it!" Sort of tingly and wide awake, alive and vital? Go back to the treasure map you made, and stand in front of it. Bring that vital, alive feeling back to your consciousness, and put that energy into your goal. Feel success as you look at the pictures on your treasure map. When the feeling peaks, take a deep, quick breath in, say "So mote it be," clap your hands together once, and in one powerful *whoosh,* exhale the energy into the treasure map—but retain the good feeling!

WATER

Water is the mist, the rain, and the snow, the streams that flow to the rivers and into the oceans, the ice that forms the glaciers, the blood that runs through our veins, and the tears that we cry. Water corresponds to our emotions, our compassion and love, and our intuition. Some people say that our emotions let us know we are alive, and intuition is our direct connection to the Divine.

Exercise: Go to a watery place—out on your porch during a rainstorm; next to a stream, lake, or ocean; or into your own bathtub, filled with clean, pure water. Take a deep breath; ground and center. Take another deep breath and let it out slowly, then meditate on water: What does water mean to you? What do compassion, love, and intuition mean to you, and how can you bring more of them into your life? Think about the luxury of clean water to bathe in, the refreshing quality of ice in your tea, and water in all its forms. Then think about emotion. Remember the last time you cried—what prompted that? Did you injure yourself? Did a good movie make you cry, or a sad song? Then switch back to that joyous feeling you accessed during the fire section, take a deep, quick breath in, say "So mote it be!" and clap your hands, and feel that really good feeling again. A true Witch can change consciousness at will—that's one of the definitions of magick—and changing your emotional state at will is a particularly potent form of magick. (How many times have you heard someone say they couldn't do something because of their emotions? Well, what if they could change their emotions at will?) Write your thoughts in your Book of Shadows.

Living as a Witch in the World: Find a good book or documentary about the hydrologic cycle, the cycle of rain and evaporation. Find out how you can help support people who are working to guarantee clean, drinkable water. Use the Internet, and get involved. Buy a water filter and a reusable water bottle, and quit sending plastic bottles to the landfill—or recycle if you must use them.

Exercise for Connecting with Your Intuition: Find the quietest place you can. Ground and center. Listen, and let the quiet soak into your soul. For a few minutes, meditate in and on silence. Find that still point within, and ask a question. The answer may not come through on the first try—you may be out of practice listening, and your intuition may be feeling shy—but keep trying. Let your inner voice know you are ready to listen; after a time it will become clearer, and it will always be reliable. Write your thoughts in your Book of Shadows.

SPIRIT

Spirit is embodied in the other four elements and transcends them as well, for spirit is the Goddess and the God, and all that they have created is imbued with their energy.

Two Exercises: Go to a place that feels sacred to you. This may be a place in nature or your personal altar. Take a deep breath and let it out, let your thoughts slow down, then ground and center. Think about the Goddess. What does the feminine energy of the universe feel like? What women do you find inspiring and powerful? Do you connect with the feminine divine as an individual goddess (Diana, Aphrodite, Danu, Quan Yin) or as the all-pervasive Goddess? If all of this is new to you, that's okay, too.

Reach out with your mind to the feminine energy of the universe and feel it surround you like a warm, soft blanket or a gentle, cool breeze, whichever feels good at this moment. Imagine a wise young woman leading you into a field of fresh flowers to dance for joy under the golden sun and the blue sky. Then imagine a loving, gentle mother cradling you in her arms and rocking you to sleep like a small child. Allow yourself to drift. Finally, imagine a wise old grandmother, with the ages in her face and compassion in her eyes, telling you just what you need to hear as advice for your journey to become a Witch. Write her words in your Book of Shadows.

Take another deep breath, and move your awareness to the God. What does the masculine energy of the universe feel like? What men do you know who are strong and inspiring? Do you connect with the masculine divine as an individual god (Zeus, Pan, Cernunnos, Odin) or as the all-pervasive God? Imagine a bold, strong youth leading you into a forest to share the secrets that he has learned through his wanderings. Then imagine a young warrior showing you how to use a bow and arrow, like magick, to hit your target. Imagine a kind father who speaks of the joy of fatherhood and family. And finally, imagine a wise old sage who answers your most important question about magick. Write their gifts in your Book of Shadows.

Living as a Witch in the World: Where and when do you feel most in touch with spirit? When do you feel awe, peace, connection, belonging, and joy? If it's a place you can go to in person, go there at least once a month to renew your spirit. If you can't go there in person, take the trip in your imagination. Feel whatever feelings come up, and take the opportunity to ask your intuition for guidance. Always write your thoughts in your Book of Shadows.

ELEMENTAL SYMBOLS AND YOUR PERSONAL ALTAR

Almost every Witch has an altar. It can be elaborate or simple, but it will probably become the focal point of your daily practice, as explained later in chapter 6. Choose a place for your altar: in the center of a room, along one wall (traditionally either the east or north), in a closet or drawer, or on a shelf. Find a quiet span of time to set up your altar. You may choose to use just one altar cloth all the time or change it with the seasons. A basic Witch's altar usually includes the following items:

- Symbols of Goddess and God or a statue or picture of one's patron deity
- Two candlesticks with candles, called "lamps of art"
- An air symbol, usually in the east (such as an incense burner or a feather)
- A fire symbol, usually in the south (such as a red candle)
- A water symbol, usually in the west (such as a seashell or bit of driftwood)
- An earth symbol, usually in the north (such as a stone or crystal)
- Small dishes or bowls holding salt and water
- A fire-making tool (wooden matches will do)
- Your ritual tools: pentacle, wand, chalice, and athame (see chapter 4)
- Working tools such as tarot cards, runes, essential oils, herbs, etc., that you may need for a particular magickal working (we'll get to these later in the book)
- And, in our tradition, a coyote (see chapter 8)

As you gather objects to represent the elements on your altar, pass each one through incense smoke and sprinkle it with saltwater to cleanse it before placing it on the altar with reverence. The objects on your altar may be changed whenever you like; your altar should be a living thing, used often and reflecting your growth as a Witch.

Once your altar is set up, sit before it and do the following exercise:

Five Elements Breath: Breathing rhythmically and slowly, visualize white clouds in a vast, sunlit blue sky, and inhale the refreshing power of air. Exhale all tension and any negative thoughts.

Now visualize the shimmering heat and white sands of a hot desert, and inhale the exhilarating power of fire. Exhale all tension and tiredness.

Next, visualize the rolling green waves of a wide sea, and inhale the rejuvenating power of water. Exhale all tension and any emotions you don't need.

Now visualize great, rocky snow-capped mountains mantled with green forests, and inhale the solid power of earth. Exhale all tension and weakness.

Then visualize your favorite goddess or god, shining, beautiful, and smiling, embracing you; inhale the exquisite power of spirit. Exhale all that is not perfect.

A personal altar

Finally, visualize a glowing pentagram radiating all the colors of the rainbow, and inhale the power of life—balanced, whole, and well. Exhale and give thanks.

The elements of the pentagram are the building materials of the universe. All that we experience can be understood as being of earth, air, fire, water, or spirit, or some blend of these.

There is a model from India, the Tattvic system, that expands upon the basic five elements. They speak of permutations such as earth of air, air of air, fire of air, water of air, spirit of air, and so on for each of the elements. Each of these also represents a metaphysical portal where one can enter and explore these deeper mysteries of the elements in combination. This is fascinating work that you can look forward to doing as you advance in your learning.

You, too, are a blend of earth and air, fire and water, filled and guided by spirit. May you be a living, shining example of the elemental balance that we see in the pentagram.

CHAPTER 4

Bell, Book, and Candle
Equipping the New Witch

Based on knowledge, filled with love,
Touching magick, wielding power,
As below, so above,
I am a Witch at every hour.

Did you think this chapter was going to start off with "Buy a pointy hat, a broom, a cauldron, and a black cat"? No? Good—because that's window dressing, and sadly stereotypical. Neither will we start with a wand like Harry Potter's, although a wand is a part of the modern Witch's toolbox, so it is a part of this chapter. A Witch's tools are aids to the mind and imagination when doing magick, but the tool doesn't make the Witch. There is a saying that an adept has the use of everything but is dependent on nothing. We would amend this to say that the Witch is dependent on nothing outside him- or herself—but what is *inside* the Witch is vital.

So what are these internal qualities? They are those attributes of self that define the Witch. Let's start with the Witches' Pyramid, a neat encapsulation of what it means to be a Witch and to do magick, captured in the following rhyme:

Knowledge as a base of stone,
Will to call the thing my own.
Imagination helps to see,
Faith to know that it will be.

The Witches' Pyramid

Silence knows what's best to hide,
Love will fill the space inside.
Spirit binds them all as one,
Now the magick has begun.[7]

The base of the pyramid is knowledge, the inside is love, and the four sides correspond to air, fire, water, and earth. Each of these four elements has a corresponding witchy tool associated with it, and so does knowledge. There is no tool specifically associated with love, but ideally all of a Witch's actions flow from the heart and love, so a separate tool is hardly necessary. We will begin with the pyramid's base, and then go around the sides in the order that they are most often used in performing magick—east (air/imagination), then south (fire/will), then west (water/silence), and north (earth/faith), finally followed by love at the center. (We covered spirit in the last chapter.) We will explore both the internal qualities of the Witch and the tool and element that correspond to each one.

THE BASE
Knowledge, Book of Shadows

The base of the Witches' Pyramid is knowledge: knowledge from this book, other books, teachers, nature, your own experiences, the Internet—anywhere you can gain knowledge about yourself, other people, and the world around you. Because Witchcraft will take you to anywhere/when/who you can imagine, the Witch needs to be well read, with a wide variety of interests and a lively curiosity to know more and more and more.

So, to become a Witch, begin by taking an inventory of your knowledge. What is your background, and more importantly, what have you learned along the way about yourself and others? About the world outside your door, halfway around this planet, or beyond this planet? What do you know a lot about; what would you like to know more about? And where do you record all this knowledge? In your Book of Shadows.

---

7 Traditional; source unknown. Our thanks to the author—we have used this for many years, with gratitude.

THE WITCHES' ALPHABET

A magickal alphabet popular in the Craft is called Theban Script, or the Runes of Honorius. It may have been first published in 1518, in a book called *Polygraphia* by Johannes Trithemius. He suggested that it was created by the legendary magician Honorius of Thebes. Today, it is used by some Witches for their Books of Shadows, as a simple cipher to protect their material from any curious muggle. Some of the fantasy Elvish alphabets look vaguely similar and may have been based on Theban.

The Book of Shadows may live on your altar, or beneath it, or elsewhere—just make sure for ease of use that it is convenient to get to.

Begin gathering more witchy knowledge from books, the Internet, and workshops. We have included an appendix of recommended readings and another of resources, including some of the hundreds of Internet sites for Witch/Wiccan/Pagan information—these make up just a fraction of the witchy knowledge available today. Once there were only a handful of books on the Craft; today dozens are published each year on Witchcraft and related subjects, and new Internet sites pop up daily. Take a stroll through the bookshelves of your local metaphysical shop, and pull volumes off the shelf that catch your eye. Buy some—support your local Pagan merchant—and start your own library.

Don't buy too many at first, though. Start with just a few, and practice what is in them before buying more, or it can get overwhelming. Eventually you will move beyond strictly Craft books to explore related subjects. You can read up on other spiritual paths, find the similarities and differences, and perhaps try practices from other faiths. Mythology is always useful for finding deities to work with, both in ritual and to walk with through life. Ancient history can give you a sense of our roots, psychology an understanding of how we think, and ecology a hope for a bright future. Grow your library carefully and tend it well, as you would a beloved garden, for it will feed your mind and soul, giving nourishment with each new book.

Search the Internet using Witch words (see the index or the glossary), and peek into some of the thousands of sites that pop up. Take workshops at Pagan festivals, online through Cherry Hill and other schools, or in person at Ardantane. Record your most interesting findings in your Book of Shadows. Then get up and do something. Witchcraft begins with knowledge, then is built on through experiences.

EAST

Imagination, Athame

Once you have a good start on your base of knowledge and the willingness to continue learning throughout your life, you can begin to build the sides of your pyramid. The first side is air, or imagination. If you can't imagine something, you can never attain it; imagination is the first step in creation, the first step in magick. Imagination and inspiration are closely linked—it's rare to find one without the other. Inspiration comes from dreams, daydreams, and things you see, hear, or feel; it is that sudden light, that spark of "I wonder..." or "I'd like to see what would happen if..." So, to begin to become a Witch, think, "What do I want?"—then imagine you have it.

Using all your senses, imagine an animal or a piece of food. What would it look like, smell like, feel, taste, and sound like? Vivid imagination includes all your senses plus your emotions. How do you feel about it—does it thrill you, scare you, make you feel all warm and fuzzy? Write it in your Book of Shadows.

The tool most often associated with air is the athame, a black-handled, double-edged knife that is used to cut through nonphysical energies. It is considered an air tool partly because air is the realm of the intellect and the imagination, and the athame can cut through illusion to get to truth. The athame helps cut through the fibs we tell ourselves and the webs of misinformation in which others want to spin us. We will talk more about how the athame is used, and about cleansing and dedicating it before use, in chapter 8. As with all the tools, the ideal way to obtain an athame is to make it yourself. Alternatively, you can find one at your local metaphysical shop, from a merchant at a Pagan festival, or, as a last resort (because you can't touch it and feel its energy before buying), on the Internet.

The athame is either worn in a sheath or placed on the east side of the altar.

THE COVEN SWORD

While each Witch owns an athame for personal use, many covens own a sword that is used to cast circles at group rituals. In earlier times, only the nobility were allowed to carry swords, but legend tells us that the Craft has always included people from the aristocracy. Some coven swords used today are heirlooms, some are decorative pieces, and others were originally well-crafted weapons that would hold up in a battle—except, of course, that a ritual blade would never be used to cut anything material, much less stab an enemy warrior.

SOUTH
Will, Wand

The second side of the pyramid is fire, or will, corresponding to the south. Will is perhaps the most complex side of the pyramid, because "will" can have many meanings. We discuss this in chapter 7, on ethics, because the Wiccan Rede says, "An ye harm none, do as ye will." In that case, *will* means your true will, not just a whim. However, in the context of the Witches' Pyramid, *will* means concentrated focus—a single-mindedness that will get you to your goal. To be a Witch, you must be able to focus on one thing until you have made it your own.

Will also implies daring and courage. Witches make change happen in conformity with will (one of the definitions of magick), and therefore Witches live with change as a constant. Sometimes change can be scary, especially changes in yourself. Yet most Witches are on a path of self-transformation to become the best they can be. Very few rest on their laurels, satisfied with the way they are.

To make internal changes, we do what is known as shadow work (more on this in chapter 8). We go within to find those parts of us that hold us back, that keep us from growing: our emotional baggage, negative thoughts, or past traumas. These are scary things to confront, and our will plays a large part in reclaiming their power. However, once imagination is fired by will, its energy and passion bring us into a whole new way of living.

Living your true will feels right in your gut, or *dan-tien* or solar plexus. A sign that you are pursuing your true will is that obstacles melt away and allies and resources appear. As Goethe said, "The moment one definitely commits, then Providence moves, too. All sorts of things occur to help one that would never otherwise have occurred...Whatever you can do, or dream you can, begin it. Boldness has genius, power, and magic in it." And nothing has more magick in it than a Witch (except possibly nature), so to become a Witch, begin to manifest your dream. Know and use your will, for will is the second step in creation.

The tool usually associated with fire, or will, is the wand. In Harry Potter's world, the wand is a necessary tool for making Harry's will come true. He can't do much magick without it. However, a real Witch doesn't need a wand to do magick; all you need is the power within you. What a wand can do is give you a focus to attract what is needed and repel what needs banishing. Why does the wand correspond to fire, to will? Partly because most traditional wands are made of wood and so will burn, but also because attracting and repelling things requires engaging your will.

If you choose to make your wand, you may simply find a stick on the ground that calls to you, then smooth and shape it. Or you may cut a branch from a living tree—but do it with respect. Find the branch that calls to you; then, touching it, ask the tree if you can have it for your wand. If the reaction feels negative, then thank it and find another branch or tree. Ask again. When you feel a yes, tell the tree you will be back in twenty-four hours; this gives the tree time to withdraw its life force from the branch so the cut will not harm it. When you do cut, do it gently, and leave a drop of your blood—or some hairs or fingernail parings—as a gift of yourself to the tree in thanks for its sacrifice. Then shape and smooth the branch with reverence, cleanse and dedicate it, and use it often. Of course, you may want to buy your wand, and that's all right, too.

The wand is placed on the south side of the altar.

MAGICK WAND

The wand is the most popular tool of any storybook magician. Real Witches do use wands, but they don't have all the powers (or special effects) that Harry Potter's does.

Traditional wands are made from fruitwood (such as apple) or one of the old sacred trees such as oak, willow, or holly. But they may be made from metal, crystal, or almost anything you can imagine.

Wands come in many styles and sizes, but most Witches are happy with a natural stick about 12–18 inches long, the length from your elbow to the tip of your middle finger.

WEST
Silence, Chalice

The third step in creation, and the third side of the Witches' Pyramid, is silence. Silence is the element of water—think of the deep silence under the ocean, of secrets that are not shared but held close. Silence means that when your magickal working is done, shut up—don't dissipate the energy. It also means discretion in general: "Silence knows what's best to hide." Being a Witch is not something you always want to broadcast. Be wary about telling just anyone. Do they need to know? Why? What will you gain (or lose) by telling them? Before blurting it out, you may want to write in your Book of Shadows, answering the three questions posed here.

Silence also relates to that old saying about having two ears and one mouth because listening is twice as important as speaking. This has to do with awareness; you can't be totally aware of your surroundings when you are babbling or planning what you are going to say next. And awareness of your surroundings, and the people near you, is one source of knowledge.

Another aspect of silence is the ability to "enter the silence within." To become a Witch, learn to listen to that still, small voice within, also called your inner bell. This kind of listening, and listening to ancestors, spirits, devas, faery folk, animals, rocks, etc., just can't be done unless you are quiet, for their voices are quiet. Listen in silence; make the silence your own. Record your experiences in your Book of Shadows.

Silence corresponds to the element of water, and the corresponding tool is the cup or chalice. The chalice also corresponds with the womb, the source of creation. The chalice is placed on the west side of the altar and may hold either water or another beverage you have chosen for your ritual.

Another set of tools corresponds to both water and earth. These are the salt and water bowls on your altar, small dishes in which pure water and sea salt are kept for asperging (cleansing) your ritual space before beginning ritual. The usual place for them is in the northwest part of your altar, with the water dish closer to west and the salt dish closer to north.

LAMPS OF ART

The candles used to illuminate a Wiccan altar were called "lamps of art" in the old days. Back when candles were rare and expensive, ordinary people might have used a simple oil or tallow lamp instead. Today we often use paraffin, although many Witches prefer beeswax tapers. In some traditions, the two main candles can represent the Goddess and the God. Often we do spells that involve candle magick, and then the color and shape of the candles will vary according to the purpose—light blue or rose for blessing, green for growth and prosperity, black for banishing, and so on.

NORTH
Faith, Pentacle

This leads us to the north side of the pyramid, the side of earth and faith. For many, this side is difficult, for faith can't be conjured on demand, though it can be inborn or result from repeated experiences that strengthen your faith.

Faith can be described as an inner knowing that is not supported by fact, usually with a good connotation of strength. We speak of having faith in something, so what do you have faith in? What can begin to build this strength within you? Start with having faith in easier things—your dog's love for you, the knowledge that spring will come again with daffodils and tulips. Then move to larger things: your partner's love, the laws of nature, the existence of Goddess/God/Deity/Divine energy. Faith in Earth herself, faith in yourself; faith that all things are connected, that magick works, that you can do magick. Write in your Book of Shadows, and be totally honest with yourself. What do you really have faith in? Where could you use more faith?

The tool associated with the north, the element of earth, and faith is the pentacle. It is a magickal shield carved into wood, made of metal, or formed of fired clay. Symbols are carved or painted on it, usually including a pentagram. So why is the pentagram/pentacle a symbol of earth? The modern answer is that it is often used on the altar as the *paten*, or plate, from which the cakes are served—and the cakes are the bounty of the earth.

Another reason the pentacle stands for earth is that the pentacle is the physical manifestation of the pentagram, which represents the totality of this world we live in, and the element of earth is all about the things of this physical world: rocks and plants and animals, all things material and solid, as well as health, abundance, and strength. According to lore, Witches made their pentacles of wax during the Burning Times so they could be thrown in the fire if the Inquisition came calling. Again, the best way for the beginning Witch to obtain a pentacle is to make one. You can go to a hobby store, get a round disk of wood, and carve your pentagram onto it (see *True Magick* by Amber K for more about the traditional symbols used on a pentacle). Or you could paint the pentagram on the wood, or make the pentacle of ceramic or metal. Or you could, of course, buy it at…you guessed it…your local metaphysical shop, or online as a last resort.

The pentacle is placed on the north part of your altar.

PENTACLE FOR YOUR ALTAR

A pentacle was originally considered to be a magickal shield, and it might have either a pentagram on it or a Seal of Solomon, the hexagram that today is often called the Star of David. Either one was a powerful protective symbol, useful to any magician who intended to call up "demons" to do the sorcerer's bidding. Since modern Witches have no interest in compelling spirits to do things they might resent, the pentacle has shifted its use. It now represents the energies of earth and the center of the material world.

THE INTERIOR IS LOVE

The interior of the Witches' Pyramid is love. The Beatles notwithstanding, love is not "all you need"—but it is essential for being a Witch. The best way to end any spell is with the traditional words, "With harm toward none and for the greatest good of all." That's a good statement of your intent to act from a place of love. It's the love inside that gives the pyramid its shape and strength, just as the love in your life gives it shape and strength. Love keeps it from being hollow and meaningless. To become a Witch, you must know that you are loved and what you love. Write about your sources and objects of love in your Book of Shadows. If you review these often, they can become a great source of power in your magickal workings.

One of the principles of magick is that all things are connected. In this context, that means that if you love anything or anyone, you are loving everything, including yourself. Likewise, if you hate something, you are hating yourself. So start loving freely—what you send out will return threefold (see chapter 7).

There is no tool specifically associated with love; because it permeates everything a Witch does, all of a Witch's tools are about love. Certainly the Goddess and God are love, represented by the light of the candles on your altar, and so the candles are symbols of love. There are usually at least two candles on the altar, and they can be any colors, shapes, or sizes you want—whatever works with the purpose of the ritual you are doing.

YOUR MAGICKAL NAME

Once you have your Book of Shadows and your athame, wand, chalice, and pentacle, you may want to choose a magickal name. It is not necessary, of course, to take a magickal name, and we know many Witches who haven't. Some see their whole lives as magickal; others don't want to seem to be hiding behind a new name; and others just haven't thought about it. However, many Witches do see several advantages in taking a magickal name. Your muggle name has past connotations—baggage—and some of that you don't want to keep in your new life as a Witch. That baggage can limit you and keep you thinking in your old patterns: "Jane is depressed, the under-dog, always the last one picked for team sports...," or whatever your past history was like. A new, magickal name can symbolize who you want to be and are becoming, or reflect an attribute you aspire to, like Lionheart for courage, Cloudcastle for more imagination, or Artemis for slenderness, agility, and a love of animals.

To become closer to nature, you might choose a name from nature. To balance your personality, choose an elemental name: for example, Fireheart could boost your will and energy. To become more flexible, you could become Willow. If you want freedom and to express yourself, you might choose Birdsong. One way to choose your name is to go through lists (see the following pages) and simply find words that speak to you, then put two or more together. Write some possibilities in your Book of Shadows, then say them out loud as if you are introducing yourself to others at a Pagan festival: "Hello, my name is Whitefeather." How does it sound? How does it feel? How it will feel in a year—is it a name you will have to grow into or one that will feel too small in a few months? If it is unusual, are you willing to always spell it out for people—A-Z-R-A-E-L—or will you get really tired of that? Try it now, and see what you come up with!

Choosing Your Magickal Name

Actions: Archer, Chanter, Climber, Dancer, Diver, Drummer, Flyer, Hiker, Hunter, Leaper, Runner, Seeker, Singer, Speaker, Spinner, Surfer, Swimmer, Traveler, Walker, etc.

Animals: Bear, Butterfly, Coyote, Crow, Dolphin, Eagle, Ermine, Firefly, Fox, Hawk, Horse, Lion, Lynx, Marten, Mouse, Owl, Robin, Salmon, Squirrel, Tiger, Turtle, Wildcat, Wolf, etc.

Archaeology: Altarstone, Bluestone, Broch, Cromlech, Dolmen, Henge, Hillfort, Holy Stone, Megalith, Menhir, Standing Stone, Tell, Trilithon, etc.

Astronomy: Aldebaran, Arcturus, Comet, Constellation, Crescent, Deneb, Diana's Bow, Ecliptic, Galaxy, Milky Way, Moon, Moondog, Pleides, Polestar, Sirius, Sol, Star, Sun, Ursa Major, Ursa Minor, Zodiac, etc.

Colors: Black, Blue, Bronze, Brown, Cerulean, Copper, Cream, Electrum, Ebon, Gold, Gray, Gules, Ivory, Lavender, Ochre, Orange, Red, Russet, Sable, Scarlet, Sienna, Silver, Tan, Umber, Verdigris, Vert, Violet, White, Yellow, etc.

Elements: Earth, Land, Loam, Mountain, Rock, Soil, Stone; Air, Breeze, Gale, Sirocco, Sky, Wind, Zephyr; Fire, Blaze, Bonfire, Ember, Flame, Niedfyr, Spark, Torch; Water, Ice, Creek, Current, Lake, Ocean, River, Sea, Spray, Spring, Stream, Surf, Wave, Wavecrest; Spirit, Lady, Lord.

Goddesses: Anahita, Aphrodite, Arianrhod, Arinna, Artemis, Ashoreth, Astarte, Bast, Baubo, Cerridwen, Danu, Diana, Epona, Flidais, Freya, Grianne, Hathor, Hecate, Hera, Iris, Isis, Lakshmi, Ma'at, Macha, Mebd, Minerva, Morrigan, Nuit, Oshun, Quan Yin, Sarasvati, Scathach, Sekhmet, Selket, Sif, Sophia, Tanith, Uzume, Venus, Xochiquetzal, Yemaya, etc.

Gods: Amon, Anubis, Apollo, Ares, Aten, Baldur, Bel, Cernunnos, Coyote, Dagda, Dionysius, Enki, Faunus, Frey, Ganesh, Ganymede, Geb, Heimdall, Helios, Hephaestus, Hermes, Herne, Jupiter, Lugh, Manannan, Mars, Mercury, Neptune, Odin, Osiris, Pan, Poseidon, Ptah, Ra, Saturn, Shiva, Silenus, Sin, Tammuz, Thor, Thoth, Vulcan, Wayland, Zeus, etc.

Herbs and Flowers: Aloe Vera, Alraun, Briony, Chamomile, Comfrey, Dahlia, Day's-Eye, Foxglove, Hagtaper, Mandrake, Marigold, Mullein, Mugwort, Nightshade, Orchid, Periwinkle, Rose, Satyrion, Soloman's Seal, Vervain, Violet, Wood Betony, etc.

Mythological Beasts: Cameleopard, Dragon, Gryphon, Hippogriff, Hydra, Pegasus, Phoenix, Roc, Sea Serpent, Sirrush, Unicorn, Water Horse, etc.

Nature in General: Autumn, Canyon, Equinox, Fall, Feather, Field, Forest, Hill, Isle, Grove, Marsh, Path, Shell, Solstice, Spring, Summer, Tor, Trail, Valley, Winter, Woods, etc.

Spirit Beings: Angel, Archangel, Brownie, Elf, Faery, Faun, Gnome, Mermaid, Merman, Nereid, Nixie, Oceanid, Oread, Pixie, Salamander, Sprite, Sylph, Undine, etc.

Stones: Agate, Amazonite, Amber, Amethyst, Azurite, Beryl, Carnelian, Citrine, Diamond, Emerald, Jasper, Jet, Lapis Lazuli, Malachite, Obsidian, Onyx, Opal, Pearl, Ruby, Sapphire, Sardonyx, Turquoise, Zircon, etc.

Trees: Alder, Almond, Apple, Ash, Aspen, Chestnut, Cypress, Dogwood, Ebony, Elder, Elm, Fir, Hawthorn, Hickory, Holly, Juniper, Oak, Olive, Orange, Pine, Plum, Redwood, Rosewood, Rowan, Sassafras, Sequoia, Spruce, Thorn, Willow, Yew, etc.

Tree Parts: Acorn, Bark, Bough, Branch, Crown, Leaf, Root, Twig, Wood, etc.

Vocations: Clown, Farmer, Fool, Healer, Hunter, Jester, Forester, Ranger, Seer, Smith, Teacher, Warrior, etc.

Weather: Breeze, Calm, Cloud, Dew, Lightning, Mist, Rain, Rainbow, Sirocco, Snow, Storm, Thunder, Typhoon, Weather, Wind, Woods, etc.

Witch Words: Amulet, Athame, Bolline, Chant, Caim, Chalice, Charm, Crone, Cup, Deosil, Incantation, Pentacle, Rede, Sage, Scry, Shadowbook, Sigil, Sign, Song, Spell, Sword, Talisman, Torc, Wand, Will, etc.

Other Ideas: North, East, South, West, Circle, Agrippa, Alchemy, Paracelsus, Athanor, Elixir, Shadow, Glow, Rune, Serenity, Radiance, Stillness, Silence, Courage, Dawn, Day, Morning, Noon, Dusk, Sunset, Twilight, Evening, Night, Midnight, names from other languages, etc.

Now you can round out your toolbox with a few of the lesser-known items that most Witches own. You may already own some kind of divination tool: tarot cards, a pendulum, a scrying bowl (a dark-colored bowl that you fill with water and look in for images), stones or bones to cast, or rune stones (more in chapter 10). Many Witches have a staff (part walking stick and part overgrown wand), a bolline (a white-handled knife used to cut material objects, like carving runes in candles, and cutting herbs), and of course a drum or six for raising power or just getting down in a drum circle.

ℬELL, BOOK, AND CANDLE

One of the early movies about Witches was *Bell, Book, and Candle*, starring James Stewart, Kim Novak, and Jack Lemmon. Though the movie's view of Witches was complete fantasy, the title is evocative of actual ritual practices. Sometimes Witches and ceremonial magicians use a bell to "alert the quarters," or inform the elemental spirits that they will soon be called to the circle. The book is a Book of Shadows, the personal or coven journal that is part of Craft tradition. And of course, candles are always the preferred lighting for magickal work, unless we can manage a bonfire.

Flutes and other musical instruments are always welcome in ritual, and incense is another tool representing air.

Then there are the tools of your specialty. If you are an herbalist, you will have gardening tools, your mortar and pestle, the pot in which you make your teas and infusions, perhaps equipment for making herbal soaps. If you are a tarot reader, you may have several decks, a cloth on which you do the spreads, and a notebook of past readings. If you are shamanically inclined, you will have a journey drum or rattles and bundles of sage or other herbs for cleansing. Don't worry about collecting these all at once; they will come to you gradually as you find your calling within the Craft (see chapter 12).

You will probably be doing most of your magickal work at home, so make your home a magickal place. If possible, your home should feel sacred when you walk in, and be a canvas on which you can paint your magickal life. If that's not possible because you share the space with muggles, or for any other reason, at least set aside a temple space of your own. You may be lucky enough to have a whole room you can devote to this; most people can't. One Witch made her "temple" in the bottom drawer of the bureau in her bedroom. She had everything set up in there, and when she wanted to do ritual, she pulled out the drawer, lit the candles, and was good to go.

THE MAKING OF A BESOM

Doreen Valiente, in her book *An ABC of Witchcraft Past and Present* (Phoenix, 1973), tells us that the traditional "besom," or broom, was made of sacred woods such as oak (strength), ash (magick), birch (purification), or hazel (wisdom). Of course, often the broom plant was also used for the brush part, or "sprays." Witches might also favor a "bune wand" (Scots for a forked stick) or a plain staff, or, on the Isle of Man, even a ragwort stalk.

You will probably find yourself collecting at least a few Witch tchotchkes—witchy things that you just want to have around: a nifty cast-iron cauldron with a pentagram on the side; a picture of the animal spirit you work with; a miniature disco ball to represent Deity in all its myriad manifestations; a Green Man mask to hang on the wall of your home office to remind you of the beauty and power of nature even when you are sitting at your computer; a collection of interesting chalices; a statue of Pan as the centerpiece of your backyard herb garden, etc. That's not even counting the books you will collect. We don't know any Witches who are not readers, and voracious ones at that. Most have five or more witchy books on their nightstand or next to their favorite easy chair.

You may get into color theory or feng shui, the Chinese art of placement for harmonious living. You may decide to make your temple room a miniature replica of the inside of the Parthenon, or paint a goddess on the wall of your garden. At some point, your home and your Witch identity will meet, and, since all things are connected, you will find your Witch life seeping into your ordinary life; it's all good.

You will also find yourself collecting clothing and jewelry—particularly ritual robes and Witch jewelry. Over the course of the years that we have been together, our taste in jewelry has boiled down to one statement: if it has no spiritual or witchy significance, we don't wear it. Every stone necklace and pendant has a special meaning or energy. Our earrings range from Isis earrings to dolphins (Amber's "younger self" animal) to carnelian drops that give Azrael strength to face new challenges. What significance does your jewelry have?

While it's hardly necessary to have a new robe for each ritual, a basic collection is not a bad thing either. We suggest one basic green, black, or white robe for general use, plus a few for the various sabbats: perhaps a brown one for the harvest sabbats, a light pastel one for the spring sabbats, and a red one for Candlemas. Others will find their way into your closet over time—we've just added a honey-gold one for a honeybee ritual we did. You may also want to have special clothing for Pagan festivals. Show up at the festival, see what other people are wearing, and stroll down merchants' row until you find something that you like.

HORSE BRASSES

It was customary in earlier times for protective talismans of brass— one or many—to be fastened on the harness of horses. These horse brasses or smaller "pony brasses" were originally shaped like suns, moons, or other symbols of good fortune, but in time many designs were crafted to commemorate interesting places or people in history, as well. Some show horses, especially the draft breeds, still wear the brasses as part of their show regalia, and many people collect them.

While we will admit we like witchy things, we hope you realize that the trappings don't make the Witch. The tools and tchotchkes speak to younger self/inner child, but it is the mind, heart, and spirit that make the Witch. Knowledge, imagination, will, silence, faith, and love together make magick happen, and your quest for these is what will make you a true Witch.

Witch Jewels for Ritual

During ritual, a high priestess may wear a necklace of alternating amber and jet, symbolizing the cycle of rebirth. She may also wear a crescent crown with the waxing, full, and waning moon on it.

A male Witch may wear a torc, a necklet formed of twisted strands of metal; there is a break, with decorative finials or animal heads at each end. This break signifies the death and rebirth of solar and harvest gods. A high priest may wear an antler crown or headpiece.

In some covens, each member has a silver bracelet or ring, perhaps engraved with a pentagram or the coven sigil.

Look, don't touch

Most Witches are very careful of their ritual tools, and some have crafted or purchased beautiful and elaborate ones. Other Witches prefer a stoneware cup and a windfallen wand from the woods. But all ritual tools have one thing in common: they must not be touched by those who don't own them without permission from the owner. We spend a lot of time investing our tools with our personal energy. Handling by another person changes the energy balance and "feel" of the tool, so it has to be ritually cleansed before it can be used again. So—look, admire, and *ask* if you may touch.

CHAPTER 5
I Am a Witch at Every Hour
Witchcraft as a Way of Life

In darkest night, in forest deep,
Touching magick, wielding power,
In broad daylight, awake, asleep,
I am a Witch at every hour.

Witchcraft is not really about wearing robes and doing rituals; it's all about how one lives. After all, any spiritual path that has no effect on one's life outside a church wouldn't be worth much. In magick, there is a saying from the Emerald Tablet of Hermes Trismegistus: "As above, so below; as below, so above." This means that everything is connected and what we do influences everything around us, just as we are influenced by everything around us. This is true in our way of life—how we live influences how we are *able* to live. If we pollute, then eventually we will not be able to breathe or drink clean water. What goes around comes around. Since the earth is sacred, Witches do our best to treat her well.

However, there is no single Wiccan "way of life"—thank the Goddess! There's no approved food list, no uniform, and no sign-on-the-dotted-line dogma. Witches are individualistic, independent minded, and often downright contrary, so this chapter will be sprinkled with a lot of "mostlys" and "sometimeses," because Witches are worse than cats when it comes to getting sorted, organized, and lined up in neat rows. We'll give you a picture of some ways that *many* Witches live—just remember, Witches love being the exception to any rule.

Those Fictional Witches

"Witches" are perennial characters in books, films, and television shows. Nasty witches abound, but we have seen some friendlier ones too. Remember Glinda of Oz, in the fluffy pink prom dress? Or Wendy the Good Little Witch, who wore red sleepers and hung out with Casper the Friendly Ghost? Samantha the nose-wiggler in *Bewitched*? Sandra Bullock and Nicole Kidman camping it up in *Practical Magic*? Almost all fictional witches have two things in common, though: (1) Their magick is unlikely and miraculous, and (2) They are powerful women. At least we can be thankful for the last part.

It Can Be Easy Being Green

It's true, most Witches are green—not their skins, their lifestyles. Pagans were the original treehuggers and dirt-worshipers, going back thousands of years. There's a chant we love that sums it up beautifully (we don't know the origin, but we give thanks to whoever is the source):

May I walk in the Beauty Way,
Dance upon the sacred path,
Always in step
With the rhythms of Mother Earth.

Witches try to live gently on the sacred earth, but precisely how is, again, up to the individual. Some, like the Reclaiming Tradition, see environmental activism as a spiritual calling. Others simply try to live as green as they can, doing all the little things that add up: recycling, using earth-friendly cleaning and paper products like Ecover and Seventh Generation, cutting down (or eliminating) meat from their diets, driving hybrid cars, and more. Not *all* Witches are perfectly green, but most of us are aware of our impact on the planet and try to reduce it as much as we can. As one chant says, "The earth is our mother, we must take care of her; the earth is our mother, she will take care of us." It's a two-way street.

WITCHES EAT FOOD

What do Witches eat? Everything. Well, not plush animals or garden hoses, but most kinds of food. Witches can be fruitarians, vegans, vegetarians, omnivores, or carnivores. We range from "I will eat only what organic berry bushes choose to drop into my lap" all the way to "Give meat to Krag, raw meat good." Wiccans are all over the continuum.

Diet and nutrition are personal choices, but Witches make those choices consciously and have to find a way to square them with the Wiccan Rede: "An ye harm none, do as ye will." (More on the Rede in chapter 7.)

More and more of the Craft are facing up to agricultural and food issues that affect the planet. Some Witches have always favored a diet that's healthy, organic, sustainable, and local. Now many more are thinking hard about food and making healthier, sustainable choices.

It's not always possible to have a perfect diet, but it's always possible to improve it. Within an omnivore diet, for example, there are choices you can make:

- Free-range chickens and eggs
- Grass-fed beef or bison instead of corn-fed
- Less red meat, more fish and poultry
- Fewer processed foods and carbohydrates
- Less salt, sugar, and high-fructose corn syrup
- More food grown or raised locally
- Plants without dangerous pesticides and fertilizers, animals without artificial growth hormones

Vegetarians, vegans, and fruitarians can buy produce that is organic and locally grown; it's even better if you can grow some of your own. A good reference for anyone who wants to eat more intelligently is *The Omnivore's Dilemma: A Natural History of Four Meals* by Michael Pollan (Penguin, 2006) or Pollan's *In Defense of Food: An Eater's Manifesto* (Penguin, 2008). A good guide for becoming a vegan gradually is Alicia Silverstone's *The Kind Diet: A Simple Guide to Feeling Great, Losing Weight, and Saving the Planet* (Rodale Books, 2009).

Before meals, you may want to give thanks. For example:

Thank you, O Lady of the Fields, Lord of the Forests,
For the Earth's bountiful harvest and this meal before us;
Thank you, spirits of those living things which now nourish us,
To our health and strength, in the service of the gods. Blessed be!

Or this version, which children will enjoy:

Give thanks to Mother Gaia,
Give thanks to Father Sun,
Give thanks for the fruits of the garden where
The mother and the father are one. Blessed be!

HOUSING
No Gingerbread

Where do Witches live? Anywhere—except gingerbread cottages. Many Witches dream of land in the country, living close to nature, planting an organic garden, and perhaps living in a communal setting. For most, this is not the reality. Witches live in cities, in suburbs, and in rural areas. It's not about where we live, it's about how we relate to the environments we do live in.

A wise man once said, "If you want to save the planet, stay put." He wasn't talking about cutting back business and vacation travel so much as choosing a long-term home, then learning to know and love that place, and living in harmony with the environment there. People who frequently change residence sometimes have no particular relationship with the natural world; their apartments, offices, commuting routes, and social connections become their world.

Sometimes life makes us go somewhere else to live. But even if you have to move often, you can still create a relationship with the environment you're in while you are there. Be there. Be conscious. Sit, walk, "dance the land." Notice where the sun rises and sets, and the moon. Pay attention to the seasons. Notice the plants, animals, and birds who share your neighborhood. Take photos often. Get to know the natural cycles. It's about consciously being in your environment instead of sleepwalking through it.

If you have the chance to build your own home, do it thoughtfully and in harmony with the land. Build with local materials, whether that's cordwood, adobe, or stone. Consider rainwater harvesting, especially in arid climates. Control erosion and conserve the soil.

If you move into an existing home, consider what kind of retrofitting makes sense. Add a sunroom or greenhouse for passive solar energy? Insulate everything better? Install photovoltaic panels? Look into your local utility's green energy program; it may cost a bit more to get alternative energy (wind, hydroelectric, solar), but it lets the utility know we want our energy to come from green sources. Do an energy audit to learn how you can reduce your energy consumption, and use Energy Star appliances.

When your home is created or re-created as you wish it, then extend your senses. What watershed are you in? What geological formations surround you? What affects air quality? What is the wildlife like? How has it changed in recent times? What is the historical climate pattern, and how is it changing?

Become an advocate for the ecosystem where you live. Find out what the environmental issues are and who's involved. Are there chapters of the Sierra Club, the Nature Conservancy, the Audubon Society, the local "Friends of Whatever River"? Join with others who care about the earth. The organizations listed in appendix C serve environmental causes and are national or international in scope. Each organization has contact information and the Charity Navigator rating, which rates organizational efficiency and financial health.

HOLEY STONES

Some stones have a hole naturally weathered through them by wind or water, or created by fossilized worm tunnels. These stones are called hag stones, Odin stones, or holey stones. Witches will sometimes tie a red ribbon through the hole of smaller ones and use them to protect a home or barn, or wear a very small one as a protective amulet. One legend says that if you peek through the hole, you will be able to see the land of Faery. These stones are most effective if you find one yourself or receive one as a gift.

A House Blessing

Every home needs ritual cleansing and blessing, especially when you first move in. The former residents may not have left ghosts hanging around, but they surely left their energy imprint. Clear it out, bless the house, and put up wards, or protective amulets. Clearing energy is simple if it is done before you move in. Don't bring your stuff in until after the space has been cleansed and blessed. If you've already moved in, do a thorough housecleaning first, then work around your furniture.

To cleanse the house of unwanted energies, bless it, and put up wards, you will need the following:

- A medium-sized bowl filled with pure water. Add three pinches of salt to it.
- An incense stick or an incense holder and incense. Don't light it yet.
- A feather.
- Pieces of rose quartz (to allow only love in) or hematite (to keep negativity out) or both, two per outside door. (These are the wards.)

Go through your home, opening every door, closet, and cupboard. Starting at the front door, pick up the bowl of water and walk clockwise through the house, keeping the wall close on your left side, in and out of every room. Sprinkle saltwater every two feet or so (and into the closets and cupboards and on the windows and doors), saying, "With earth and water, I cleanse this home so that it may become a place of comfort and love." Say it over and over as you go through the house. When you return to the front door, end with, "So mote it be!"

Next, light the incense. Pick up the feather in your left hand and the incense in your right, and follow the same path throughout your house. This time, touch the feather to the wall by the front door at about shoulder level, and keep it touching the wall all the way through the home. Say, "With air and fire, I cleanse this space so that it may become a home of happy thoughts and vitality." When you return to the front door, end with, "So mote it be!"

Finally, dunk the rose quartz and/or hematite in the saltwater and pass them through the incense smoke, saying, "I charge thee to guard and protect this home from this day forward; so mote it be!" Then go to each exterior door in turn, ending with the front door, and place the stones on the floor on either side of the door. Say, "May only good things, thoughts, and people pass this threshold; so mote it be!" and close the door. Visualize a warm pink and golden glow surrounding your home, protecting it and you from harm. Leave the incense to burn out in the living room, and wash your hands with the rest of the saltwater.

A simpler home blessing may become a part of your daily practice. Visualize the pink and golden glow remaining strong and bright, and strengthen it each day by saying, "May this home be protected and safe. So mote it be!"

$\mathcal{B}$LUE BEADS FOR PROTECTION

Ceramic beads in a vivid blue color provide luck and protection,
especially for horses and other animals, according to the old stories.
This custom seems to have spread from the Middle East—
perhaps a bit of folklore that the European crusaders
brought back from the Holy Land.

HEALTH FOR HEALERS

How do Witches differ from cowans as far as taking care of their health? Well, Witches come from a long line of healers. Many Witches seek health and wellness rather than just the absence of pain or other symptoms. Exercise, nutrition, clean air and water, rest, and relaxation are priorities. Most Witches respond to illness and injury with a combination of modern medicine and traditional, noninvasive cures.

We are open to many different branches of healing: energy work, herbs, Chinese medicine, Ayurvedic healing, aromatherapy, soul retrieval, and much more. Witches may use Feldenkrais, yoga, Pilates, the Alexander Technique, reiki, and a host of other modalities. Most Wiccans are not totally averse to allopathic medicine—drugs and surgery—but we see that as only one part of the healing realm.

Mental and emotional health therapies are just as diverse: we may try psychoanalysis, but we're just as likely to go for music therapy, art therapy, equine therapy, Jungian, rational-emotive, humanistic, or mead-around-the-bonfire therapy.

And to get really witchy, we'll use divination, ritual, and spellwork as part of our wellness program. Witches know that the body is more than a flesh machine: the

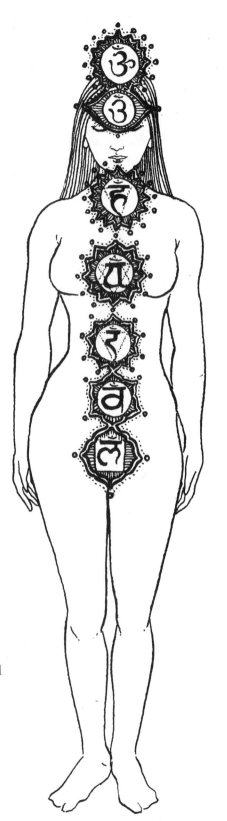

The chakras: from top, crown (rules
higher knowledge), third eye (rules
higher intuition and psychic skills),
throat (rules communication), heart
(rules love), energy/navel (rules vital
energy), spleen/sexual (rules sexual
desire and passion), and root (rules
survival)

mind, energy field, emotions, and spirit are all essential to wholeness and harmony. A large part of this is your energy field, so a chakra check, or "running the energy," may be just what you need. Chakra? We'll explain.

The fire part of you is your will, desire, and passion, but also your energy field.

The human body is permeated and animated by electromagnetic energy. The human aura is the glow from that field that can be seen visually or sensed in other ways. Everyone has an energy field, even the dead. But yours, assuming you are not dead, is very obvious and easy to work with. Your energy field is essential to life and health, so it deserves quality time and attention.

Within the human energy field, the places where the power concentrates are called chakras. There are seven major ones (see illustration, opposite page) and many minor ones.

The simplest way to sense your energy field, including both aura and chakras, is to be still for a few minutes, ground and center, and become consciously aware of your energy. It's a little like a regular breast self-exam (or the guy equivalent) in that you have the chance to notice if something is wrong and treat it.

Many people can see the energy field, some in color, some in shades of gray. Look at any living thing; it's easiest when the subject is in front of a neutral background and not too brightly lit. Or look at yourself in a mirror. You may first notice an overall glow extending out for a couple of feet, or perhaps a brighter, inner layer that surrounds the body close to the skin.

"But I've tried, and I can't see auras!" No problem. Some people sense auras in other ways. You may feel the aura kinesthetically. Close your eyes and feel the outside of your skin, then extend your senses out about an inch. You may feel a warmth or sense a thickening of the air. When you hold your palm over a chakra, there may be a slight tingle or pressure.

If you're very auditory, then imagine the note that your aura is humming; is it clear, strong, and even? Move your hand over different chakras, and listen to the hum change. Over time, you can learn what the changes in pitch, volume, and timbre tell you about the health of each chakra.

To be more thorough, focus on each of the seven major chakras and evaluate them in turn. Trust your intuition, your "inner bell." If a chakra feels weak or painful, breathe healing light into it: take a deep breath and imagine it as light suffusing the area, then exhale any imbalance or negativity you find there. Meditate on how that chakra is reflecting events in your life and what you need to do to heal. You can also pick colors that will balance your energy field. Mentally check each of your major chakras and choose a color to support the weakest one:

- If the root, or base, chakra is weak, wear red, brown, or black for survival, basic material needs, and grounding.
- If the sexual, or sacral, chakra is weak, wear orange for creativity or procreation.
- If the energy, or solar plexus, chakra is weak, wear yellow for power and the ability to manifest your goals.
- If the heart chakra is weak, wear light green or rose for love and emotional health.
- If the throat chakra is weak, wear blue, aqua, or turquoise for communication and clarity.
- If the third eye chakra is weak, wear indigo or dark blue for intuition, psychic ability, and perceptivity.
- If the crown chakra is weak, wear violet or white for spiritual enlightenment, wisdom, and connection with the Divine.

An elaborate, powerful exercise called the Middle Pillar involves visualizing the chakras, "running energy" through them, breathing, and intoning the names of Deity. This is explained in detail on pages 96–99 of the fifteenth anniversary edition of *True Magick: A Beginner's Guide*, among other books.

RELATIONSHIPS
Sacred Connections

Every living thing is an aspect of Deity. When you interact with any other being, that relationship is Deity face to face with Deity. Some beings are highly intelligent; some are not. Some are consciously aware of their own divinity; most are ignorant. Some are in harmony with their own sacred nature and live as perfect expressions of the Divine; some are damaged, alienated, and filled with fear and hatred.

But all are sacred, whether they know it or not. Therefore, from the Witch's perspective, all relationships must include respect, acceptance of differences, and recognition of immanent divinity.

Adults in relationships should be able to look at each other and realize "Thou art Goddess, thou art God." When adults make a commitment, they may participate in a handfasting; this is sometimes called the Wiccan equivalent of marriage, though it is not identical to a mainstream marriage. A handfasting ceremony may include a woman and a man, or two people of the same sex, or three or more adults. The partners may commit for "a year and a day," and then decide whether the commitment should dissolve or be renewed. However, they may also handfast for "as long as love shall last," for a lifetime, or for eternity. Sometimes relationships end, and then a handparting ceremony is held, if possible; each party is released and sent forth with as much gratitude and good feeling as possible.

Another special relationship common to Witches is that of covenmate, or coven sister or brother. This will be explained in more depth in chapter 11. There is also a bond of loyalty and goodwill between all members of the Craft.

SEXUALITY
Love and Pleasure

Sexuality is a blessing from the Goddess and part of the celebration of life. Yet if one party is exploited or coerced, or a promise to a partner is betrayed, or a woman becomes pregnant but is not happily so, then the gift has been tainted by human cruelty or foolishness.

"All acts of love and pleasure are my rituals," says the Goddess. Generally, any relationship is acceptable when it is between consenting adults and does not harm them or others. What about premarital sex? The same standard applies: will it harm anyone? If it results in guilt, anger, disease, or an unwanted pregnancy, it violates the Rede (see chapter 7).

What is NOT okay are power-over, exploitative relationships. Sexual activity between an adult and a child or young person is wrong—it cannot be a relationship of equals. Sexual activity with someone else's partner is wrong unless all parties have consented to open relationships. Sexual activity is wrong if one partner knowingly conceals having a sexually transmitted disease and imperils his or her sexual partner. Sexual activity is wrong if you are not ready and willing to care for children and yet fail to use birth control.

The freedom to be and to choose is paramount within the boundary set by the Rede. Our community welcomes straight people, gay people, bisexual people, transgender people, and those who cannot or will not identify themselves in any category. Many of our most respected leaders and teachers have some alternative sexual orientation. Are we totally free of bias and bigotry? No. We still have work to do. But most often, we judge a person by their character and accomplishments, and not by their sexual orientation.

Some conservative covens do focus on the male-female pairings that are central to any fertility-oriented religion. Many others are not worried about promoting human fertility, since we seem to be rapidly overpopulating the planet.

The general attitude toward human sexuality in the Craft is very open and positive. In the past, Witches have been accused of everything from "carnal knowledge of the devil" to "mass orgies by moonlight," and we want to be sure those ridiculous stereotypes are not spread any further. Joyous sexuality and responsible, ethical behavior can coexist; in the Craft, they come as a package.

CHILDREN
To Love and Protect

The care of children is a special and sacred responsibility. Parents, teachers, and anyone in a position of authority over children—pretty much all adults—must respect and protect children and young people.

Lots of Wiccans have children, and they are precious to us. One might expect a Witch-raised young person to be a little different from the average kid, and we think they are. They tend to take after their parents: independent-minded, individualistic, resourceful, and strong. Most Wiccan families encourage their kids to follow their own dreams and to think for themselves when it comes to religion.

Beyond this, it's quite difficult to generalize about Pagan children and youth. Only a few decades ago, most people who came to Wicca had been raised in a mainstream faith. Now we are seeing a generation of young people who were raised in the Craft.

They are teaching us, the elders, what that means and how they will tackle life's challenges. Stay tuned as an extraordinary new generation brings Wicca to the next level of evolution.

Pyewacket and Fido
Animal Companions

Some Witches do have black cats around the house…and so do some Methodists. Many Witches have cats of other colors, and many Witches are really dog people. Some Witches put up bat houses, but more put up birdhouses. The occasional Witch will enjoy the companionship of a snake or six. There are even Witches who live with hamsters and gerbils and poodles.

Virtually every Pagan loves and respects animals, both wild and domesticated, and will share their homes with the tamer ones wherever possible. A shaman friend rehabilitates injured raptors and always has a few owls and hawks and crows around the house. Another friend supports a sanctuary for wolf hybrids, and many have made their back yards into mini wildlife sanctuaries.

Note: Our family dog, Kyoshi, has read and approved this message.

What familiars do

A Witch's familiar can be any animal, but often they are cats, dogs, or toads. In some of the old Burning Times stories, they have names like Pyewacket and Greediguts.

Technically, a familiar is an animal that helps the Witch in her or his magickal work and is not "just" a pet. Because animals have keener senses than humans, they can act as sentries and let a Witch know when a spirit being is close by or whether the energy is positive or negative. Some familiars can help with grounding energy, and some can even assist with divination or love spells.

GODS AND ANIMALS

Many or most of the Pagan deities have their favorite critters.
For example, cat lovers will want to talk to Freya, the Norse
goddess of love and war, or Bast, an Egyptian sun goddess in a
cat's body. Like dogs? Hang out with Hecate or Artemis. Horse
people will have much in common with Epona (Celtic), Rhiannon
(also Celtic), or Poseidon (a Greek sea god). You can read
about Athena and her owl, or Odin and the Morrigan and their
ravens. Brigit loves boars, foxes, and farm animals…and so on.
Seems like most Pagans, divine or mortal, are animal lovers.

WITCHES IN THE WORKPLACE

What do Witches do for a living? Almost anything, but we do seem to be strongly
represented in two areas. One is health care: doctors, nurses, doctors of oriental medicine, chiropractors, massage therapists, medical technicians, naturopathic doctors,
herbalists, reiki masters…the list goes on. After all, we do have a very old tradition of
healing, originally as the wise women and cunning men in rural villages.

The other field that has lots of Witches is technology: computer programmers,
Web designers, online networkers, and so forth. Just because we are treehuggers
doesn't mean we are technologically backward—quite the contrary!

Wiccans can be found in almost any field. Whatever field you're in, work consciously, with respect for the planet, knowing that all people and creatures you interact with are sacred.

Does your employer have a recycling program…promote energy conservation…
use healthy cleaning materials…and do environmental impact studies? Do they treat
all people well, regardless of race, religion, gender, ethnicity, sexual orientation,
and so on? If your employer is way out of line with your values, can you help them
become greener or more respectful and compassionate?

If that's not possible where you work, why are you in that job? And if your job is
not the work you dream of doing, what *is* your dream job and why aren't you doing
it? As far as your vocation or livelihood, what is your true will?

WITCHES AND WEALTH

Most Witches believe in the abundance model of the universe: "The Goddess provides." She will give you what you need, or a lot more. (However, it won't be handed to you on a platter—work with the gods of abundance, then do the work to make it happen.) This contrasts with the common scarcity model, which proclaims that resources are finite, competition is natural to humanity, that it's a dog-eat-dog world.

The abundance model doesn't mean you can be careless or spendthrift with resources. It means that with wise planning, careful use, and minimum waste, there will be enough. We should reduce, reuse, and recycle, because it's kinder to the planet. If everything is sacred, so is abundance—to be used well.

Truthfully, there is also a "poverty is spiritual" mentality among some Wiccans. This has been a recurring theme in religion for millennia. However, poverty means inadequate housing, poor nutrition, lack of health care, limited education, and crime…none of which promotes spiritual growth.

Now in some circles, wealth has a bad name because people see it misused. We see a lot of conspicuous consumption in our society: presidential candidates with seven houses, corporate executives who make millions every year even as their companies fail, people who have several fancy cars, folks who gamble away thousands in an evening, and so on. We find that rather revolting.

But, in fact, money is neither good nor evil; it's just a tool, another form of energy that can be used or misused. Remember that a Witch has the use of all things but is addicted to none. Money is fine to have and spend when it is in service to the Goddess-in-all; it's not fine if it addicts you or corrupts you into a greedy, selfish, wasteful person.

A custom popular with some Witches is tithing, the ancient idea of donating ten percent of one's gross income to Spirit, usually in the form of charity. It makes us think about what is really important and deserves our support. It encourages us to be more careful with the income that's left. And it doesn't even require a sacrifice, because according to the Law of Return, our generosity will return to us three times over.

Many people feel they don't deserve abundance—maybe you're one. Your beliefs create your reality. Work on believing that you are sacred and deserving, and that it's perfectly fine to gather abundance *if it's well used*. Be a rich Witch.

Pagans and Consumerism
Buy This, Buy That!
New! Improved! On Sale Now!

Buy more clothes, more food, more cleaning products, more cosmetics, more electronic communication gadgets so you can share inane comments with your friends 24/7—are all people in industrialized societies first and foremost consumers of products? How do Witches relate to this buying and selling frenzy?

There is no simple way to explain Wiccan attitudes toward material possessions. On the one hand, we like to enjoy the material world and all the sensual pleasures associated with it. We have no belief that earth is sinful and heaven is pure, or that there is a division between the material and the spiritual. So eat, drink, and be merry, and enjoy things while you are here, as long as no one is harmed.

But that's the tricky part—"as long as no one is harmed." On an overpopulated planet, if some people have more than they need, does that mean that others have less than they need? Or is there plenty of everything—food, water, energy—to go around? More and more, people have to think about the impact on the earth of manufacturing, transporting, and possessing *stuff*. Witches too are asking the tough questions:

- Where does the product come from?
- What is the cost to the planet (including the carbon footprint involved in gathering the raw materials, manufacturing, and transport)?
- What is the impact on the workers who make it, move it, and sell it?
- What does it do to the planet during its operation or functional lifetime?
- What happens when it's no longer usable? Can it be recycled or do we "throw it away" (except there is no "away")?
- If we did not have a certain product, or made and used it only locally, what would be the effect on the planet and humanity?

For a one-stop website that explores these questions, go to www.GreenAmerica Today.org.

Maybe there is a clue in the little marketplaces, or merchant rows, that are part of every Pagan festival. There you can find brightly colored, festive clothing; jewelry; books; polished stones; drums and flutes; and ritual tools. Rarely are there mass-produced products of plastic. Many of the goods for sale are handmade and unique. Yes, Witches like stuff…but they *really* like stuff that is beautiful, practical, and can be made with little or no harm to the earth.

TRANSPORTATION
My Other Car Is a Broom

What do Witches drive, or do they? Sadly, we can't really fly brooms, apparate, or use floo powder as Harry Potter does.

Owning a vehicle is a trade-off between convenience and the cost to yourself and the earth. Do you really need to own a car? Do you live in midtown Manhattan and hardly ever travel outside it? Use public transportation and rent a car when necessary, or pool ownership with family or roommates. City dwellers in Europe ride bicycles and use buses, trains, and subways; what a concept!

If you live in the country, do you really need a Hummer? Maybe you need a car and a truck, but do you need a gas hog or can you drive a hybrid, or at least something fuel efficient? Whatever you drive, keep it tuned, watch the emissions, inflate your tires properly, and minimize trips. Mother Earth would prefer we ride brooms, but when we can't, let's do the alternatives responsibly.

Purchase carbon offsets to balance out the carbon your lifestyle puts into the environment. Search the Web for "carbon offset."

FOR GODDESS' SAKE, GET SOME CLOTHES ON (OR OFF)

Can you recognize a Witch by his or her clothing?

Well, at rituals the robes and stag crowns probably give us away. And in areas with privacy, the nudity of some traditions provides a hint.

But in public, don't expect Witches to walk around in ritual gear or raggedy black robes and pointy hats (although we might at parties, just to mock the stereotypes). And not many Witches are really suit-and-tie or skirt-and-pantyhose types. In the range between, anything is possible.

GOING SKYCLAD

Skyclad means "clothed by the sky" and is the Witch word for "naked" or "nude." Some covens and individuals perform their rituals skyclad for various reasons. Some say they can raise power more easily without clothing in the way. Others like the feeling of utter freedom and the wind on bare skin. Many say our bodies are a gift from the Goddess and should be honored, not hidden.

After one gets used to it, and especially among coven sisters and brothers, it seems quite normal. However, many covens simply do their rituals in robes.

Most Witches, most of the time, don't stand out from the crowd. We have had centuries of practice in blending in, looking ordinary and harmless. Some Witches will wear pentagram jewelry out in public; more wear magickal jewelry that doesn't look particularly witchy. But most of the time, a Witch will look like—anyone.

Only the Witch will know that clothing colors have magickal meanings. Almost the first thing you do each morning is choose your clothes for the day—and that can be a decision based on magick. Select your outfit according to the magickal significance of colors and materials.

Colors can be chosen for the day of the week, each of which corresponds to a planetary energy and one or more deities:

Sunday (the sun; solar deities of light, healing, energy, and intellect): Gold, yellow, orange. *Corresponding metal:* Gold, vermeil, gold-washed.

Monday (the moon; lunar deities of magick, change, and intuition): Silver, silver-gray with black. *Corresponding metal:* Silver.

Tuesday (Mars, Tyr/Tiw; deities of action, assertiveness, and war): Red. *Corresponding metal:* Iron or steel.

Wednesday (Woden, Odin, or Mercury; deities of the hunt, the harvest, war, victory, wisdom, poetry, prophecy, and magick; guides of the dead; and, in

Mercury's case, trade, abundance, travel, and communication): Rainbow, any and all colors. *Corresponding metal:* Bronze or mixed metals.

Thursday (Thor, Jupiter, and deities of thunder, lightning, and weather in general; strength, rulership, protection, the sky and the heavens): Purple, red, and gold. *Corresponding metal:* Tin (tin is hard to find; use pewter).

Friday (Venus; deities of life, love, and creation): Rose/pink, aqua green. *Corresponding metal:* Copper.

Saturday (Saturn; deities of limitation, discipline, organization, and time): Black. *Corresponding metal:* Lead (however, we do not recommend wearing lead jewelry, even if you could find some; hematite and pewter are safer substitutes).

Of course, you may not have a huge wardrobe in all the colors of the rainbow. That's okay; your chosen color for the day can be represented by an accessory such as a scarf, tie, vest—even your socks!

Where the Pointed Hat Came From

Why do Witches wear pointy black hats? Well, real Witches don't, unless they're having fun mocking the stereotypes. But why do fantasy witches almost always have them?

At least three theories exist: (1) The hats represent the "cone of power" raised by Witches at their rituals. (2) The hats are like women's headgear that was out of style centuries ago—think about princess hats—and were a way to belittle Witches for being hopelessly old-fashioned. (3) They are a distant descendent of tall, conical metal crowns with magickal and astrological symbols on them worn by the priest-kings of early civilizations.

Who knows?

Many Witches wear magickal jewelry with stones of the appropriate colors, or simple amulets such as a holey stone or shell, or even elaborate talismans designed to store particular kinds of energy. The metals used in jewelry correspond to different deities or energies, as described in the list. In choosing jewelry for the day, you can think out the appropriate correspondences, use the charts in the appendices, or simply go with your instincts.

THE SOCIALLY AWARE WITCH

The majority of Witches tend to be progressives, socially and politically, but there are certainly exceptions. Almost the only broad issues where the Craft is unanimous are (1), that the environment is sacred and must be respected and protected (exactly how is not always so clear), and (2), that freedom of religion must be defended.

But let's look at a few other hot-button issues and see, if we can, where Witches stand.

War and Peace: Many Wiccans serve honorably in the military, but they are no flag-waving warmongers. In keeping with a "live-and-let-live" attitude, most would rather leave other nations alone unless our homes are directly threatened.

Abortion: Discussing abortion seems to be a no-win proposition, which is perhaps why there is very little real discussion of the issue and a great deal of rigidity and anger surrounding it. As with most issues, Witches have no official position or dogma as a religion. Doubtless there are sincere Witches on both sides of the issue; the majority (if numbers mean anything) would probably say that abortion should be a woman's personal choice, with input from her family and physician. The Rede says harm no one, and this may be a case where choosing the lesser harm must be left to the individual Witch's higher self.

Drugs and Alcohol: Most Witches would rather keep their faculties unclouded by drugs, and develop their psychic and spiritual abilities without that complication. However, there are certainly some who like recreational cannabis, and a few others who will carefully experiment with entheogens—plant substances that are said to trigger religious experiences, such as peyote and certain mushrooms. We would caution anyone exploring this path: first, be aware that such use can be dangerous, especially if it's not guided by someone very experienced in such practices.

Second, if the practice is illegal, are you willing to pay the penalty for violating the law? Remember too that a Witch arrested on drug charges harms the entire Craft community by association. It's unlikely that a headline would read LUTHERAN ARRESTED FOR DRUGS, but you can bet you would see the headline WITCH ARRESTED FOR DRUGS. This alone is enough to keep us, the authors, far away from illegal drugs.

Alcoholic beverages are legal for adults to consume, and their effects are better understood. However, we know Witches who never touch alcohol, Witches who will only take a sip of wine in the circle, Witches who drink lightly and socially, and some who really, really savor a good bottle of mead. A Witch who truly lives by the Rede may not drink to the point where her health is damaged, nor may she drive a vehicle if alcohol impaired. Under the Rede, a Witch who drank so much that he lost control of his thoughts, his tongue, or his reflexes would be creating the potential for harm. A Witch who does overindulge too often may want to take advantage of Pagan 12-step programs. Almost every festival hosts meetings, and you can find more information by searching "Pagan 12-step" on the Web.

Civil Rights and Race Relations: Witches by their very nature support civil rights, because if civil liberties and personal freedoms are threatened, we are among the very first targets. Regarding race, skin color is irrelevant to us. The majority of Witches are Caucasian, because Wicca originated in Europe and many are drawn because of their ancestral connections. Sometimes it is simpler for whites to connect with their European roots, blacks to connect with their African roots, etc. However, the Craft is open to anyone who is called to it, and we are fortunate that some people of color have found their spiritual home in the Craft community. Many folks of Hispanic heritage are discovering the Craft as well, which seems quite natural, since Spain (and Central and South America) were very Pagan places before the Catholic Church became dominant there. To repeat: we judge a person by their character and accomplishments, not by their race or cultural heritage.

We could explore a hundred more social issues, but in most of them the conclusion would be the same: Witches are free to choose the position they hold under the guidance of the Rede: harm no one, and follow your true will.

Alara lives in a restored Victorian mansion covered with gingerbread woodwork and runs her own veterinary practice, where she uses reiki healing and crystals as well as modern drugs. She loves Japanese manga (comics) and is dating a Druid physicist.

Wolfy lives in a small town outside Seattle and works in a bakery. In his spare time, he raises exotic tropical plants and designs Internet games that boost the players' psychic skills. He socializes with Luanne, a retired long-haul truck driver who paints giant Goddess murals.

Rita and Vixen run a bed-and-breakfast in the mountains, and have been partners for twenty-seven years. They also make wands to sell to Witches worldwide, and they have three dogs and a large snake as companions.

Torrin, Murf, and Petal are transforming some overgrazed grassland into an organic truck farm and selling their produce to fancy restaurants in three states. Murf is developing new mushroom hybrids, Petal likes to rebuild muscle cars from the sixties, and Torrin works online part-time as a financial analyst. They have been in a polyamorous relationship for seven years.

Joan and Marty are married with three children and have converted an old barn into their model energy-efficient home. Joan is a magistrate judge, Marty writes science fiction novels, and the whole family takes care of the hamster colony together.

Terra lives in a high-rise in the center of a large city and works for the Animal Control division of the police department. She wonders when the owners of her apartment building will notice the raised-bed herb gardens on the roof.

They're all Witches.

Every Witch's lifestyle is unique and personal, but the foundation for all is the Wiccan Rede, a great love of the earth, and the ability to see Goddess and God in all things.

As a Witch, you will represent the gods and the Craft to the other inhabitants of this planet. Your life will express one more facet of the infinite and sacred diversity of all things. So be yourself, and live the way that only you can live while seeking wisdom, love, and power within.

And yet, we haven't really covered how Witches live until we look at one more thing. Most Witches have certain things they do each day to help them along their spiritual and magickal path—a daily spiritual practice. We'll explore that in the next chapter.

DEEPENING YOUR PRACTICE
Exercises Toward a Wiccan Way of Life

- On separate sheets of paper, list the various aspects of life we have discussed:

  Sustainable living • Food • Housing
  Health care • Relationships • Sexuality
  Children • Animals • Work/Career
  Money/Wealth • Consumerism • Transportation
  Clothing • Social involvement

  Now think about your life in each of these areas. Which feel as though they are genuinely witchy in style already? In which areas do you feel like you have a very muggle lifestyle? Rank them from "most witchy" (magickal, spiritual, natural) to "least witchy" in your life.

- List three priorities for improving your life in each area, and write down a plan or series of steps to achieve them.

- Brainstorm a list of the people you most admire and respect. What is it about them and their lifestyles that you would like to be and do yourself? Write your observations in your Book of Shadows.

CHAPTER 6
Spiraling Into the Center
Your Daily Practice

At your altar, seek the way,
Touching magick, wielding power,
With Spirit start and end each day,
I am a Witch at every hour.

To become superb at anything, be it tennis or art or starship design, you must practice. To become a great Witch, you must practice. Many Witches do, in fact, have a daily practice in order to grow magickally and spiritually—but because we are so incredibly individualistic, what we do to hone our skills and nourish our spirit varies dramatically.

Here are some examples:

- Rosewood meditates on positive questions each evening and spins fire poi.

- Aventurine lights incense on her altar, thanks the gods for the new day, and selects one tarot card to study.

- Cybele visualizes a great pentagram and then mentally moves from point to point, checking the energy of each element within her life.

- Twig walks in a forest grove by his house and greets the trees and wild things.

- Lyonesse works to clear and balance her chakras, then chants to the Goddess.

- Blade does breathing exercises, then practices his martial art, dedicating his bo staff work to Scathach, his patron goddess.

- Amethyst chooses a stone that intuitively feels like the energy she needs that day from her large collection of gemstones and crystals; she greets it, thanks it, and places it in her pocket.

- Catnip visits her garden during the warm months, shares energy with each plant, and talks with the deva of that species. In the winter, she converses with a different plant deva each morning before her altar.

Some have done essentially the same thing for years, at least outwardly, deepening the experience as they mature spiritually. Most of the others have changed their practice as they felt the need.

Choose a personal daily practice that serves your needs. You may want to energize yourself each morning for the day's tasks. Perhaps you want to get some quick guidance for the challenges you are going to face each day. You might feel the need to express thanks each evening for all the blessings in your life. Your sessions could be designed to keep your magickal skills honed and ready for action. Your practice could help you balance the elements in your life. Maybe you just need to ground, center, and gather your resources.

We will discuss some of the infinite options for your daily practice as a Witch, but first, some basic decisions need to be made. Will yours be a completely personal activity, done in solitude? Will you work with your spouse or partner? If you have children, will they be involved? Or will you do some combination of these, perhaps working alone in the morning, having a bedtime ritual with the children, and giving thanks later in the evening with your partner?

Of course, if you don't share your home with other humans, it may just be you and the cat, or dog, or iguana—whomever.

Think about timing as well. Morning practices are fine to energize and seek direction for the day. Your schedule may allow a daily practice at any time during the day, perhaps during your lunch hour or breaks from work or study. And many Witches like to do progressive relaxation and meditation just before bed.

Your daily practice will evolve into something unique because you are unique. But you will probably want some suggestions to get started; experiment with these techniques until you find the activity or combination that fulfills your needs. Write the results of your experiments in your Book of Shadows.

YOUR CHANGING ALTAR

A personal or family altar can be an ever-changing work of art *and* part of your daily practice. A basic altar is described in chapter 3. However, you can get very creative with your altar arrangement—and you can redo it daily, weekly, at each moon cycle, or for every sabbat.

For some Witches, it feels appropriate to change the altar each day, to reflect the energies and goals for that day. You would not have to change every part, only as much as feels helpful. Simply changing the candles to a different color is enough to change the focus: for example, orange for energy if you feel sluggish, or pink for healing if you feel a cold coming on. Or you might have one central magickal object that changes according to need: a quartz crystal for clarity, a rose in a bud vase for romance, or a chunk of hematite or tiger iron for stamina. Tarot enthusiasts might place a different card in the center each day, while others may prefer a carefully select-ed runestone. (For more on tarot and runes, see chapter 10.)

On any special occasion, take the time to redo the whole altar; you don't have to wait for a sabbat or a new lunar cycle. Job interview? Health crisis in the family? Looking at a new project? A fresh altar will help you be ready.

WORDS OF POWER

Witches are careful with their words, because words have power to heal or harm. They can become part of your daily practice if you craft them carefully into a tool for self-transformation.

You have probably heard some of the affirmations floating around the New Age community: "I am a child of the universe, filled with rainbow light…" Most are harmless, but perhaps they could be more powerful.

Here are some simple guidelines for writing or choosing a powerful affirmation:

- State your intention in the positive: "I am strong" rather than "I am no longer flabby and weak." Your younger self will focus on the adjective, such as "strong" or "flabby," and has difficulty understanding a state of not-being.

- State it as something that exists now or is coming into existence, rather than in the future tense. For example: "I am the balance of the elements…" or "I am becoming more balanced every day…" Don't say, "I will become…," because that's always in the future and can't manifest now. And don't say, "I am trying"; remember Yoda: "Do or do not; there is no try."

- Keep it simple. Concentrate on what you need most right now.

Write affirmations you like in your Book of Shadows, whether you create them or find them in your research. Carry around three-by-five-inch index cards, and when you come across a well-phrased statement that is especially meaningful to you, write it down (transfer it to your book later) and tape it to your bathroom mirror.

Apart from affirmations, you can read passages from an inspirational book, favorite poems, or anything that has power for you. You can choose things that are appropriate to the season and sabbat if you wish.

Sometimes you may want to switch from a positive statement to a question, to broaden the possibilities. For instance, if you don't know what you want to be doing, instead of saying, "I have a great new job," you may want to ask a question: "What wonderful financially abundant opportunities are coming my way?" This adds the opportunity for a financially abundant non-"job" to come to you. Meditate on this question, and unexpected answers may pop up!

Remember, all words are Words of Power.

THE BREATH OF LIFE

Breathing is good. We highly recommend it as part of your daily practice.

Well, yes, you breathe all the time—but do you often breathe *consciously*, in a particular pattern, for a definite purpose other than survival?

If your daily practice includes a balancing activity for each element, then intentional breathing is one way to include the element of air. Hindus have a name for the practice of intentional, controlled breathing: *pranayama*. Here are three different styles, from many possibilities:

Energizing Breath: Boosts your oxygen and clears your lungs of stale air. Either stand up or sit tall. Inhale deeply, all the way down into your abdomen, then expel all the air. Now inhale three times quickly through your nose without exhaling: three deep sniffs. Immediately open your mouth wide and blow out all the air through your mouth quickly, making a *ha* sound. Do it again: three quick inhalations through the nose, one explosive exhalation through the mouth. Do five to seven complete breaths; then pause, and breathe normally. You should feel energized and clear-headed.

Relaxing Breath: Inhale deeply through your nose to a slow count of four, then exhale through your lips to a slow count of four. Make sure you inhale all the way down into your belly. Relax your neck, shoulders, and facial muscles as you breathe out, and try to expel the very last dregs of old air from the bottom of your lungs. Do ten complete breaths, and focus only on your breathing. With each exhalation, allow your whole body to relax more. You will feel calm and relaxed.

Earth and Sky Breath: Breathe slowly and regularly, with your inhalation the same length as your exhalation. Now visualize a beautiful place on the earth: mountains, sea, or forest, whatever you choose. Breathe in the beauty and strength, and at the same time allow love for the earth to fill you. Do this several times. Then, as you breathe out, send your love for Mother Earth into her heart. Then feel her love returning to you, enfolding you, and inhale it. Breathe more love back to her. Do this several times.

   Next, visualize the starry heavens or the brilliant sun in a blue sky if you prefer. Breathe in the beauty and power, and allow love for the heavens to fill you. Do this several times. Then, as you breathe out, send your love for the sky into Father Sun. Then feel his love returning to you, filling you, and inhale it. Breathe more love back to him. Do this several times. You may feel connected, loved, and even exalted.

You can read books about breathing techniques and experiment with different types until you have a collection of favorites that are especially powerful and effective. Continue using them in your spiritual practice and whenever you need them during the day.

MEDITATION
Still Moments

When most people think of meditation, they imagine sitting quietly and releasing all thoughts, letting the mind be still and empty. That's a fine practice, but there are many other styles of meditation to choose from.

Meditation is a mental discipline used to get beyond the "thinking" mind into a deeper state of relaxation or awareness. Different meditative disciplines emphasize different goals—from achieving a higher state of consciousness to greater focus, creativity, or self-awareness to simple relaxation and serenity.

Meditation is also a good way to connect and harmonize with Deity. Many Witches have a statue or picture of their favorite god or goddess on their altar, and spend a few quiet moments daily just contemplating it. By the way, this is not "worshiping idols" any more than when a Christian looks at a picture of Jesus. No one believes that a statue of Athena is alive, but it can be a powerful visual focal point for meditation.

Practice your meditation in a quiet room or peaceful outdoor setting with few distractions. It can be done seated, lying down (stay awake), or during any repetitive activity such as walking or swimming. Saying the rosary or using mala beads involves rhythmic touching and movement as well, and these are also forms of meditation.

During meditation, you can focus on a statue or artwork, or on your breathing, or on a flower, candle flame, affirmation, mantra, passage from a holy book, or the names or attributes of Deity. In a walking meditation, you might focus on the play of your muscles, the rhythmic movements, and simply being in your body. In Chinese qigong, the practitioner concentrates on the flow of energy within the body; in hatha yoga, on the kundalini energy rising through the chakras; and in bhakti yoga, a goddess or god is the object of devotion.

One popular form of meditation is to concentrate on a question. Zen Buddhism provides mind-bending koans, such as "What is the sound of one hand clapping?" You could choose a passage from one of your favorite authors. Programs such as Access (AccessConsciousness.com) ask things like "How does it get any better than this?" Then there are the Big Questions, such as "Why am I here?"

In another type of meditation, you do not focus on one thing, but open your awareness to the environment around you. A walking meditation in nature is natural for Witches; just let the breeze, the light, the bird songs, and the colors flow around and through you; this is relaxing, cleansing, and energizing at the same time.

COMMUNING WITH THE GODS

Direct communication with Deity or an aspect of Deity is the core of many Witches' daily practice. (Of course, you can also talk to spirit guides, animal allies, plant devas, ancestors, faery folk, trees, stones, and other people.)

We are all familiar with prayers, which are one way to communicate with Deity. At any time you may talk to Deity either as the Goddess or the God, Mother Goddess or Father God, Lady and Lord, or as a very specific aspect such as Oshun, Hermes, or Freya.

Witch customs differ from Christian prayer. Witches do not generally kneel to pray—we respect our gods without subservience. Nor do we rely only on prayer—simply asking God to put some favor in our laps feels much too passive to us. We are more likely to do a spell for something and invoke the powers of a deity or other ally as we do the work, then follow up with practical action.

Witches are always aware that we are communicating partly with Deity-within, not with a separate being who is Out There Somewhere. Thus, when you pray "to" the Chinese goddess Quan Yin, you are invoking all the compassion you have in your own heart and mind, as well as the divine compassion that permeates the universe.

It is simple courtesy to give thanks frequently, rather than just whining to heaven whenever we want something. This can be a specific expression of gratitude—thanking a particular tree for shade on a hot day—or a more general one, as in giving thanks to the Goddess for life. You might give an offering: a drop of wine as a libation, a stick of incense, a silver coin for a tree that gives wand wood, or perhaps a dance, song, poem, or ritual.

Talking to the gods, with or without words, is fine, but it's also a great idea to be silent and listen. The divine powers don't always speak to us as clearly and directly as we would like: "This is God. You should eat more—you're too thin—and that cigarette can't be good for you. By the way, the winning lottery numbers for Saturday are…"

The messages often will be both simpler and subtler—hope in the sunrise, comfort in a warm bed, or persistence from the tiny, tiny barrel cactus spotted while walking today in the high desert. Or the messages may come through the words of others, in a quiet conversation with a friend, the words in a book, or the lyrics of a song. One purpose of meditation is to teach ourselves to be still and listen, for the Goddess and the Old Gods are always speaking.

JOURNALING
The Mighty Pen

Journaling can be done together with dreamwork or divination, or separately as a meditation on the day ahead or the day that is closing. If done in the morning, it is a way to prepare your mind, emotions, and spirit to create the kind of day you want. If it is an evening exercise, it can be used to remember, absorb, and integrate the events of your day.

Journals do not have to be in perfect English, or even complete sentences, to be valuable. Sometimes phrases, impressions, or poetry can best express your thoughts and feelings.

Writing about your life should be a disciplined effort to record and understand it, not merely stream-of-consciousness babble. Return to your earlier journal entries from time to time, and see how your views and attitudes have evolved. Then you can consciously choose to continue your life in the same direction, accelerate, slow down, or choose another path.

MUSIC HATH CHARMS
And Songs and Chants

If you already sing or play a musical instrument, then naturally you will want to include that part of your life in your spiritual practice.

But what if music is not really part of your life? What if you've never been part of a band or chorus, or have never learned to play anything? What if your musical talent is limited to sliding a CD into a boombox?

In his *Bill of Musical Rights*, David Darling said, "There are no 'unmusical' people, only those with no musical experience." Deep inside you there is ability. Your heartbeat tells you that you could make rhythmic sounds with a drum or rattle; your breath says you could breathe into a wooden flute. You may never be an opera singer or world-famous pianist, but you can make music.

How does music fit into your daily practice? Think about it. If you meditate, why not have beautiful music playing softly in the background (here's where that slide-in-the-CD skill is handy). Or play recorded music and dance—or breathe—to it.

But you can also make music to celebrate your life and blessings, to give thanks to Mother Earth or the Hornéd God of the Wilds. The music you make does not have to be someone else's song, printed in proper notation and played correctly. It can be totally spontaneous and free, whatever comes out of you. Pound that drum, dance and shake those rattles, blow those pipes! There are no music critics listening. Maybe it's just a joyful noise, and that's fine. Maybe over time you can make something more complex and pretty to the ear, and that's great too.

And if you are already a skilled musician, then create and play and sing as an offering to the Old Gods and just to make your spirit happy. Here are some Pagan chants you can learn, if you want. Just remember that your music never has to come out of a box or stay in one.

Chants for a Daily Practice

Unfortunately, due to increasingly strict copyright rules, we can't give you the words to some of our favorite chants, even with attribution. However, we can list them with websites where you can get the words and the tune, so that's what we'll have to do. All websites were accessed on Samhain 2010. Websites change and disappear, but if you put the words of the title in quotes, you can find websites that have the lyrics and tune. All songs can be accessed at www.bornpagan.com/upca /song_cycle, unless specified otherwise.

Circle Chant (We Are a Circle) by Rick Hamouris, Kate West, or Unknown, depending on your source.

- http://www.youtube.com/watch?v=EQQWwFnk198 (alternate tune, wonderful pictures)

Goddess Chant by Deena Metzger, the chorus in "Burning Times" by Charlie Murphy on *Rumours of the Big Wave* CD, EarthBeat Records, Redway, CA, 1992, 1993.

We All Come from the Goddess by Zsuzsanna Budapest

Elemental Chant (Air I Am) by Andras Corbin Arthen

Air Moves Us by the Reclaiming Collective

The River Is Flowing by Diana Hildebrand-Hull

The Blood of the Ancients by Charlie Murphy

Hecate, Cerridwen by Patricia Witt

Silver Shining Wheel by Peter Soderberg

GARDENING

Many Witches have gardens that they tend with great love. This is one of the best ways to attune with nature, to see the wonders that sun, rain, and fertile soil can bring to the world. Consider planting a garden, or even a small pot of herbs, and caring for it every day.

There are as many kinds of gardens as there are unique gardeners. Some people enjoy the classic English flower garden, one that's bound to have some faery folk playing in hidden corners. Or you may prefer to grow herbs for healing and magick; just be sure you are well trained before you use them medicinally! If your soil allows, it's always wonderful to have a vegetable garden; you can eat something absolutely fresh and organic that you grew yourself.

A xeriscape garden is perfect for dry areas. Create beautiful groupings of drought-resistant native plants among rock formations, and support it with a water-catchment system on your roof. You can also design gardens based on the elements, the zodiac, chakra colors, certain periods in history, or other cultures. Be careful not to plant invasive species that will crowd out the locals, and of course avoid chemical pesticides and fertilizers.

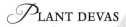

Every plant species has a deva, which might be called the soul of the species. People who work closely with these spirits can learn about the plants from the source and become amazingly adept gardeners, farmers, or foresters. A modern example of this relationship between humanity and the plant kingdom is the Findhorn community, where the founders created lush gardens on a salty beach in northeastern Scotland. Though we certainly have no monopoly on this art, many Witches work closely with the devas in their own gardens.

SPIRIT IN MOTION

Never assume that spiritual practice has to be passive or still. Sure, you can sit and meditate—but you can also move, and isn't that almost the very definition of being alive? Go for a walk, and just be with nature; dance, and play with mudras. Mudras?

Mudras are sacred body postures, or arm and hand positions, associated with yogic practice. However, lots of religious traditions have something similar. Christians assume a particular position to pray, Muslims bow toward Mecca and touch the earth with their foreheads, and so on.

Are there particular postures associated with Witchcraft? Yes. Most of them don't involve kneeling or bowing, though. (Witches are generally not good at humility.) Instead, we stand in a circle. A priestess may stand with her arms out and up to her sides, forming a human chalice, in the "Drawing Down the Moon" position (see illustration, next page). Then she fills herself with the energy of the Goddess. The male equivalent is standing with feet together and arms crossed over the chest and is known as the Osiris position; it honors the god of death and resurrection.

You can also create your own special mudras to honor the spirit or deity of your choice. You can even do elements with your body: sway like a tree in the wind (air), let your hands flicker and dance like flames (fire), make hula-like side-to-side gestures

The "Drawing Down the Moon" position

like waves (water), or stand strong, feet apart, like a mountain (earth). If you have a power animal or ally, honor it by moving as it moves, or dancing its spirit: ramble like Bear, soar like Eagle, leap like Salmon.

And now we have moved into dance, one of the most ancient forms of celebration and worship. Your dance can be spontaneous and creative or elaborately choreographed and stylized. You can learn the folk dances of your ancestors or just swirl around in circles or hop up and down in one place.

No matter what the rest of your daily practice looks like, make sure your body gets in on the action.

RITUAL

In a sense, any daily practice can be a ritual, a planned and purposeful activity. One thing that distinguishes a formal ritual from, say, a simple spell or a daily walk is that rituals are normally done in sacred space, intentionally created. Which is to say, you will "cast a circle," or define sacred space, as explained in chapter 8. Many Witches like to do their daily practice within a circle, even if it's cast in a quick and simple way.

Others feel that there is always a circle protecting their temple or altar space simply because they have created one there so often. They do not feel the need to make it official every morning or evening.

If you wish, you can do a more formal ritual each day, complete with cleansing the space, casting, calling the quarters, and invoking Deity. Of course, this takes time, and it may extend the period you need to set aside each day. There is also a risk that doing the process every day will result in mindless repetition instead of a spiritual experience. You are the only one who can decide whether formal ritual should be part of your practice—daily, occasionally, or rarely. As always, trust your intuition, your instincts, your inner bell.

Designing a daily practice can be daunting; there are so many different ways to do it, and there is no single right way. Your daily Witch thing must be tailored to what you need at this time in your life. Now, part of what you need might be stability and continuity, in which case you may pick a practice that feels right and do the same thing for weeks or years. (To avoid getting stale, you might do that thing and occasionally add something very different.)

You might want to experiment with all the things we've discussed here, one at a time, to see how they affect the quality of your life. Perhaps you could try meditation for a week or longer, then try music and chanting for a while, and just go through the list. Write your experiences in your Book of Shadows. Favorites will emerge.

It's fun to try to design "the perfect daily practice," which we think would involve all the elements of you: physical movement, mental challenge, emotional exploration, energy work, and connection with spirit—and, of course, it should be doable in less than eight hours! Brainstorm a list. Read the myths and legends of Deity in all its forms. Write poems and invocations, sing and chant, dance, perform mystery plays in ritual, wear colors or jewelry that have significant meaning, learn about the gods and goddesses, redecorate your altar, do a quick divination.

Then ask yourself, "What else could I do?" Get creative, even wacky. Remember, "An ye harm none," you can try anything. Walk outside and focus on a different element each time. Meditate on a mind-expanding question like "Who am I?" or "What function do I serve as one tiny part of Gaia?" Try a new sensual experience each day, to honor your body. Massage your own feet. Explore the contours of your ears. Taste a food you've never tried before. Smear raspberry jam on your tummy and lick it off—good luck. (Is this a religious practice? That depends on your frame of mind and your approach to it.)

The keys are to be consistent, creative, and fully present. *Consistent* in doing something in a spiritual context every day, even if not the same thing. *Creative* in trying new things whenever you become bored or too comfortable. *Fully present* in body, heart, mind, will, and spirit.

You are finding time and making the effort to re-create yourself daily. You are worth it.

Deepening Your Practice
Exercises in Creating a Daily Practice

- Try the activities suggested in this chapter for a week each. Make notes in your Book of Shadows as to how each one felt and how it influenced your day.

- Ask yourself if there is anything that you *already* do every day that could be done in a more mindful or spiritual or satisfying way.

- Ask your friends if they have any daily practice to help them face the day or bring it to closure. You may get some good ideas.

- Explore the idea of a combination of brief activities that could be done daily to strengthen and focus you physically, mentally, energetically, emotionally, and spiritually. (A single activity might accomplish more than one of these.) Try a different combination each day for a week, and choose the one you like best.

CHAPTER 7

Are You a Good Witch or a Bad Witch?
The Rules of Witchcraft

An ye harm none, do as ye will,
Touching magick, wielding power,
Heal always, never kill,
I am a Witch at every hour.

Wiccan ethics can be summed up in eight words:

An ye harm none, do as ye will.

This is the Wiccan Rede. The old Anglo-Saxon word *rede* means "counsel" or "advice." Though it is short, the Rede contains much more than meets the eye. Let's begin with a rough translation: "As long as you harm no one, act as your true will leads you."

One word at a time:

An = An archaic word meaning "if" or "as long as."

Ye = The individual Witch, you.

Harm = Anything that causes lasting damage.

None = No one, yourself included.

Do = Act. The Rede is not concerned with thoughts, attitudes, or beliefs except as they influence our actions.

As = In some versions, the word "what" is substituted.

Ye = You. The responsibility for how you act is yours alone.

Will = Your true will, the part of you that flows from your higher self and has a deep understanding of right and wrong. "Will" never means just "want" or a whim.

No one can follow the Rede perfectly. On some level, we do harm just by living: we eat plants and perhaps animals, we make waste, we disturb habitat by building houses. But we are allowed to survive—the aim here is to minimize harm to anyone, including ourselves.

Lately it has become crystal clear that humans are doing immense damage to the environment: harming the planet we live on, and the other residents, in ways that are not necessary to our survival. As a species, we strip-mine the land, release poisons into the air and water, and cause other species to become extinct.

Fortunately, many people are becoming aware of this and taking action. We are finding ways to live with less damage to the earth and its life. Recycling, solar and wind power, organic farming, habitat conservation and restoration, eating locally grown foods—all are ways to survive with less harm.

Ultimately, who decides what "harm" is? Well, for the environment, Mother Earth speaks clearly enough to us; we just need to pay attention. The disruption of local ecologies and the dwindling of other life forms is a clear signal that we're doing harm. In human society, we know that stealing, assault, and murder almost always constitute harm. Beyond that, Witches generally let each individual decide what "harm" means to them.

The next part of the Rede that causes confusion is trying to define "none" in relation to harm. In order to survive, to eat, most people harm something. Are you willing to eat sentient animals, like dolphins and octopi? What about cattle and pigs? Should you exclude all animals from your diet? Can you ethically eat vegetables that have been pulled from the earth or cut from their roots? Depending on where you draw the line, you may choose to be an omnivore, a fish and poultry eater, a vegetarian, a vegan, or a fruitarian. The choice is yours, and your conscience is the only authority you must answer to—but be clear about why you eat the things you do.

Aside from the definitions of "harm" and "none," the other challenging part of the Rede concerns your will. How can we know what our true will is? Well, first of all, our true will cannot cause unnecessary harm to ourselves or others, or else the Rede would contradict itself. Secondly, it is a question of trust. Do you trust yourself to know the difference between right and wrong—not just in your head (because our minds can rationalize all kinds of nonsense), but in your heart and spirit?

Many people don't even try to figure out what's right and wrong. They simply turn to an authority figure, like the law or the church, and say, "Tell me the rules." They assume that as long as they follow the Ten Commandments or the statutes of their community, they're living a moral life.

That works—sometimes. But what if you are a German citizen in 1940, and the law is controlled by the Nazi Party? What if you are a good Christian during the Inquisition, and the church says to burn the heretics?

Either you trust yourself to know what is right or you trust someone else. For a Witch, the authority is always your true will, which always reflects the will of nature and the gods.

Naturally enough, people make mistakes—and not only Nazis or Inquisitors. You might want something very badly for purely selfish reasons and persuade yourself that it's your true will. Fortunately, there are some checks and balances:

- The first part of the Rede: *harm none*. If someone would be harmed, and it's not preventing a greater harm, the proposed action is not your true will.

- Your community. If the people you love and respect are opposed to your action, you need to rethink it. Often several heads are better than one.

- Your elders. Who are your teachers and your role models? Who do you respect for their wisdom and compassion? Ask for their counsel.

- Your divination. Sometimes the tarot cards or runes help us see consequences that we would otherwise overlook.

- Your inner bell, or gut instinct. If it feels wrong, it probably is. Keep looking for a better way.

In the end, it's about responsibility to yourself and others. You have to make the hard choices, and the buck stops with you. You can't excuse yourself by saying, "I was ordered to do it" or "So-and-so (a person, institution, or law) said it was all right"— not if you're a Witch.

The Eight-Line Rede

The Rede has not only an eight-word version but also an eight-line version. Many Witches like that it includes the ideal of "perfect love and perfect trust," as well as the Rule of Three, or Threefold Law, as explained further on. (There is also a very poetic version that is longer still, written by Adriana Porter as a gift to the Craft decades ago. You can find it in appendix E.)

Bide the Wiccan Law ye must,
In perfect love, in perfect trust.
Eight words the Wiccan Rede fulfill:
An ye harm none, do as ye will.
And ever mind the Rule of Three:
What ye send out comes back to thee.
Follow this with mind and heart,
And merry ye meet, and merry ye part!

The Ordains
Traditional Laws of the Craft

The eight-line version of the Rede begins with "Bide the Wiccan Law ye must." What law is this? The Rede itself is "only" advice or counsel, even though it is taken extremely seriously by most Witches.

The "Law" refers to the Ordains, or Ardaynes, a rather mysterious list of laws whose origin has been lost. The version that seems oldest has 162 sections, most of which comment on coven operation and the correct uses of magick. It is written in archaic-sounding language and includes words that have left common usage such as "skith" (harm), "bales" (technically, evils or sorrows; in context, probably dangerous herbs), "apies" (opiates), and "appenage" (land, revenues, or property in general). Yet some of the phrasing sounds suspiciously modern as well.

There are a few clues as to its time of origin. One phrase says, "in some future time…the persecution may die and we may worship our gods in safety again." This, and the emphasis on secrecy and discussions of Witch-hunting and torture, imply that it was written during a time of persecution, i.e., roughly the period 1400–1700 CE. But another section mentions that "in England and Scotland, 'tis now many a year since a Witch hath died the death," so perhaps it is post–Burning Times. Perhaps some parts are old, and other parts are much newer.

Whatever its origin, most of it seems applicable today. Because Wicca is a folk religion and has never claimed to have the revealed word of God, most Witches don't care where the Ordains came from as long as they are consistent with the spirit of the Craft and work well. The late Lady Galadriel wrote an updated version that is very well received by many modern Witches, *A New Wiccan Book of the Law* (Grove of the Unicorn, Moonstone Publications, P.O. Box 13384, Atlanta, GA 30324, USA or through http://www.abaxion.com/bbb7.htm). An even simpler, more modernized version can be found in appendix A-2 of *CovenCraft: Witchcraft for Three or More* (Llewellyn, 1999).

Following are some key ideas from the Ordains:

- It violates the Ordains to reveal anyone as a Witch. Every member of the Craft has the right to decide whether or not he or she will be "in the broom closet."

- We are forbidden to boast or threaten, much less use magick to harm others. Any of these could bring attention or persecution to the Craft. The Craft must be preserved.

- If the community agrees, we can use magick to bind others from doing harm, but that's the most we can do when using magick to influence others.

- We cannot use magick to harm others, but above and beyond that, we must oppose anyone who works evil magick and depose any leader who has violated the Law.

- We do not take money for doing magick, period. It is done freely or not at all.

- There's nothing wrong with magick for your own benefit—say, for healing or protection or prosperity—as long as it is really needed and no one is harmed. But it must be debated and endorsed by the coven if there is any doubt.

- In conflict between Witches, the laws of the Craft and the leaders of the Craft are to be used to resolve the dispute. Taking an issue to public courts can only harm the Craft (unless someone's safety is threatened, such as in domestic abuse). If the people involved are from different covens or solitary, they can agree to arbitration by respected elders.

The Ordains have the weight of tradition and common sense behind them. If they didn't work in the real world, Witches would ignore them. But they contain a great deal of wisdom and are honored by most who know them.

THE NEED FOR INFORMED CONSENT

As a guideline, we assume that unwanted interference in a person's life may constitute harm. Thus, for example, we do not perform magick for an individual unless they request it—or give their informed consent.

If Aunt Molly is ill, we might think, "Oh, I'll do some healing magick for her." Not without her consent! Her body may need that illness for reasons we don't understand—to cleanse toxins from her system, to force her to get some rest, to enable her to get love and attention. So we may *offer* healing magick but not proceed without her understanding and permission.

About the only exceptions to this rule are magickal workings for your children and magick to defend yourself. Because you have responsibility for your child until they come of age, and you presumably have more wisdom or experience than they do, you are allowed to set rules for them—and perform magick if you feel it's in their best interest. Needless to say, this means magick for healing, protection, wisdom, and other positive aims.

Magick for self-defense ordinarily doesn't require that you act against another person; shielding yourself and your loved ones is normally enough. But in emergency situations, you may have no choice but to bind an attacker or disable them using magick. This should never be done for trivial reasons, such as because you are miffed or embarrassed; but to protect your life or the lives of your loved ones, do what you must.

An older version of the eight-line Wiccan Rede makes this clear:

Bide the Wiccan Law ye must,
In perfect love, in perfect trust.
Eight words the Wiccan Rede fulfill:
An ye harm none, do what ye will.
Lest in thy self-defense it be,
Ever mind the Rule of Three.
Follow this with mind and heart,
And merry ye meet, and merry ye part!

LAW OF RETURN/RULE OF THREE/THREEFOLD LAW

There is a law that is called the Law of Return. It is a natural law, not an arbitrary rule invented by humans, and it has a great bearing on human ethics. Sometimes it is stated this way: "Whatever you send out will return to you." But other people explain the same concept in different ways:

"What goes around, comes around" (Folk wisdom)

"A liberal man will be enriched, and one who waters will himself be watered" (Judaism)

"What proceeds from you will return to you" (Confucianism)

"Whatever a man sows, that he will also reap" (Christianity)

"If a man sow poison, he cannot expect ambrosia" (Sikhism)

"You cannot gather what you do not sow; as you plant the tree, so it will grow"
(Hinduism)

If you act with honor and kindness, this is what you will receive from the universe. That's simple enough. But Witches understand this somewhat differently from other traditions: we believe that what you send out returns magnified as much as three times. There is some universal force or structure that multiplies the energy you get back called the Law of Return, the Rule of Three, or the Threefold Law.

In northern New Mexico, there is a place called Echo Amphitheater, a great stone cliff with a giant semicircular scoop out of the side, created by wind and water. If you stand in front of it and call out, your voice echoes back to you again…and again…and again. It's very much like the Threefold Law. The only difference is, at the amphitheater you get the results immediately and in the same medium you sent them (sound), whereas your karmic actions in life might return to you later on or in a different form.

So don't expect to hand ten dollars to a homeless person and have an angel appear a moment later to give you thirty dollars. The return usually doesn't happen that quickly and may not be in the same coin.

Although *sometimes* it works very fast and clearly. A covenmate of ours once was stuck in traffic and wanted to turn left but realized too late that the street was barricaded in that direction, so she turned on her right-turn signal and waited for a break in traffic. The driver behind her, who couldn't see the barricade, honked furiously. Finally, our friend managed to slide into the right-hand lane and get clear. Through her rear-view mirror, she saw the angry honker make a whipping left turn—and squeal to a halt in front of the barricade, blocking three lanes of oncoming traffic… who all started honking at him.

Because your actions are magnified, you have the power to affect the world more than you know. A single act of kindness can spread and grow until many lives are changed—but an act of cruelty is also multiplied.

Modern Witches get tired of seeing nasty, green-skinned, warty-nosed
"witches" in fantasy movies. But the movie writers get one thing
correct: the Law of Return. Invariably, the witch-villains experience that
karmic backlash within ninety minutes of performing their evil deeds.
In Oz, the Wicked Witch of the West gets melted by a bucket of water;
Snow White's queen/witch was made to dance in red-hot iron shoes (in
the original fairy tale, not the Disney version); and Hansel and Gretel's
witch was shoved into the oven. Yep, the Law of Return works.
So why would any intelligent Witch do evil to others?

A SAFETY VALVE FOR MAGICK

Sometimes you may work magick with all kinds of good intentions but wind up
making a situation worse. This isn't surprising; we are not omniscient and cannot
see every outcome of our acts. Half the comedies (and many tragedies) in books and
movies are based on this premise:

- Good-hearted people face a problem.
- People think of a scheme to fix everything.
- Unforeseen results make it worse.
- Good-hearted people scramble to repair the bigger problem, and so on.

Witches have a kind of safety valve that we attach to most magickal workings, just
in case. After the intention has been stated, we add the phrase "With harm toward
none and for the greatest good of all." This essentially gives the gods (and our deep
minds) permission to deactivate the spell if it would cause harm.

A Note about Love Spells Particularly

One question we are asked by new Witches is this: "So, how do I do a love spell and still be ethical?" This, at least, recognizes that there is an ethical question here: "How can I do a love spell without interfering with the other person's true will, which would violate the Rede?" Indeed, a typical love spell (pink candles, rose essential oil, and a couplet that includes "and bring Johnny to me") *would* violate the Rede, since you are asking the gods to override Johnny's true will. Instead, hard as it may be, change the rhyme to say, "bring my true love to me." This changes the spell to an ethical working, and you may discover that Christopher (or Marilyn) is truly your love.

The Golden Rule

We've all heard of the Golden Rule, which almost seems like the ultimate moral and ethical standard. Many faiths have versions of it:

"Do unto others as you would have them do unto you" (Christianity)

"What is hurtful to yourself do not to your fellow man" (Judaism)

"Do unto all men as you would wish to have done unto you, and to reject
for others what you would reject for yourselves" (Islam)

"Hurt not others with that which pains yourself" (Buddhism)

"What you do not yourself desire, do not put before others" (Confucianism)

"Treat others as thou wouldst thyself be treated; do nothing to thy neighbor
which hereafter thou wouldst not have thy neighbor do to thee" (Hinduism)

There's nothing wrong with the spirit of these moral imperatives; they are designed to help you act with empathy toward others and treat them well. The only difficulty, from a Wiccan perspective, is that other people may not want, need, or object to the same things you do. Some people like juicy steaks; some like crunchy vegetables. Some people go bungee jumping; others would rather read a good book. Some people cover their skin with tattoos; others do not like sharp needles poked into them repeatedly. You can't assume someone else's needs, desires, or objections are the same as yours.

For Witches, the imperative is "do no harm," not "do as you would have done to you." What's the difference? Well, treat other people as *they* want to be treated, not the way *you* want to be treated, but only up to the point, in your best judgment, where harm may be done. You are not obligated to assist anyone in something that seems risky or harmful, no matter how much they think they want it.

IF YOU DO WRONG

Despite our best efforts, we all occasionally mess up. We act carelessly or let negative emotions control us, and someone gets hurt. What then? Do what any honest, responsible, ethical person would do: admit your mistake and do whatever you can to heal the situation. Witches take responsibility for our own actions—if we make a mess, we clean it up.

Occasionally the person (or group or animal or place) you harmed is out of your reach and you cannot remedy the situation directly. Then you can work magickally to mend whatever can be mended, sending positive energy for healing—not forcing it on the individual but making it available to their higher self for them to use in whatever way seems best.

As an additional way to balance the scales, find someone to stand in for your original victim and then do something positive for them. Maybe you were cruel to a dog long ago, and it has since passed on to the Summerland. You can't help that animal except by sending good energies to its spirit self, but you feel the need to make up for what you did in some tangible way. Well, adopt a puppy from the nearest animal shelter, and give it a good home. If that's not possible, volunteer at the shelter and help care for the homeless animals, or dog-sit for friends and give their animals lots of attention, affection, and good care.

Someday, in the afterlife or another incarnation, you may have a chance to meet face to face with the one you hurt; until then, do all you can to balance your mistake with love here and now.

In case it isn't clear, Witches do not believe that simply apologizing is enough. It's a start but must be followed by practical action to repair what was broken. Acts of contrition, like apologizing to God or saying prayers as penance, seem irrelevant to us. Guilt is also useless, unless, pathetically, it's the only thing that will motivate you to take positive action. As the Hawaiians might say, if you steal a pig, don't tell God you're sorry while you enjoy roast pork. Give the pig back.

WITCHES WITHOUT THE REDE

Some who claim Witchcraft as their path (non-Wiccan Witches) do not choose to follow the Rede. We think of them as "Old Testament Witches"—if they feel they have been attacked, they will demand "an eye for an eye." Some will not hesitate to do binding spells or active curses if they feel their enemies deserve it.

We wonder whether such magicians are aware of the Law of Return or have any idea that their negative magick will come home to them, grown into something bigger and more destructive than what they originally conjured. A few may believe that they can shield themselves against the Law, but that's like trying to shield yourself against gravity. You can fly for a little while, but gravity is still waiting when the wind dies or your fuel tanks are empty.

The fact that we support Wiccan ethics will cause some of the Redeless Witches to dismiss us as "fluffy bunny" Pagans, obviously not dark, edgy, or fierce enough to join their club. If that's the choice, we would rather be bunnies than hunters who repeatedly shoot themselves in the foot. That just doesn't seem wise to us.

Or perhaps we are more like wolves, who behave more ethically than many humans and never get into magickal feuds or revenge trips.

ETHICAL BEHAVIOR AND THE CRAFT COMMUNITY

How does the Craft community respond to unethical behavior? There are many Craft communities throughout several countries, all different. In some areas, local Witches are able to live and work in harmony almost all the time.

In others, conflicts may be settled by appealing to a council of elders, respected Craft leaders who will hear both sides of the dispute and make a decision according to the traditions of the Craft and common sense. Their work may lean toward mediation or toward arbitration. Not everyone may like the outcome, but it would certainly damage one's reputation to participate in the process and then defy the decision of the elders.

In extreme cases, where an individual misbehaves badly and cannot be guided to a more positive path, they may be shunned by the local Craft community. Shunning is an ancient and powerful technique; it means that the person is totally ignored. No one in the Craft community will speak to them, do ritual with them, or invite them to sabbats or festivals; it is as if they no longer exist. They have to start over in a different community.

What about bringing in secular law enforcement—the police? The Ordains do say to keep Craft disputes within the Craft, but if there is a serious crime, most Witches would invite the police and courts to do their work. Once someone has seriously violated the Rede as well as the laws of the state, they can no longer expect the protection of the Craft community.

Witch ethics are not simple or easy to follow. *Simple* rules, codes, and laws often don't work well for human communities, because people are inventive enough to get around the spirit of the law while they follow the written rules to the letter. Wiccan ethics require perceptiveness, knowledge, thought, and judgment—wisdom, perhaps. This is, after all, called the Craft of the Wise.

Where the wisdom of the individual is not enough, we look to the wisdom of our elders, our community, and our traditions. Beyond that, we look to the wisdom of the human species as expressed in teachings throughout many cultures and ages; we know that Witches do not have a monopoly on wisdom.

And always, we look to the wisdom of the Goddess and the Old Gods as expressed all around us, in nature—which is the embodied wisdom of the divine Spirit.

With guides and teachers such as these, we can hope to live well and ethically.

More Resources

An Ye Harm None: Magical Morality and Modern Ethics by Shelley Rabinovitch and Meredith Macdonald (Citadel, 2004)

When, Why…If: An Ethics Workbook by Robin Wood (Robin Wood Enterprises, 1997)

CHAPTER 8
When the Moon Is Full
Witchcraft and Magick

I cast the circle, raise the cone,
Touching magick, wielding power,
And pour the wine when magick's flown,
I am a Witch at every hour.

Magick has many definitions, including causing changes to happen in conformity with will, the art of changing consciousness at will, and using psychic energies to transform oneself and one's environment. In each case, knowing your true will and applying energy to that goal is the basis of magick.

Witches have adopted the shamanic practices of our ancestors and the forms of ceremonial magick and its correspondences because they work. Witchcraft is a very *practical* practice—if something works, we use it again to achieve the same result. If it doesn't work, we try something else. Not everything works the same for everyone.

Magick is a huge and complex subject that could take lifetimes to explore, and what follows is only a brief overview. For those who want to know more than can be included here, we have explored the subject more deeply in our books *True Magick* and *RitualCraft*.

THE USES OF MAGICK

One of the oddest things about magick is that few people seem to know what it's for. In the movies and fantasy novels, magick is either a way to accomplish totally trivial tasks like washing dishes and changing costumes, or it's used to curse people and battle hordes of malicious wizards and monsters.

No. Real magick is not a way to avoid doing chores, and very few people are attacked by sorcerous enemies or mythical beasts.

In fact, there are two great branches of the Art Magickal: thaumaturgy and theurgy. The first is sometimes called low magick or practical magick, and includes workings for health and healing, prosperity, safe travel, finding jobs, protecting your home, and such. While magick can help in all these areas, they can all be handled by mundane means as well. Sick? Get some rest and drink plenty of fluids. Your house doesn't feel safe? Install a new lockset and deadbolt. Magick is not a replacement for commonsense measures; it's a powerful booster.

The other branch of magick, theurgy, is not nearly as simple. This is magick for spiritual growth and self-transformation, what the alchemists called the Great Work—perfecting oneself. Theurgy helps you expand your consciousness, balance the elements within, illuminate your shadow, create the sacred marriage of your masculine and feminine principles, aspect the gods, and develop the whole and splendid potential of your humanity and your divine self.

This is magick's best and highest purpose, and the tools of magick are uniquely suited to the task.

THE POWER BEHIND MAGICK

Where does magick's power come from? Fictional magick always seems to have a Ring of Power forged by dwarves under a mountain, or some invincible sword—a thing. But where would such an artifact get all that energy, that juice?

The power is not just in the thing. The power is all around us. We live in a sea of energy and can tap into it at any time. Think of all the forms of radiation invisibly sleeting through you right now. Think of the light and heat of the sun, the great movements of winds and tides, the constant pull of gravity, the momentum of planets in their orbits. Think of matter, which, at its core, is energy.

It is power that we can concentrate by simple means, like breathing or singing or playing drums. And then it can be sent to a goal by thoughts, images, words, and actions. Focused intention is the key to effective magick.

Most people swim in power—or flounder—without even knowing it. They dribble their power away in thoughtless words, unfocused whims, and mindless behaviors. And they accomplish little.

Witches know that every word has power—and so does every thought, emotion, and movement. Witches know how to make choices, to desire, to focus, and to achieve. That is magick.

STYLES OF MAGICK

Not every magician works in the same way, any more than every musician is a classical pianist. There are some broadly different approaches to magick, and if you pursue the art, chances are you will lean toward one of them. Briefly:

The Kitchen Witch does practical magick concerned with daily life and often uses ordinary household tools to do simple spellwork. Her magick might be aimed at cooking healthful and tasty meals, protecting her home, or helping children fall asleep at bedtime.

The Nature Magician works outdoors, using the energies of sun and wind and rain, working with animal allies or plant devas, using a stick or a rock as tools. His magick is often used to attune with nature and know the Goddess and the God as expressed in nature.

The Shamanic Magician works with nature but also ventures more deeply into the spirit realms through journeys, trancework, shapeshifting, and the like, to heal people and perform soul retrievals and other magick that requires a trance state. She has a few specialized tools such as drums and rattles.

The Simple Ritualist does ritual with a formal outline at particular times or seasons, with an array of specialized ritual tools and with the aim of celebration or self-transformation. This describes what most covens do.

The Ceremonial Magician takes ritual to a deeper and more complex level. He is known for his costumes, highly decorated ritual tools, use of symbolism and correspondences, and formal language, degrees, and titles, but more importantly, he is almost entirely focused on theurgy.

The Intrinsic, or Inner, Magician works only with her mind and body, using will and imagination to manipulate energy. Because she requires no robes, altar, props, or tools, it looks more like simple chanting, yoga, or silent meditation than magick. It is powerful and transformative nonetheless.

Just reading these brief descriptions, you probably feel more attracted to one style or another. Experimentation and practice will reveal which style works best for you. Write your experiences in your Book of Shadows.

SPELLCRAFT

A spell is generally defined as a word or phrase supposed to have magick power, such as a charm or incantation. To most Witches, it is any magickal operation and may or may not involve words. Simply imagining a desired outcome could almost be considered a spell; if you intentionally put additional energy into that image, it would definitely be one.

AMULET VS. TALISMAN

Many people say that the difference between an amulet and a talisman is that an amulet is sacred or powerful because of what it is (a holey stone or a crystal, for instance), while a talisman is sacred or powerful because of what has been done with it (like inscribing a pentagram on an otherwise inert piece of silver). Others say that amulets are for protection, while talismans draw a particular planetary energy to the maker.

Spells always involve imagination, will, energy, and action, but the forms and materials are limitless. Spells can be constructed with images, symbolic actions, songs, chants, poems, prayers, affirmations, incense, candles, poppets (dolls that represent individuals—with their permission), cords, stones and crystals, potions, elixirs, drums or other instruments, wands, athames, tarot cards, fire, runestones, amulets, talismans, and a host of other witchy paraphernalia.

Herbs in Witches' Potions

In the play *Macbeth*, the three crones add "eye of newt, and toe of frog, wool of bat, and tongue of dog" to their potion. Why would anyone boil up such unappetizing ingredients?

Long ago, most herbs had interesting folk names. "Eye of newt" was a common name for mustard seed, and "tongue of dog" was otherwise called hound's-tongue; "toe of frog" could have meant bulbous buttercup leaves.

Healing herbs were used by the wise women and cunning men of the villages. This knowledge was known as *wortcunning*, meaning "plant knowledge." Many modern Witches still study plant lore and use herbs.

Want to do a magickal spell? Okay, here's your first one. Imagine something you need—nothing that could harm another, of course (besides, you don't need your friend's very cool sports car, you just want one like it). Let's say you need some money and plan to use it for legitimate purposes, like paying your debts or saving toward a new home.

Take a deep breath. Say aloud, "Gods and goddesses of prosperity, I call upon you. Grant that financial wealth may flow to me, *X* thousand dollars or more; may it be with harm toward none and for the greatest good of all." Now imagine the feeling you will have when the money arrives. Inhale deeply, and as the air flows into your lungs, pour energy into that image of a delighted and prosperous you, and make the image brighter and larger and more detailed. Inhale twice more, and charge the image again each time. Now send the image out into the world, and say, "So mote it be" (witchy for "So it must be").

That's a spell. Will it work? Yes. Could it be more powerful and effective in any way? Oh, yes! There are a hundred ways to make it stronger: preface it by giving a tithe to a good cause, do the spell on a Sunday at noon, raise more power by drumming, make and charge a talisman with a wealth bind-rune on it, light some golden candles, visualize and name specific deities such as Lakshmi and Fortuna…and much, much more.

Then act in accord: take practical action that will support the spell on the material plane. You've heard the joke about the person who pleads with God to let them win the lottery but forgets to buy a ticket? Well, do your money spell, but then act: ask for a pay raise from your boss, invest intelligently in a new business, rent out your spare bedroom—whatever your divination or intuition tells you might work.

ℬELLARMINE JARS

Bellarmine jars (or "Beardman jugs") are salt-glazed, stoneware bottles created in the sixteenth through eighteenth centuries. They have a fierce bearded face molded on the side. It supposedly depicted Cardinal Bellarmine, a well-known church leader, but the face was actually the Old God, Woden.

These bottles were sometimes used for magick, either protective or baneful. They were filled with such things as bent pins, rusty nails, and human urine, then buried under porches and gates. They could serve as traps for evil spirits, or possibly as curses on someone's enemies.

Since most modern Witches never do curses, the bottles are rarely used today.

While a spell can certainly be worked by itself, it will often pack more power if worked within a sacred circle, as the centerpiece of a ritual.

RITUAL MAGICK

Ritual is a very important tool for Witches everywhere. There are three kinds of ritual, broadly speaking, in the modern Craft:

Celebratory Rituals: Sabbat celebrations, some moon rituals, anything that marks the turning of the seasons or a special event.

Transformative Rituals: These involve magick to change yourself or your world. Often they are performed at esbats, but they can be done whenever needed.

Rites of Passage: These mark a turning point in an individual's life such as a baby blessing, coming-of-age ceremony, handfasting, initiation, or croning. They are partly celebratory and partly transformative.

Ritual can be as simple as lighting a candle or a stick of incense or as complex as casting a full circle and including many other activities. But normally we are talking about a process with the following steps:

Defining the Purpose: Never do ritual just because it's on someone's calendar. The purpose may be to celebrate the Summer Solstice, join two lovers in a handfasting, or "perform whatever practical magick each covener needs this night, drawing the power of the full moon." Sometimes the purpose is simple, and sometimes, with self-transformation or social change, it can require much thought and careful phrasing to be clear.

Gathering Tools and Supplies: In chapter 4 we talked about the magickal equipment and supplies you may want to obtain. Some Witches use a few simple tools in ritual; some go all-out for the most ornate and expensive. Either can be effective, for it is the will that makes the Witch, not the tool.

Setting Up the Altar: Decorate your altar with items that reflect the sabbat, the season, the phase of the moon, or otherwise enhance the purpose of your ritual. Use your imagination, and have fun!

Self-Preparation: Begin the process that moves you mentally and emotionally into sacred space. This may include a ritual bath, putting on robes (or removing your clothes), wearing special jewelry, meditating, chanting, or anything else that puts you in the mood and mindset.

Gathering: If you work with a group, decide what will help everyone make the transition. In some covens, members gather in a circle and hold hands. In other traditions, a leader casts the circle, then invites people to enter through a gateway, where they are purified and welcomed.

Attunement: This can be any activity that helps participants connect and harmonize with one another mentally, energetically, emotionally, physically, and spiritually. Chant together. Hold hands and hum. Have a short drumming circle. Listen to a brief guided meditation. The activity should help everyone feel fully present and in touch with everyone else. If you are working solitary, ground and center, then think about the work you will do. You may also want to chant, drum, or dance.

Cleansing: Remove all negative or distracting energies by sprinkling the circle with saltwater, carrying incense around the edge, smudging each person with burning sage, or sweeping the circle with your ritual besom (broom).

Casting the Circle: This is also called creating sacred space or establishing the temple. You will create a spherical shell of energy around the participants (or just yourself), using an athame or sword to direct the power. The circle contains and focuses the energy you raise until you are ready to send it to your goal, and it keeps away energies or entities that might disrupt the work. To cast the circle, walk deosil (clockwise), pointing your athame where you want the circle to manifest, and will the circle to come into being. Say aloud words like these:

> *I conjure thee, O circle of power, that thou beist a boundary between the world of humanity and the realms of the Mighty Ones, a guardian and a protection, to preserve and contain the power we (I) shall raise within; wherefore, do I bless and consecrate thee!*

Visualize a ring of blue fire springing up where you point, and when the circle is complete, see the energies rising up and extending down from the ring until they touch at top and bottom, creating a translucent blue sphere (partly below the floor) with you in the center. When done, state, "So mote it be!" to strengthen the sphere.

$\mathscr{W}$HICH WAY AROUND THE CIRCLE?

Deosil is the Wiccan word for sunwise, sunward, or clockwise, from the Druid term *deiseal*. It is pronounced "jesh'-ul" and is the direction that Witches move around the circle when we cast the circle or raise energy. *Widdershins,* from Lowland Scots, or *tuathal*, from Scots Gaelic, mean counterclockwise, and we move that way when doing magick for banishing or releasing.

Calling the Quarters: Facing each cardinal point of the compass in turn (usually east, then south, then west, and finally north), invite the elemental powers to attend. For example: "Spirit of Air, I call upon you to be present this night and lend your powers to my / our work." It might also involve mudras, music, dance, or song. It serves a dual purpose. First, it reminds you to be present and engaged in every way: mentally, emotionally, energetically, and physically. Second, it brings the spirits of air, fire, water, and earth to the edge of the circle to empower your magick. (*Note:* Do not invite the elements *into* the circle, or the air will blow out the candles after the priestess's sleeve catches on fire, and she knocks over the chalice, drowning the cakes, etc.)

Invoking Deity: Your deities may be general or specific, from "Great Spirit" to "Lady and Lord" to "Athena and Apollo." You may simply invite them to be present. But a trained and experienced Witch may aspect Deity (also called "Drawing Down the Moon [or Sun]," or "assuming the God-form"). This means that a specific deity—for example, Athena—is invited to enter the Witch's body and speak through her or his lips. Goddess and / or God becomes incarnate; this is theurgy in its purest form.

Stating the Purpose: Because all words are Words of Power, it helps to focus energy if you speak your purpose aloud. This is especially important in group rituals, to make sure that everyone understands the purpose and supports it.

Core Activity: In a sabbat or celebratory ritual, this might involve dancing the maypole, singing songs, or playing a game. A transformative ritual will require raising power and directing it to a goal. To raise power, you can sing, chant, dance, clap, or drum until you feel the energy rise. When the power reaches its peak (you will feel it surging around and within you), direct it to the goal. You can raise your arms and let it flow through you to an image you visualize, or you can cup your hands around a talisman and let the energy flow into it. After the power ebbs, ground any extra energy by touching the earth, while any remaining power flows back to the Mother.

Cakes and Wine: The sharing of food and beverage enables us to give thanks for the earth's gifts and begin transitioning back to the usual world. Eating also helps you ground.

Farewells to Deities and Quarters: Thank whatever deities were invited and release them. You may say something like, "Thank you, _____, for your presence and power in this ritual. May your wisdom, love, and power stay with me. Stay if you will, go if you must, and if you must go, I bid you hail and farewell!"

Then release the quarters similarly, thanking them for their presence in your ritual and bidding them "hail and farewell" as you imagine them retreating from the edge of your circle into the distance where they came from.

Opening the Circle: The energy sphere is taken down, and the area returns to normal space and time. Walk widdershins (counterclockwise) around the circle, pointing your athame at the ring of blue fire. Imagine it being pulled back into your athame as you walk. For a traditional closing, say: "The circle is open but never broken. Merry meet, and merry part, and merry meet again!"

Acting in Accord: Follow up any magickal working by taking practical action in support (like sending out résumés for a new job, installing those deadbolts for a more secure house, etc.). You may also repeat the ritual later to reinforce the magick.

WRITING RITUALS
And a Word about Coyote

We believe in the value of writing your own rituals rather than trying to memorize and perform "canned" rituals written by someone else. Your and your life are unique, and no one else can fully understand your circumstances when writing rituals in a book. A book ritual can be an excellent place to start and a source of really witchy wording, but do personalize it. (A sample self-dedication ritual is included in the appendices. We do not expect you to say it word for word, just use it as a starting point. It can also serve as a template for other rituals.)

In your Book of Shadows, write out your rituals as you envision them—and be ready for the Goddess and the Old Gods to stick their fingers in and stir things up. No ritual ever goes exactly as written if the energy is alive and moving.

Sometimes, things can get really out of whack; the Trickster has appeared. He is called Old Man Coyote in the Southwest. To acknowledge this trickster energy, we usually place a small coyote on the altar—either a tiny statue of an actual coyote or anything funny (Wile E. Coyote and Snoopy come to mind). Thus we honor the trickster energy, which otherwise may manifest in spectacularly disruptive ways. Ignore the Trickster at your peril.

A Sample Ritual for Samhain

Every ritual is unique; even if the same outline is used, different participants and lunar and seasonal energies will guarantee that one ritual cannot duplicate another. Differing traditions, goals, and styles make the range of variation even more enormous, so it's difficult to present anything like a typical ritual. Nonetheless, here is one just to give you a glimpse.

October 31, Samhain. Outside, children have wandered the neighborhood in costume, being deliciously scared and gathering great bags of Halloween candy. But the hour grows late, the streets are dark and deserted, and now an ancient holy day will be celebrated.

"Why do they schedule Halloween on the same night as Samhain?" grumbles Oak Shadow, the high priest of Twilight Coven. "Did someone turn off the porch light?"

"Done," says Velvet, the coven maiden. "And the altar is ready. Where's Summerlight?"

"Here." The high priestess seems to flow into the room, her black robe swirling. "Gather the clan, please."

When all eight members are gathered, Summerlight invites them to place mementos of their beloved dead on the altar, and each comes forward to place a framed photo, piece of jewelry, or once-treasured possession between the black candles.

"We have prepared ourselves for this night with fasting and meditation," says Oak Shadow. "Let us begin. Velvet, will you lead us in an attunement?"

Soon, all are holding hands and chanting: "Hecate, Ceridwen, Dark Mother, take us in…" Afterward, all but Summerlight and Oak Shadow step into the next room.

At the altar, Summerlight murmurs quiet words over a dish of salt and a bowl of water, then combines them. Then she moves slowly around the room, flicking saltwater to purify the space. Oak Shadow follows her, the coven sword in his large hands. In his deep voice he intones, "I conjure thee, O circle of power…" and continues until the circle is cast. Then he cuts open a portal, and he and his high priestess move to flank the invisible entrance into the circle of energy.

Now the coveners enter one by one; they are purified with the smoke of incense, then welcomed, kissed, and spun to the left of the gateway, according to the old custom. When all have been "spun into the circle," Oak Shadow closes the gate with the sword.

Now the coven moves in unison, facing east, then south, then west, then north; at each direction, they salute with their athames and then simultaneously draw the appropriate element-invoking pentagram. At each quarter, one invites the appropriate power: "Spirit of air, guardian of the watchtower of the east, join our circle this Samhain eve…"

When the elemental powers are present, Oak Shadow invites Osiris, lord of the Underworld, and Summerlight calls Isis, the great healer.

Summerlight continues. "Six months ago, we came together at Beltane and danced the maypole in celebration of life. Now the Wheel has moved halfway round, and we are gathered in this sacred circle to acknowledge the end of life, to mark the third and final harvest of the year, and especially to honor those whom we have loved and who have gone before us to the Summerlands. If you wish, step forward now and offer tribute to your dead." One at a time, the Witches speak heartfelt words: to a departed grandmother, to a friend who lost his life in a highway accident, to a family cat who passed on after fourteen years of companionship.

The next hour is reserved for solitary meditation or quiet divination on the coming year. Singly and in pairs, the coveners find nooks and corners. Some draw tarot cards or cast stones or bones on the carpet. One sits before the altar and looks at a photo, communing silently with his departed friend.

Later, a soft chime brings them together. Summerlight lifts a plate of small cakes and asks the blessing of the Goddess. Oak Shadow raises a chalice of dark, rich wine and thanks the God. With whispered blessings, the food and drink are passed around the circle.

Finishing, Summerlight thanks Isis for her presence, and Oak Shadow does the same for Osiris: "And if go ye must, we say, 'Hail and farewell!'" The coveners echo the "hail and farewell."

Soon the elemental powers have been thanked and released, and the circle is formally opened. Food appears, and Summerlight cries out: "I have a bottle of Estelle's pomegranate mead, can you believe it? If you're not driving later, help me savor it!" With a mixture of somberness for those who are gone and celebration of their lives, the meal and conversation continue late into the night.

Resources for Ritual

How do you learn to design and perform ritual? You've already started just by reading this chapter. You will want to read more, starting with *True Magick: A Beginner's Guide*, which is used by many covens as part of their training programs. When you're ready to go deeper, find a copy of *RitualCraft: Creating Rites for Transformation and Celebration*. The reading list in that will take you as far as you want to go with ritual magick.

However, reading is never enough. This is the Craft; it's about practicing the Witches' arts. So attend as many Wiccan (and general Pagan) rituals as you can: public sabbats, festival rituals, any coven rites you can get invited to. At every one, watch, listen, and feel. Afterward, make notes in your Book of Shadows. What parts were powerful and moving? What parts, if any, seemed flat or unnecessary? What would you have done differently? Imagine that you are the ritual leader, and direct the whole event in your mind.

WITCH BALLS

An old custom says that it's wise to place a shiny glass ball in your window or in the ceiling corners, where negative energy can collect. These "Witch balls" will either trap or scare away any negative spirits that might wander into your home. Some people use old glass fisherman's floats, but there are also mirrored balls and glass art balls designed for the purpose. Even a Christmas tree ornament can do the job.

In the meantime, you can practice rituals at home, as a solitary or with family or friends. At first it will seem awkward, almost like reading lines out of a book. Soon it will flow more smoothly, and you can really concentrate on the power, the meaning, and the spirit of the ritual.

In time, you will also have chances to volunteer for parts in an open ritual. Most ritual leaders are happy to have help and glad to share their knowledge and experience. You might begin by helping set up the altar, or calling a quarter, or even leading a chant if you are musical. It won't be long before you can design and lead a large public ritual like a master.

SHADOW WORK

Just as a large part of the year is filled by the darkness of winter, an important part of our magick is shadow work: exploring those areas of our own hearts and minds that are difficult, painful, and largely unknown—hidden in shadow.

To understand what we mean by shadow work, you first need to understand the Witch's attitude toward light and darkness. To us, these are two essential polarities that balance each other in the universe. Night and day, light and shadow, winter and summer—each is part of the natural pattern. A world with only light or only darkness would be unbalanced and lifeless.

Note that we do not assign moral values to these polarities. In mainstream Western thinking, it is common to speak of light as good and darkness as evil. The knight in shining armor glitters in the sunlight, while the nasty dragon lurks in a dark cave. The cowboy hero wears a white hat, the villain wears a black one. The Star Wars Jedi wear white tunics, the evil Darth Vader wears black. And so on.

To a Witch, night and darkness are not associated with evil. They are simply one side of reality, as necessary and right as day and sunlight. They are opposites, but not moral opposites. We understand that good things can happen in the darkness: from the dark, fallow soil of winter, new life emerges in the spring. On the other hand, evil can flourish in the light. A politician can make noble-sounding speeches even as he leads his nation into an unnecessary war. A forest watershed can be bulldozed in broad daylight to make way for tract housing.

So, shadow work is not about black magick or anything harmful. In shadow work, we confront those uncomfortable parts of ourselves that are usually hidden in the subconscious. They reveal their presence in our feelings. When we experience fear, anger, hatred, shame, guilt, grief, or even irritation or embarrassment, we can be sure that a shadow issue has been triggered.

Shadow issues also manifest in negative attitudes, such as self-loathing, prejudice and bigotry, pessimism, and even indifference. And ultimately, they reveal themselves in harmful behaviors: addictions and other self-destructive acts, sloth, mindless con-formity, discrimination, recklessness, or violence. Unresolved shadow issues also fre-quently lead to emotional, mental, and physical illness.

All these things stunt our potential. They limit our ability to be joyous, creative, lifegiving, and healing individuals. They not only prevent us from being positive forc-es in the world but can cause us to harm others, even those we care for deeply.

As Witches, we face our shadow sides, work to understand their sources and roots, then reframe, transmute, and harness the power that resides in the shadow. This is in huge contrast with those who want only to ignore, avoid, or escape anything to do with the shadow.

Of course, we are dealing with the same issues that one encounters in counseling or psychotherapy. And Witches are quite willing to seek counseling when it seems appropriate. It is simply that we have different perspectives and tools than the average therapist.

Shadow work is not comfortable or quickly done. But those who will not shine a light into the shadowy recesses of their own hearts are destined to be controlled by whatever lurks there unseen. And Witches submit to no control except that of the divine spirit within.

Doing shadow work requires three steps:

- We admit and take responsibility for our negative emotions, attitudes, and behaviors.

- We choose *not* to stuff them, avoid them, ignore them, blame them on others, run away from them (through alcohol, drugs, etc.), or let them control our behavior (act them out in destructive ways).

- We work with them until we understand their sources and can bring them into the light and release them, or transform them into something positive.

Take care of your basic physical health, because negative feelings can be caused by, or worsened by, a physical condition. Check with your doctors and healers to see if there might be a physiological cause for feelings or behaviors that distress you. A chemical imbalance in your brain can lead to manic depression, a shortage of serotonin can lead to clinical depression, and the list goes on. These can be treated with improved diet, control of your blood sugar level, medication, and other approaches.

Of course, there is usually a synergy between physical illness and emotional, mental, energetic, and spiritual problems, so you can approach it from both sides. We believe that very few problems are strictly physical or emotional; we are each a complex interaction of many parts, and the whole person must be treated for any imbalance or disease.

Many magickal or ritual tools or techniques can be used in shadow work:

- Meditate until you understand why that shadow was necessary in your life; then thank it, say farewell, and do a releasing spell.

- Do magick to discover whether you are affected by an outside agency or person; for example, see if energy cords from other people are attached to your chakras. Ask yourself, "Is this my 'stuff' or does it belong to someone else?"

- Work with animal allies, elemental spirits, and spirit guides who have balancing strengths; if you are fearful, get help from one who is filled with courage, like Lion or a fire elemental.

- Imagine a version of yourself who has transcended the shadow issue or transformed it; raise power and draw it into yourself or a poppet (doll) representing you.

- Rename or reframe the shadow; look at it from another perspective that is positive and useful, and pour energy into that image.

- Make and wear a talisman based on an element, planetary energy, or deity that can heal, release, or transform the shadow.

- Think how you could be without that shadow, then act in accord, "as if" it were already healed or released, until it becomes reality.

- During meditation, go inside and meet your shadow self. (It may be an earlier version of you from a traumatic time in your life.) Talk and listen to it, then do healing for that wounded self.

- Do a ritual cleansing to release the shadow and embrace the pure you.

- Do self-blessings and affirmations frequently; affirm the former need for the shadow and release it from your life now.

- If you have harmed another or yourself, seek atonement. Balance the scales: restore, heal, or replace what was lost or damaged.

You need not face the dark alone. Work with deities who understand shadow issues; these are only a few of them:

Persephone, the maiden who was taken to the Underworld but returns to the world of life and light each spring for a while. She understands both light and darkness. And remember that she is Queen of the Underworld—that's where she gets her power.

Hecate, the torch-bearer who guides Persephone through dark tunnels to the light and her mother, Demeter.

Inanna, the Sumerian goddess of life who voluntarily went to the Underworld to learn to understand death, and there met the dark queen Ereshkigal.

Rhiannon, the Celtic goddess who was forced to suffer and bear many burdens before she achieved her freedom.

Ceridwen, another Celtic deity, who has the sacred cauldron of transformation and rebirth.

Osiris, Odin, Tammuz, Mithras, and the gods of sun and grain who die and are reborn.

Quan Yin, the compassionate goddess of the East "who hears the weeping world."

Isis, Brigit, Apollo, Hygeia, Aesclepius, and all the healer goddesses and gods.

Ganesh, the loving Hindu god who can remove all obstacles.

You need not face the dark alone. Work also with people who understand shadow issues; these are a few of them:

- An elder Witch who has worked through these issues.

- Your coven sisters and brothers, who may be able to lovingly point out an issue or help you gain clarity.

- A counselor; after all, most of the behaviors you may question will have a nonspiritual side to them. An NLP (Neuro-Linguistic Programming) practitioner won't even necessarily need to know your issue, just the behavior or thought you need to change. (Search the Web for "NLP" and your state.)

- And don't neglect the many really good books that are available on many different aspects of self-help. Browse your local bookstore until one or more speak to you. They can add structure to your quest.

PRACTICAL MAGICK

The Arts Magickal can easily be seen as very serious stuff, only to be used in a properly cast circle for important issues. That's true for theurgy, the branch of magick that helps us connect with the divine powers. However, thaumaturgy has a more immediately practical slant. Witches use mini spells and incantations all the time to deal with ordinary life: for traveling safely, finding a parking spot, healing a cold, getting calm before a test or interview...these little magicks help us get through the day. Now, to wash the dishes instantly by wiggling our noses...

Ritual is a vessel for magick, a structure that has proven effective for a long time. Magick itself is the heart, and it is more difficult to understand than the steps of ritual. You may have doubts about magick. You may have been programmed for your entire life to believe that magick is irrational and superstitious—even sinful. Your first task may be to simply open your mind and give it a chance.

Magick has been practiced for untold thousands of years by people from many cultures. They were not all fools. Magick is real, even if much of it is still a mystery. Magick is a tool, and like any tool it can be used for good or evil, and wielded for great purposes or small ones.

If you are one of the few who really become adept, use it with wisdom and love, for magick truly does have power.

Deepen Your Practice
Energy Exercises

- Imagine a ball of energy in your hands; compress it until you feel it tangibly, then shift it from hand to hand. Play with it for a while, bouncing it, stretching it, and compressing it again. Now gently release it into the earth.

- Do the same again, but before you give it to the earth, allow a little energy to flow into any part of your body that is stiff or weak or painful.

Ritual Exercises

- Begin by becoming familiar with the steps of ritual as outlined in this chapter and expanded in appendix F, the self-dedication ritual.

- Asperging and casting: every week for six weeks, come up with a different way to asperge and a different way to cast the circle, and do a ritual using your ideas. By the end, you will have six new methods in your toolbox. *Hint:* think of how you could asperge and cast using visual cues, sounds, touch, taste, or smell. Also, try one way that you would use in an air ritual, one for fire, etc. Write the results in your Book of Shadows.

- Calling the quarters and invoking Deity: every week for another six weeks, come up with a different way to call the quarters and a different way to invoke Deity. Do a ritual calling and invoking that way. By the end, you will have six new methods in your toolbox. Remember that these are the parts of ritual most suited to poetry—so put on your poet's hat, and have fun!

- Moving energy: every week for six weeks, come up with a different way to raise, send, and ground energy, and do a ritual using them. Then you will have six more new techniques in your toolbox.

- Cakes and wine: every week for six weeks, come up with a different way to do "cakes and wine" and to say your farewells to the quarters and the Lady and the Lord. For the farewells, go back to your quarter calls and invocations, and make matched sets of calls and farewells. Do a ritual each week using your new farewells, and make sure your entire ritual hangs together stylistically.

- Create a water-based ritual as a house blessing, so that all the parts of ritual have something to do with water. Do likewise for a fire-based ritual for raising your own willpower, and include something fiery at every step.

Shadow Work Exercises

- Get several sheets of paper, and write a negative emotion at the top of each: anger, fear, shame, guilt, and so on. Then ask yourself questions and write down your answers for each. Example: *anger*. When do I feel angry? How does it feel? Where did that feeling come from? What would my life be like without it? Who could I be without the anger but with the energy and intensity of it? How can I transform it into something positive?

- Use an idea from the list of tools and techniques discussed starting on page 160, under shadow work, and try it. Discover whether it helps you release or transform a shadow you have grappled with. Write your experiences in your Book of Shadows.

CHAPTER 9

I Am the Soul of Nature
This Sacred Earth

Work your will, but earth revere,
Touching magick, wielding power,
And every creature living here,
I am a Witch at every hour.

Imagine a world where slender, faerylike beings exist in colonies, connected underground with a fine web of nerve and tissue; each one whispers and flutters in the sun for forty to 150 of our years, then dies, but the colony may survive for eighty thousand years…

Imagine a planet mostly covered with oceans, some deeper than six terrestrial miles. Deep below, in darkness and freezing cold, black tubes rise from vents in the sea bottom, spewing acid at 750 degrees F into the blackness—more than 370 trillion gallons as this watery world makes one orbit of its star. Imagine that gastropodlike creatures crawl about the base, some with venomous fangs, some with scales of iron. Other bizarre life forms live on the methane and sulphur compounds all around them. Nearby, drawn to the warmth, float huge-eyed monsters whose tentacles are covered with swiveling hooks…

Imagine a beautiful world of waterfalls, where you can stand in one high place and see giant, foaming torrents of water plunging down on three sides, or 275 large falls within a space of less than two miles, or water cascading in a single vast sheet more than a mile wide and three hundred feet high, and another where the liquid cascades

165

three thousand feet straight down, or a titan where more than three million gallons of water per second thunder over the edge…

Imagine another world, where great living creatures rear three and four hundred feet in the air and contain more that fifty thousand cubic feet of mass; these elder life forms may thrive for two thousand years and more. However, mutant albinos of their species, only sixty feet tall, survive vampirelike by sucking the fluids from the living bodies of their elder brothers…

Imagine a planet where vast systems of tunnels and caves snake underground, filled with delicate sculptures of stone and occasionally crystals more than thirty feet long. Envision a tunnel three hundred miles long, or another seven thousand feet deep, or a subterranean chamber 2,300 feet by 1,300 feet, more than 260 feet high. Imagine this deep world filled with blind, pale creatures that have never seen the light of their distant sun…

Imagine a cold world, partly covered with ice more than a mile thick, ice so heavy that it has crushed the land beneath for tens of millions of years; a planet where more than 70 percent of the fresh water is locked immovably in frozen ice, and where a thermometer from your house might show 120 degrees F below zero—if it could register coldness that deep…

Imagine a planet crackling with wild electric storms, sixteen million lightning storms every single year. Bolts of lightning streak through dark skies at 130,000 miles per hour, each one soaring to 54,000 degrees F, hot enough to fuse sand into hollow glass tubes that reach deep into the ground, ignite vast fires, or deafen the little creatures that scurry about under the chaos…

Can you imagine these exotic and wonderful places? Welcome to Earth, a single planet that encompasses all these worlds, and many more. A colony of aspen trees in Utah. The Mariana Trench in the Pacific. Thermal vents in several seas. Giant squid. Victoria Falls, and Iguazu and Angel Falls. The Sequoia redwoods of California and their mutant cousins. Mammoth Cave and other caverns worldwide. Antarctica. Lightning storms. It's all real, and it's all part of your home.

And it's all filled with life—living things that dwell inside hot rocks deep under the earth's surface, or cold rocks in a frozen desert. Organisms that are happy with a little iron to eat; or surviving thousands of feet underwater; or floating in salty sludge, dissolved arsenic, or nearly boiling acid; or who can dry up and blow around in the dust for a few thousand years, then pop back to life when there's moisture. And one special creature that seems to thrive on constant noise, stress, pollution, and overcrowding. These are all called extremophiles, except the last, who are called New Yorkers. They are all residents of planet Earth, along with us.

We have talked about nature as composed of earth, air, fire, water, and spirit. Now explore further: nature as the foundation of our health, as our teacher, as the source of magick. And most of all, nature infused with spirit, the sacred body of the Divine, the incarnate Goddess.

APPRECIATING THE REAL WORLD

In modern society, especially among city dwellers, there is a temptation to get comfortable in an artificial environment and venture from it only rarely; to separate ourselves not only from wilderness but from the countryside, even from the outdoors.

This would be understandable in a moon colony. On Earth, it means that we begin to see air-conditioned high-rises and fluorescent lighting and frozen, packaged food as normal—as more real than the natural world. Nature becomes a fantasy world in books and movies. This world is simultaneously harmless—a cartoon backdrop of perpetual sunshine and green trees—and scary, when we see TV specials about hurricanes or tsunamis deluging distant lands on the news. We see snapshots, some fictional and some not, and have no comprehension of the whole.

Thus we forget what gives us life and sustains us.

Forgetting this, we forget to honor and protect the living biosphere, and the earth becomes nothing more than a repository of raw materials for our use.

A whole generation of urban children are more in touch with their iPods, smartphones, and computer notebooks than they are with the stunted little Charlie Brown tree down the street. What kind of stewards will they be for our planet?

Richard Louv has written about this in *Last Child in the Woods: Saving Our Children from Nature-Deficit Disorder* (Algonquin, 2005). He points out that unstructured free play outdoors has been replaced by indoor hours spent with electronic media; not only does this alienate children from nature, but it contributes to depression, anxiety, attention-deficit disorder, stress, and childhood obesity. He calls for a "nature-child reunion."

The remedy is simple. More children outdoors, more of the time: walking in the woods, building forts, fishing, climbing trees, hiking, bird watching, taking photos, growing gardens, walking the dog, camping with their families or Scout groups, and playing in a creative, completely unorganized way.

Obviously adults need nature time too, either outdoor adventures (backpacking, kayaking, skiing) or more gentle pursuits like gardening, neighborhood walks, and outdoor photography.

To appreciate anyone, you spend time with them. It's true for the natural world too. You don't have to enjoy mosquitoes and mud and cold, gray days as much as rainbows and bunny rabbits. But you may learn in your gut what you probably know in your head: that all parts of nature are necessary elements of the cycle…and that this whole, vast, complex earth is splendid just as she is.

NATURE FOR HEALTH

We mentioned that kids who spend time outdoors may be healthier. It's true for us too. Natural sunlight helps our bodies produce vitamin D. When breathing fresh air, we avoid inhaling household chemicals, gases from plastics, and airborne germs. When moonlight floods our bedrooms, we attune to natural lunar sleep cycles. Working and playing outdoors stretches our muscles and conditions our bodies.

Yes, there are natural hazards: sunburn, hypothermia, allergens, poisonous plants, snakes, and bugs, plus the occasional blizzard, earthquake, or tsunami. But probably many Witches would rather face sunlight and snakes than the traffic, crime, and pollution of any major city. We (the authors) live in the country. We have a coyote pack that runs our land, and diamondback rattlesnakes close at hand, and the occasional tarantula and scorpion. We have high-altitude sunshine, an arid climate, and flash floods, lightning storms, and gale-force winds in season. Guess what? Still alive, still kickin', wouldn't trade it for anyplace else. Partly because our environment is mostly free of artificial radiation, chemicals, pollutants, and the like. Partly because it's constantly, magnificently, awesomely beautiful. And partly because we live with the land and have come to a relationship with it, and we work to keep it healthy, even as it keeps us so.

NATURE AS TEACHER

Learning happens in classrooms or from books and the Internet, right? Well, sort of. But so much of that is thirdhand knowledge, gathered by other people from the experiences of still others and packaged as factoids for us to memorize.

Firsthand knowledge from personal experience is *real*, and it not only fills the head but climbs into our bodies, our guts. What we do and touch and smell helps us understand reality and stays with us. This is why great teachers love field trips, because they want their students to smell the sawdust at a lumber mill or discover a beetle creeping through the grass, not sit passively and look at pictures or read letters that together make up words that symbolize real things.

That's why nature is such a great teacher. It's real. What do Witches learn from nature? As we just said, you have to experience it for yourself. Though we can't put it in words, not really, maybe we can give you a glimpse:

- From a frosty winter's night, at the dark of the moon, we learn the power of silence, stillness, and cold.

- From a rounded chunk of golden sandstone, drowsing in a canyon under the desert sun, we learn patience and restfulness.

- From the yellow stare of a coyote padding across a forest road, we learn self-sufficiency and the will to survive.

- From a red-tailed hawk circling high in a cerulean sky, riding thermal drafts between looming stone formations, we learn freedom.

- From an ant wrestling a grain of sand out of its anthill, we learn persistence and the power of tiny things.

- From a gnarled and ancient juniper leaning on the edge of a bluff, half its roots exposed over the precipice, we learn to love life.

- From a trio of fox cubs tumbling and playing in front of their den under a mossy tree, we learn joy.

- From the changing patterns of light and shadow that move across an ancient red-rock mesa, we learn of constant change and enduring strength.

- From the feathery patterns of white cirrus clouds high above the earth, we learn peace.

We can learn so many more things—sudden insights and deep wisdoms—but most of them are unique to one person at one special place at one moment in time. That person is you, and the place is somewhere outdoors, and the time is for you to choose.

NATURE AS POWER SOURCE FOR MAGICK

Some kinds of magick work directly with the elements and powers of nature. For example: energy to fuel a magickal spell can be drawn from the generalized field that permeates all things, but it can also be a more specialized "flavor" of power drawn from wind and air currents, sunlight, the currents and tides of the sea, or from lines of power deep within the earth. These are common sources of energy; an adept might also draw from lines of magnetic force, moonlight, or even starlight for certain special magicks.

Natural materials such as wood, stone, metal, or herbs have their own special properties and are used in amulets, talismans, and ritual tools. Rowan for protection, willow for flexibility, oak for strength. Amethyst for moderation and sobriety, turquoise for joy and emotional uplift, lapis lazuli for strengthening psychic sensitivity. Copper for love, iron for action, silver for change. Valerian to calm, mugwort for magick, and peppermint for alertness.

Animal spirits can be guides, protectors, teachers, totems, or allies. When incarnate, some serve as familiars to Witches, as psychic sensitives, or as guides in healing or divination work. Familiars can be cats, dogs, owls, ravens, toads, mice, ferrets, or other creatures. You can dance your power animal and gain some of its strengths, or communicate with animals psychically. Some Witches can mindshift, or "ride along," in the consciousness of an animal, sensing all that it experiences. To mindshift, take a deep breath and exhale, ground and center, and imagine the animal. Remember all you know about it, then see it in front of you. Ask if you may join minds with it for a while; tell it you mean no harm and will simply follow where it leads. Then gently extend your mind to meet its mind, and allow yourself to be carried along, seeing what it sees, feeling what it feels, smelling what it smells. When it's time, thank it and return to your own body and mind. Write about your experience in your Book of Shadows.

Plant devas, the collective spirits of each plant species, can also host our consciousness but are especially expert at guiding us in our work with gardens, orchards, vineyards, and farms. They are the spiritual gateways to the kingdom that provides us with beauty, food, medicinal plants, soil retention, carbon removal and oxygen production, materials for building and crafts and clothing, shade, and more. Even the plants normally dismissed as weeds have valuable gifts for us once we begin to understand their mysteries.

Weatherworking is one form of nature magick with a mixed reputation. In ancient times, some Witches were said to control the winds and could capture their spirits in a triple-tied bag. Release one knot, and a gentle breeze would spring up; two knots, and you would have a brisk wind; three, and a violent storm would strike. Today, Witches are very cautious about interfering with natural weather patterns, though our coven has occasionally done successful rain magick to break a drought.

There are many ways to work divination with the aid of nature. Dowsing, or "witching," for water is traditionally done with a forked hazel stick. Some can read future events in the patterns of clouds, the flights of birds, or by scrying in a still pond. Astrology reveals much by the positions of the stars and planets in relation to the zodiac and each other. The magicks of nature are as varied as Mother Nature herself, and many Witches prefer these powers to the cerebral and abstract arts of the ceremonial magician. Both have their place.

THE ELDER TREES

Witches are known for their skill at glamoury, or creating an illusion so they look like something else. Some elder trees in particular are supposed to be Witches in disguise. A famous thorn tree in East Anglia, England, is called "the Witch of Hethel" and was first recorded as "the old thorn" in the thirteenth century. It is the oldest living one of its species. She has been there for more than 800 years and must hold the record for the longest-running glamour. But any tree might be a Witch, so be careful how you treat your tall green neighbors.

NATURE AND SPIRIT

"In wildness is the salvation of the world," said naturalist and philosopher Henry David Thoreau. You know already that Witches don't feel the need to be saved from original sin, but we do think the living earth needs to be saved from human folly and overuse.

Partly, this is a matter of simple survival, since destroying Earth's ecosystems is a certain road to species suicide for *homo sapiens*. However, it's even more than that for Witches. Nature, including our home planet, is the body of the Divine for us—the embodiment of the Goddess and the God.

We don't believe the mainstream notion that all "creation" is just something God made, separate from him, to be wisely stewarded or trashed, depending on whether you believe the Rapture is imminent. We don't divide the material world (nasty, where the devil hangs out) from the world of spirit (nice, belongs to God). For us, nature *is* the gods incarnate.

> *By the air that is her breath,*
> *By the fire of her bright spirit,*
> *By the waters of her womb,*
> *By the earth that is her body…*

This Pagan chant from the Reclaiming Tradition of Witchcraft sums it up. The wind, the rocks, the trees, the critters with fur and feather and scale and skin—all are part of the sacred body of Deity. Nature—which is, simply, everything—is spirit-filled, ensouled, holy, sacred. When you strip-mine, dump toxins in rivers, or pollute the air, you are doing that to your Holy Mother and Divine Father and your sacred self.

GAIA

Alias: Mother Earth

Our bodies are made of many elements and systems, interconnecting and interdependent. And we have company: we are host to living things such as bacteria, fungi, archaea, yeasts, and protozoa. There are a lot of them; though we have about ten trillion cells in our bodies, there are ten times that many bacteria in the intestines alone. Many of our tiny passengers are "friendly"; they compete with pathogens, manufacture vitamins, or remove toxins. Others have no known effect on us. Occasionally some go "rogue," like cancer cells.

As above, so below. As below, so above.

You have heard of the Gaia Hypothesis, now called the Gaia Theory, first widely noticed when James Lovelock explained it in the 1970s. He suggested that the earth behaves like a giant, complex living organism that could regulate its atmosphere and oceans to create and sustain an environment friendly to life. Lovelock defined Gaia as "a complex entity involving the earth's biosphere, atmosphere, oceans, and soil; the totality constituting a feedback or cybernetic system which seeks an optimal physical and chemical environment for life on this planet."[8] There was perhaps the implication that Gaia was both purposeful and friendly to life.

Well, yes. In 1971, Oberon Zell, the well-known wizard and author, wrote about "a discovery so vast that its impact on the world's thinking will ultimately surpass the impact of the discovery of the Heliocentric structure of the solar system. This is the discovery that the entire Biosphere of the Earth comprises a single living Organism."[9]

But Lovelock may have been surprised when certain people took the next step and said, "Yes, living, self-regulating, friendly to life—*and* intelligent, conscious, and enspirited."

"No scientific evidence for that," said Lovelock's supporters. "That's mysticism!" True, but it's exactly what Witches believe; we are science- and technology-friendly, but are also willing to journey beyond into spiritual matters.

Our relationship with Gaia, the earth, is that of living, sentient, enspirited beings to a greater such being of which we are part. One could also say that we humans, all almost seven billion of us, can be compared to some of Gaia's bacteria, or cells in her nervous system. Some authors have suggested that the human species is analogous to Gaia's brain. For Gaia's sake, we hope she has a better brain somewhere, because *homo sapiens* is not behaving intelligently in our relations with the rest of the planet.

---

8   James Lovelock, *Gaia: A New Look at Life on Earth* (Oxford University Press, 1979, 2000).
9   Oberon Zell (Otter G'Zell), "Theagenesis: The Birth of the Goddess," *Green Egg* vol. V, no. 40 (July 1, 1971). The entire text can be found at http://original.caw.org/articles/theagenesis.html.

In fact, some argue that we are now a cancer on the Gaia organism. Oberon Zell said: "When in the human body some cells start multiplying all out of control and excreting toxins into the bloodstream, we have a cancer....At this moment, humanity...is multiplying wildly out of control and excreting vast quantities of deadly pollutants into the air, water and soil...If our own cancerous population growth is not halted—indeed, drastically reduced—our numbers and poisons will severely cripple or kill our planetary organism, Gaea."[10]

Scientists from global research programs meeting in Amsterdam in 2001 noticed the problem. They stated that

> Human activities are significantly influencing Earth's environment in many ways in addition to greenhouse gas emissions and climate change. Anthropogenic changes to Earth's land surface, oceans, coasts and atmosphere and to biological diversity, the water cycle and biogeochemical cycles are...equal to some of the great forces of nature in their extent and impact. Many are accelerating...Human-driven changes cause multiple effects that cascade through the Earth System in complex ways...that are difficult to understand and...to predict...Human activities could inadvertently trigger [abrupt] changes with severe consequences for Earth's environment and inhabitants...that may prove irreversible and less hospitable to humans and other life...The nature of changes now occurring simultaneously in the Earth System, their magnitudes and rates of change are unprecedented.[11]

According to the Millennium Ecosystem Assessment, a four-year study of the world's ecosystems by 1,360 scientists:

> The Condition and Trends Working Group found that over the past 50 years, humans have changed ecosystems more rapidly and extensively than in any comparable period of time in human history, largely to meet rapidly growing demands for food, fresh water, timber, fiber and fuel. This has resulted in a substantial and largely irreversible loss in the diversity of life on Earth. In addition, approximately 60 percent (15 out of 24) of the ecosystem services it examined are being degraded or used unsustainably,

---

10 Ibid.
11 The Challenges of a Changing Earth: Global Change Open Science Conference was held in Amsterdam, The Netherlands, July 10–13, 2001.

including fresh water, capture fisheries, air and water purification, and the regulation of regional and local climate, natural hazards, and pests.[12]

The Earth Policy Institute spotlights just one of the problem areas: "Three quarters of oceanic fisheries, a major source of protein in the human diet, are being fished at or beyond their limits, and many are headed toward collapse."[13]

Fifteen of the earth's twenty-four primary "ecosystem services" are being "degraded or used unsustainably." Things like forests and fresh water. That's no way to treat your mother.

If we are acting as a disease instead of an organ or a symbiotic species, the possible outcomes are pretty limited:

We may damage the earth to the point where it cannot sustain human life. In the process, we will kill many other innocent species, but Gaia will eventually rebalance and life will continue without us.

We may damage the earth to the point that climate change and other disasters take an enormous toll in human life, as well as on other creatures. The process may cull millions or billions of humans from the gene pool, but our species would survive and have another chance at learning to live sustainably on a changed planet.

We may change our ways and learn to live sustainably and responsibly on the earth before more irreversible damage is done. This would mean great changes in our way of life: food production, energy, manufacture, transportation, housing, more birth control, you name it.

The authors would prefer to see our species survive and grow up, but instant action is required. For most Witches, this is a sacred duty as well as a pragmatic strategy.

GREEN CONSCIOUSNESS AND HOPE

There is great cause for alarm, but there are also hopeful signs that people are waking up to the dangers. We have come a long way since the 1950s, when environmental concerns were on the fringe of public awareness. In 1962, Rachel Carson warned about pesticides and pollution in *Silent Spring* (Houghton Mifflin). On April 22, 1970,

---

12 The Millennium Ecosystem Assessment, 2005.

13 Lester R. Brown in "Learning from Past Civilizations," *Plan B, 3.0 Book Byte* (Earth Policy Institute, July 29, 2009, http://www.earth-policy.org/books/pb3).

Senator Gaylord Nelson organized the first Earth Day demonstrations. In 1990, Earth Day mobilized over 200 million people in 141 countries around the planet. By 1997, the Kyoto Protocol on climate change was first launched, and a total of 184 nations have now ratified it—the United States being one of the few holdouts. In 2009, the Climate Conference at Copenhagen passed resolutions that may lead to binding treaties and will certainly lead to increased cooperation between the developed and developing nations on green policy issues.

Today, people are mobilizing. Corporations are responding to public demand with hybrid cars, energy-efficient appliances, and household products free of toxins. The city of Albuquerque, New Mexico, has created more than four hundred miles of bike paths in the last few years. Texas now generates enough electricity from wind turbines to power about 1,760,000 homes. High-school students in Hingham, Massachusetts, built a greenhouse and learn about organic gardening, locally grown produce, composting, and endangered plant species. A man in Steamboat Springs, Colorado, is organizing his community to plant twenty thousand trees. The Brazilian government has set ambitious targets for reducing deforestation and carbon dioxide emissions, and four of the world's largest meat producers have agreed not to buy cattle from newly deforested areas of the Amazon rainforest. Wildlife corridors are being organized: the Paséo del Jaguar in Central and South America, a wolf corridor in Alberta, eighty-eight identified elephant corridors in India, and many others.

We could fill a book with stories of individuals and organizations who are taking action for conservation, wildlife, alternative energy, green building, and other facets of environmental sustainability. Many Witches are on the front lines of ecoactivism, but more importantly, people of many faiths and cultures are acting together to protect our common home. Maybe you are one of them.

It's a beautiful world out there. Experience it, savor it, appreciate it. Resolve to live in harmony with the earth and her living creatures. Become active in the quest to make our whole civilization and species more aware, more caring, and wiser in our relationship to Gaia. You don't have to be a Witch to do all this; but if you don't, you can hardly claim the title priestess, priest, or Witch.

DEEPENING YOUR PRACTICE
Exercises in Nature

- Find a secluded square foot of grass—on a lawn if you must, but wild is better. Take your Book of Shadows with you. Watch this area until you can describe the life within it. Describe it in your book—thoroughly. Offer your blessing, and leave without touching it.

- Walk the land around your home until you begin to feel more than acquainted. Describe it in elemental terms in your Book of Shadows, and tell how it has changed your view of the world. For example, Ardantane is a place of earth (rocky mesas and canyons) and fire (bright sun). Yet occasionally air appears in the form of fierce winds driving a thunderstorm before them, water comes roaring down Cañon Cercado, and the dry arroyo is suddenly a turbulent river!

- Visit places where each element reigns almost supreme: a windy mountain peak or windswept grassy plain; a desert, volcano, or hot spring; a stream, river, lake, or seashore; and mountains, rocks, or a forest. Take time to just *be* there.

- Do meditations in which you seek out the spirits of a favorite animal, tree, and herb or flower. Give them energy and blessings, and record their messages in your Book of Shadows.

- Go on a meditation quest in nature for several hours up to a couple of days. (Make sure you are properly equipped for the terrain and weather, and tell someone exactly where you are going.) During this time, ask Gaia / Mother Earth what is the best way that you can help her. Work against air and water pollution? Lobby for laws to preserve wilderness? Replace your vehicle with something more eco-friendly? Put solar panels on your roof? Give time and money to save an endangered species? Make a commitment, and fulfill your promise.

Chapter 10

Worlds Beyond This One
Divination, Dreams, and More

Soar upon the astral planes,
Touching magick, wielding power,
Visit woodland faery fanes,
I am a Witch at every hour.

We create our personal realities out of the infinite possibilities of the universe around us.

Consensual reality—what our society generally agrees is real—is a subset of All That Is. Our society says that toasters are real and trolls are not. We behave as if that is true; we put bread into shiny boxes, but we don't hire guards to watch for trolls. For most of us, that is just—reality.

Our personal realities are also a subset of All That Is and are made of those beliefs, perceptions, and experiences that we allow into our consciousness. Every individual's reality is unique. Maybe you believe in ghosts, but your neighbor doesn't. He believes in the Christian hell, but you don't. You both base your actions, your whole lives, on what you believe to be real. And from the infinite resources of the vast universe around us, you can each find some evidence to support your reality—or believe you can, which amounts to the same thing.

No one understands the totality, the mega-reality, except the Creator/Supreme Being/Great Spirit. We have models of reality, ways to organize our ideas about it.

The Norse have Yggdrasil, the enormous ash tree with the halls of the gods high in its branches, our world of Midgard at its base, and great roots twining through the realms of the dead. The ancient Greeks had the Underworld, where Hades and Persephone reigned, and our world, and the gods' home on Mount Olympus, and the Elysian Fields for the more fortunate souls. Jewish mysticism has the Kabbalah and the Tree of Life, with the ten sephiroth, or spheres, representing the different levels of reality, the emanations of the Divine.

Many philosophies have the idea of planes of existence, which range from the Underworld, through the dense, material, embodied physical plane, up through finer states of energy and consciousness, all the way to God. All these subtle worlds inter-penetrate the physical universe; they exist here but are so ethereal that they cannot usually be seen or felt by us dense, gross critters. The Rosicrucians have seven Cos-mic Planes, from the World of God down to the Physical World. Sufis, Buddhists, Muslims—everyone has a model or cosmology.

Modern secular civilization generally ignores such esoteric stuff and focuses on the physical universe: we have the earth, our solar system, the Milky Way, and a hundred million galaxies beyond that.

THE WITCHES' UNIVERSE

Witches don't argue with the scientific view of the cosmos, we just think it's a bit limited. Witches believe that there are more realities—"planes of existence"—than most muggles understand or experience. Science has not discovered most of these realms, mostly because they aren't looking for them (consensual reality: they aren't there, why look?). Here's one Wiccan model:

- The physical universe, as described above.
- The Summerland, where human souls go between lives to rest, reflect, and prepare for the next incarnation.
- The shamanic Lower World, a "spirit world" where we can meet animal spirits and other discarnate beings, and do inner work and healing.
- The Astral Plane, a "higher" realm where thought is reality and even more discarnate species live. We create stuff by putting a thought or concept on the astral, then pouring energy into it until it becomes denser and manifests in the

physical universe. We can, however, create special places there and leave them on that plane.

- The realms of the gods, the divine creative energy.

Many Witches have a slightly different model or work with additional planes of existence, and that's fine. There's room for everybody. Use the model that works for you.

The Witches' cosmology is not just an airy-fairy idea. Witches can not only perceive the planes, but go there. Astral travel gets us to the more subtle planes, shamanic journeys let us travel to the Lower World, and aspecting the gods gives us a glimpse of the divine plane. All these are advanced skills that should be learned face to face from someone with experience; we're not going to explain in detail here. But someday you too can travel to those other mysterious realms—and when you do, you will meet the inhabitants.

THE OTHER INHABITANTS

Who dwells in these realms beyond our everyday world? Let's begin with our ancestors, the mighty dead. Many cultures, including Wicca, believe that our ancestors and deceased kin can watch, protect, and guide us from the afterlife. Each year at Samhain, we contact those who have passed on in the past twelve months, as well as those who have been "gone" longer but are still beloved. Some Witches set up shrines to their departed, either just at Samhain or for year-round remembrance.

And yes, we do believe in ghosts. Besides those special to us, many other discarnate human spirits appear in our world. Some so-called ghosts are mere revenants, images or memories impressed into a place by extreme emotional energy; for example, at the moment of death. These have no consciousness; they are psychic recordings. Real ghosts are conscious entities who either choose to stay on this plane for reasons of their own, are trapped here, or are simply lost and confused, sometimes unaware that they are dead.

The elemental spirits are the essences of the great building blocks of the universe: earth, air, fire, and water. In Pagan lore, they are traditionally visualized as gnomes, sylphs, salamanders, and undines. However, sometimes they are represented as animals (in one tradition, as Black Bear, Golden Eagle, Red Lion, and Silver Dolphin).

Among ceremonial magicians, they appear as archangels: Uriel, Raphael, Michael, and Gabriel. The elemental spirits are always invited to be present and lend their power at magickal circles.

The faery folk, also called Good Neighbors, the Sidhe, the Fair Folk, elves, etc., are controversial. Some say they are folk memories of the aboriginal inhabitants of the old countries in Britain and Europe. Others believe they are a race of highly evolved beings who exist on another plane but sometimes materialize and interact with humans. For some, they are more like the quaint, cute "flower fairies" that were popular in Victorian England. Ask one.

THE FAERY FOLK

Faeries were not always portrayed like Peter Pan's Tinkerbell, as tiny flying sprites dressed in flower petals. Some say that the real faery folk, or fair folk, were the aboriginal inhabitants of the British Isles. They were smaller than the later invading Celts and Anglo-Saxons. Some lived in turf-covered dugouts, later called "hollow hills," or the underground Faery realm. They had Stone Age technology but were skilled at woodcraft and plant lore. Scots lore says that they sometimes intermarried with the newer immigrants, so many people living today do have faery blood.

Plant devas are the species spirits, or oversouls, of each type of plant. With courtesy and sensitivity, we can communicate and receive guidance for tending our gardens and crops.

Animal spirits, likewise, are the species overspirits of each kind of animal. We call them, for example, Wolf or Wolf Spirit, as distinct from the soul of an individual wolf. They are highly intelligent and epitomize the chief strengths or virtues of each species, such as memory and wisdom for elephants or healing and playfulness for dolphins. Sometimes they are willing to guide and protect us, or grant insights into a situation. Many Witches work with one or more as allies, guides, or power animals.

We discuss the gods and goddesses in more detail in chapters 1 and 12, but suffice it to say they have their own realm and influence all the planes below them. We often envision their homes as great halls, palaces, or temples—the closest analogy that human minds are comfortable with.

Other entities who fit into none of these categories dwell beyond our world. They have their own lives and needs and desires; some are intelligent, some are not. Some are benevolent toward humankind, many are indifferent, a few seem malevolent. Christians call them angels and demons, but that is a huge simplification. They *could* also be the reality behind alien visits, some "ghost" sightings, and encounters with legendary creatures like yetis, mermaids, and monsters.

The universe is more full of life than we can dream. But much of it is invisible and exists in other planes of reality that barely intersect with ours—or on micro- and macro-levels of reality that we cannot yet perceive. But some of these are realms that Witches know of and, with courage, can even visit.

ASTROLOGY

Not all Witches are astrologers, but most understand the basics. Astrology may not be what you think; the daily horoscopes in the newspapers and on the Internet are mostly entertainment, too brief and facile to reflect the true depth and complexity of this art.

Fortunately, there are many books and tools on the subject, so you can use it as a divinatory tool without spending a lifetime learning far beyond the basics. To begin, get your natal horoscope (birth chart) done by a good astrologer, and ask her or him to explain it to you in some detail. Many services online will also provide your chart when you give them your date, time, and place of birth.

With that foundation, you can check tools like *Llewellyn's Astrological Calendar*, *Pocket Planner*, or *Moon Sign Book*. *The Witches' Calendar*, *Witches' Companion*, and *Witches' Datebook* also contain lots of good astrological information for each day. Check one each morning to know the basic energies you will encounter during the day ahead. This enables you to work with or around those energies, unlike people who are totally unaware of them and often work against the current.

For example, what if your astrological calendar says that Mercury is retrograde (said when Mercury appears to be moving in the opposite direction from its usual

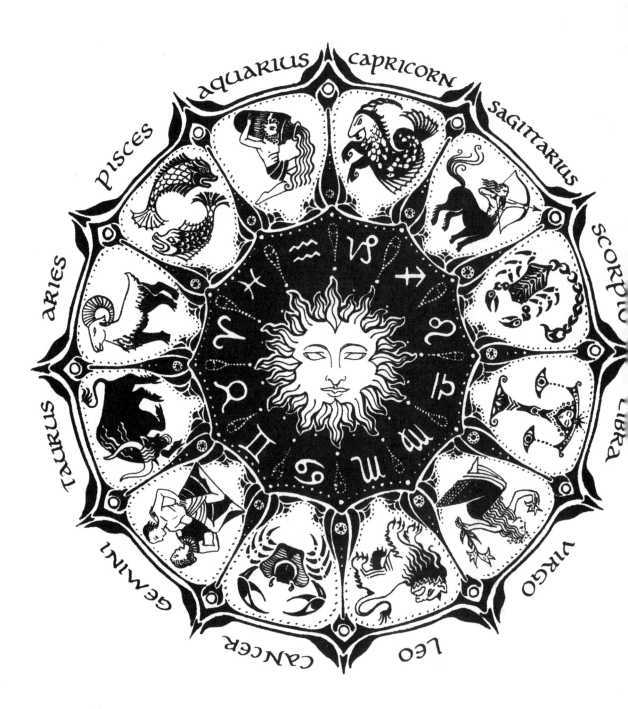

The zodiac

one)? Traditionally, this means it's a difficult time for travel, communication, and commerce, which Mercury rules. If you have something important to communicate, during Mercury retrograde, it might not as clarity as if it weren't be off the octopus. Right. In other words, be extremely careful how you communicate, or just wait until Mercury goes direct again.

Another example is a moon void-of-course, as discussed in chapter 2; you can save yourself a lot of trouble if you don't start anything major during those periods of time.

Those are only two examples out of thousands of possible celestial events that mysteriously seem to affect or reflect human events. You can study astrology for a lifetime and still discover new aspects of this ancient art and science, or you can learn the basics and check them each day as part of your practice.

DIVINATION

Along with magick, ritual, and healing, one of the major skills of a Witch is divination. Divination is a method of gaining information and understanding that is not normally available at the conscious level of the mind. Witches practice many, many forms of this art; we'll discuss some of them shortly.

As with healing or any other art, some Witches are naturally gifted in this area, and others have to work harder. But any Witch can find some divinatory method for which they have a talent.

Just as magick is divided into theurgy and thaumaturgy (high and low magick; spiritual and practical), so divination can be used to learn information about the external world, or to give you understanding and clarity about your inside world.

But how does it work? To most nonmagickal folks, divination seems like fortune-telling, almost supernatural. Is it all a hoax, or do some people have amazing psychic skills, or do spirits feed us information through a deck of cards or a handful of chicken bones?

None of the above. One of the principles of magick is that everything is connected. Hindus call this connected universe "Indra's web"; think of cords of light or energy that run from you to every other object and entity in the cosmos. Since whatever information you need is out there somewhere, you are connected to it. The idea of the Akashic Records, which hold all knowledge (past, present, and future), has also been around for a very long time. Think of them as a Super Internet.

More recently, psychologists have introduced us to the concept of the collective unconscious, a storehouse of human knowledge and memory deep beneath the subconscious mind of any individual. Divination taps into what the universe or our species knows that you are not consciously aware you know.

And fortunetelling? In forecasting events, divination does not "tell the future" because the future is not preordained. Divination can only show trends, patterns, projections, potentials—the flow of events as they will occur if nothing diverts them.

Divination can help you discover insights about yourself that are hidden to normal waking consciousness: who you are and could become, your themes and potentials, your deep motivations and hidden strengths.

Here are some common methods of divination and examples of how they may be used. Since this is an introductory book, we will go into depth only on one basic tool: the pendulum. You can find detailed techniques for the rest of these in specialized books.

Tarot: Many, many beautiful sets of tarot cards are available today; some people collect them because they are so diverse and colorful. The first decks, from about 600 years ago, were Italian, but there are decks with Egyptian, Mayan, Celtic, Goddess, and Native American themes, and a hundred other variations. Many are based on the Rider-Waite Tarot, designed by occult scholar A. E. Waite, which set a new standard when it was published by the Rider Company in 1909. (Today it is often called the Rider-Smith or Waite-Smith deck to acknowledge the artist, Pamela Colman Smith.)

There are three primary approaches to reading the cards. First, each card's meaning can be assigned in advance, usually by the deck's designer in an accompanying book. Second, the reader can tap their psychic sensitivity to understand what a card means for a particular client (or "querent") at that moment. Third, the reader can ask questions to help the querent find their own understanding of each card, so the meaning becomes intensely personal and will vary at each reading.

You can read a single tarot card or choose several and arrange them in a pattern called a spread. Books on tarot are full of spreads, requiring anywhere from two cards to dozens. In any given spread, each place in the pattern has a meaning that will affect how the card is read. For example, suppose you want to know about a potential love relationship, and you do a five-card spread with earth, air, fire, water, and spirit positions. The cards in those positions may answer these questions, respectively:

(**Earth**) Are we a good match physically and sexually?

(**Air**) Are we mentally compatible? Will we communicate well and understand each other?

(**Fire**) Is it a high-energy relationship? Is there passion?

(**Water**) Is there a heart connection? Is there romance?

(**Spirit**) Will we find common ground in terms of our religious beliefs or spiritual paths?

If you have no tarot experience, start with a basic deck like the Rider-Smith and work with it. Once you understand the basic structure of the deck, you can seek a deck, reading style, and spread that work well for you.

Tarot for the Nobility

Tarot cards were probably first invented in the Middle Ages, and originally every card in each deck was hand painted, and sometimes gold leaf was added. Each deck was unique, and only the very wealthy could afford them. One of the earliest decks is called the Visconti-Sforza Tarot, commissioned by two noble families in fifteenth-century Italy. Replicas have been printed in recent times, though four cards were missing and modern artists had to create new ones in the same style.

Other Card Sets: Some wonderful card sets other than tarot decks are very popular for guidance and divination. Among them are:

- Goddess cards of several varieties. We really like the *Goddess Guidance Oracle Cards* by Doreen Virtue, for the quality and intensity of the art.
- *Medicine Cards: The Discovery of Power Through the Ways of Animals* by Jamie Sams and David Carson
- *The Druid Animal Oracle* by Philip and Stephanie Carr-Gomm
- *The Celtic Tree Oracle: A System of Divination* by Liz and Colin Murray
- *AORA Gemstone Oracle Cards: Cards to Explore the Crystal Realms* by James McKeon and Roberta Carothers

If you have a special connection with a specific culture or with animals, trees, stones, or some other aspect of nature, you can find a deck to suit you. Look for them at your nearest metaphysical store or find them online.

Runestones or Runes: These are the (usually twenty-four) letters of Old Norse and Germanic alphabets inscribed on stones or small pieces of wood—a bit like Scrabble tiles but more elegant. You could make your own set out of clay or wood, or purchase sets that are carved on gemstones, polished bone, wood, glass, or ceramic.

Several forms of the runes exist, but the best known is the Elder Futhark. Each letter has a name and meaning apart from its functional use as a letter. Raidho, for example, looks like a stylized capital R and means travel, journey, movement, or change of perspective.

If you draw a rune as part of your regular practice each morning, it can tell you what energy lies ahead for the day. With thought and interpretation, you can use the runes to answer any question.

Casting the Stones: Several methods of divination involve tossing stones onto a cloth or the earth and looking for the relationships among them. Generally, each stone has a particular meaning (news, love, luck, home) or energy related to astrology (sun, moon, Venus, etc.).

Because sets are composed of several stones—thirteen is a favorite number—and they can land in an infinite number of patterns, interpreting the message is challenging. However, it is possible to use them in a simpler way by choosing one stone to represent yourself and two others to symbolize yes and no. Toss the three, and the one closer to the primary stone gives you the answer.

Doreen Valiente, a British Witch and elder who worked with Gerald Gardner, presented one popular version of casting the stones in *Witchcraft for Tomorrow* (Robert Hale Ltd., 1993).

Scrying: Here, the Witch looks deeply into a dark or clear surface in a focused, almost trancelike state of mind and allows images to appear to the inner eye. This technique has been popularized as the "crystal ball" or "magic mirror" sort of fortunetelling.

Real Witches might use a crystal sphere or make a dark mirror for the purpose, but some use a black bowl filled with water. Amber uses a polished slab of obsidian.

Scrying can be used to contact a friend or family member who has passed over or for any other question where an image may bring guidance.

Ouija Boards: Perhaps you have seen these or even used one. The board has the letters of the alphabet and "Yes-No" printed on it, and there is a rolling planchette that you hold lightly while "the spirits" spell out a message. Ouija has a bad reputation, and it's probably deserved. You can ask to communicate with the spirit of Thomas Jefferson or Saint Francis, but the answers may come from someone (or something) else altogether. There is no controlling who responds or who they claim to be. We can't recommend the Ouija board, especially for beginners.

Pendulum or Radiesthesia, Dowsing or "Witching": This is a fairly simple way to get information. Your pendulum can be any small object on a thread or fine chain. Pendulums made for divination are often semiprecious gemstones or lathed from exotic woods.

The pendulum taps into subconscious information and can answer yes or no questions very quickly. Is the road over the mountain passable? Would I enjoy that concert? If I return to school, will I find money for tuition? Is this cantaloupe ripe?

Obtain a pendulum from a metaphysical shop or just tie a thread on a heavy button. Calibrate the length by holding the thread between thumb and forefinger until it swings freely—allow about six inches between your gripping point and the object.

Now ask the pendulum to show you its signal for yes. It might begin moving in a circle, deosil or widdershins. It might swing from side to side or forward and backward. Then ask it to show you the signal for no. Once you have these, any other signal probably means "The issue is in flux" or "You're asking the wrong question." Check the signals by asking questions for which you already know the answers. "Am I sitting down?" "Are my eyes purple?" "Is my name Pyewacket Pigglebones?"

Some questions cannot be answered yes or no. Then you can ask something like "Show me the effectiveness of this herb for healing my cough," or "Show me the relative safety of driving this route today." The strength and distance of the pendulum's motion will give you a relative answer, and you can compare it to a different herb or route.

You may begin every session by requesting your favorite deity or spirit guide to help. Then ask: "Can I get accurate information on (this issue) right now?" If not, try again later. End by thanking the pendulum and any spirit being you asked for help.

Closely related is dowsing, where the diviner walks an area with a forked stick or other simple device to find water, pipes, minerals, etc., underground. When you locate a well site, it is called "water witching." (There is a town in Arizona named Witch Well because the well there was discovered this way.)

Unusual Forms: You may want to try other intriguing forms of divination. The Chinese I Ching has a reputation for great wisdom and depth. Tea lovers can explore tasseomancy, the art of reading tea leaves. A traditional shamanic practice involves collecting, casting, and reading bones from various creatures. You can open a book at random and pick a line (bibliomancy), read ordinary playing cards (cartomancy), look at the lines on people's hands (palmistry), or gaze into a fire (pyromancy).

Some forms of divination, such as reading the entrails of a freshly sacrificed ox, are more cumbersome and messy. Seriously, Witches do not perform any kind of divination (or sacrifice) that would harm an animal! However, the movements and natural patterns of animals and birds can be omens, and you can learn to read them if you watch closely.

Psychic Skills
Talents Beyond the Everyday

Because we are connected with all things and beings, humans have psychic skills. With rare exceptions, like the studies by J. B. Rhine and a few Russian scientists, they are ignored by science. However, that doesn't mean they aren't real or cannot be developed with practice. Witches are very open to such things, since they dovetail with the magickal arts. Let's look at several.

Intuition: This is a water element quality, as discussed in chapter 3. It is the most common, basic psychic skill of our species. Everyone has hunches, a sense that something is dangerous, or a feeling that someone can be trusted, or that the weather will change soon. Do you know when you're being watched? Can you sense trouble waiting to happen? Do you hear a little voice say "uh-oh"?

Here's one explanation: we take in more data than we consciously process or are aware of—but the subconscious keeps correlating data and finding patterns, even as our conscious minds are busy thinking about something else. You walk into an Old West saloon where there's an ambush set: they's a-layin' fer yuh. Your mind is on whiskey, but your subconscious picks up subtle danger signs: the sudden drop in conversation, the bartender's tension, covert glances from the card players. Suddenly you feel it: message from subconscious, "Danger, danger!" Trusting your instincts, you drop, roll, and come up with six-guns a-blazin' at the varmints who just appeared on the balcony.

Pay attention. Trust your intuition, what Marion Weinstein called your "inner bell." When you get a message, listen and act. Later, note it in your Book of Shadows, along with your response and the outcome.

Messages from your subconscious may come through your body: queasy stomach, tight shoulder muscles, a tingling on the back of your neck. Ask yourself: does this situation, person, or object psychically feel warm or cold, heavy or light, bright or dull, smooth or rough, perfect pitch or off-key?

You will probably misinterpret some of the signals, especially if you're very intellect-oriented and in the habit of ignoring "mere feelings," but over time you can hone your intuition to a fine edge.

Reading Auras: As we explained in chapter 5, everything has an energy field that emanates from it and surrounds it. With practice you can learn to sense the aura and tell high energy from low, health from illness, joy from anger, and much more. This particular psychic skill is very valuable to healers.

Healers will sometimes hold a pendulum over each chakra and interpret health from its movements. Some will hold their hands over a chakra and receive colors or images, as though they were scrying. You may sense auras by seeing, feeling, or hearing them hum.

It's sometimes useful to read the auras of others, to get a sense of their emotional or physical state, but your main concern should be your own energy field, because it reflects your state of health and well-being.

Psychometry: This is the art of receiving psychic impressions or information from an inanimate object. You have done this a thousand times without realizing it. You have picked up a piece of clothing, or a book, and felt drawn to it—it just felt warm, inviting, or friendly. You may have touched some other object and recoiled—it had a bad energy, hostile or sad or pained.

Touch or hold something very old, with a lot of history. Center, allow your mind to relax and open, even go into a light trance; you may get impressions that are clues to its past. The object may be holding an emotional charge or a vague sensation of a place where it was kept for many years. You may receive a sense of light or darkness, moisture or dryness, heat or cold, trauma or peace. Smells may come to you, or sounds. You might even get a vivid image of a place or person associated with the object.

Shielding: You can arrange your energy field to protect you from negative energies, either random ones or those directed at you with harmful intent.

This latter situation is rare; there are very few magickal adepts around, and probably none who wish you harm. Yet there could be an occasional person, without any magickal training, who is angry at you and projects her or his feelings strongly. It's not comfortable, but you can ward off that angry energy until you resolve the situation.

A greater concern is the undirected negative energy that floods the ether and affects anyone who is psychically sensitive. The emotions of fear, despair, frustration, guilt, anger, and hatred are very powerful. Most people are not very sensitive to such free-floating emotional toxins or have developed natural filters and shields. Sensitive natural receivers for emotional energy are called telempaths (as opposed to telepaths, who hear thoughts) and can be affected badly until they learn to shield.

A simple way to protect yourself is to ground and center, then inhale deeply and draw energy from the earth through your root chakra; inhale again and draw energy from the sky through your crown chakra; keep breathing and let the energies pool in your solar plexus chakra. Then mentally send the combined energies into your etheric body, the layer of energy that extends just beyond your skin. As that layer becomes stronger and denser, push it out an inch or so, and let it stabilize there. Do this often, until you have trained yourself to hold a strong, expanded energy field.

You can also shield somewhat with a protective amulet or talisman; for example, charge a silver pentagram pendant and wear it over your heart.

Many techniques exist for shielding, but your best protection is to keep yourself healthy and fit, keep a positive attitude, and avoid areas or situations that are toxic. A strong and healthy Witch sheds negativity and deflects hostility automatically.

Precognition: Precognition is the direct knowledge or perception of the future, obtained through extrasensory means. The existence of precognition seems to demonstrate that time is not linear but simultaneous; we only experience events in linear time because our brains would be overwhelmed otherwise. Witches are not necessarily more precognitive than anyone else, and most use divination to understand future probabilities. Two aspects of precognition are clairvoyance, the ability to see things removed in space or time that are not accessible to normal vision, and clairaudience, which refers to hearing sounds from the past or future, or at a great distance.

Time Travel: Though we don't send ourselves bodily into the past or future, Witches do occasionally bend or transcend time when necessary. We use psychometry or past-life recall to gather information from the past, and divination to see future trends, and have been known to move a magick circle forward or backward in time for healing purposes or to avoid doing ritual at an astrologically difficult moment.

Past-Life Recall or Regression: Most Witches believe in reincarnation because they have experienced past lives. *Recall* indicates that one has recaptured memories from an earlier incarnation, usually fragmentary and with little emotion attached. *Regression* is a much more intense and complete experience, where one is immersed in that earlier life and can see, touch, smell, and hear everything around him or her, and relive the emotions that were part of that moment.

Because reincarnation is foreign to the Christian mainstream in the West, things like random flashbacks, déjà vu experiences, vividly realistic dreams of distant times and places, or unaccountable, obscure knowledge are shrugged off. However, a competently guided regression can be very convincing.

Exploring past lives can give you insights into personal issues with origins from before this incarnation. Past-life work can help heal lingering emotional scars, such as phobias or irrational prejudices. But it's not a game to discover if you were someone famous centuries ago; you probably weren't, because most of us have spent many lives as peasants, goatherds, or galley slaves.

If you choose to explore this hidden part of yourself, find a priestess, priest, or clinical hypnotist who knows what they're doing. They will guide you into a trance state and, hopefully, ask objective, non-leading questions to help you be aware of the experience and gather information. Then it's up to you to use that data to improve yourself here and now.

Necromancy: This branch of magick involves communication with the dead. Witches often do so at Samhain, contacting friends and relatives who have passed over. Some people seem to have a particular talent or calling for this. Occasionally a Wiccan priestess or priest will receive messages from the departed so consistently—and insistently—that they know they are called to be a psychopomp, one who helps guide the dead to the next life. Several techniques can be used for communicating: the pendulum, automatic writing, or providing energy to help the spirit manifest visually. Though most "ghosts" are not dangerous, it is a good idea to have an experienced Witch around if you try these.

Telekinesis: This is the ability to move objects with your mind. Although some people can move tiny, light objects, few—if any—have the power to do useful physical work with mind alone (even with a good wand—"Wingardium leviosa!"). If you want to try it, take a small, square scrap of paper and fold it crosswise and diagonally until it becomes a sort of umbrella shape. Balance it on a pin or needle stuck upright in a candle or lump of clay. Focus, and rotate the paper with your mind (make sure your breath can't reach it). What this accomplishes is unclear, but it can be a fun exercise!

DEFORMING UTENSILS WITH MIND POWER

The famous psychic Uri Geller claimed to be able to bend
a metal spoon with the power of his mind; magician James
Randi said it was merely a trick, a clever stage illusion.

Amber once tried it and, indeed, mentally bent a spoon. She
discovered later that one is supposed to use a comparatively
soft silver spoon, not stainless steel (no wonder it took so
long). Her conclusions: (a) it's quite possible to psychically
bend a spoon; and (b) why would anyone want to?

Dreamwork: Dreams are one of the easiest of altered states to enter (we all do it), and good information can be brought back to the conscious world if you work at it. You must build a strong intent to remember your dreams, and have a journal to write them in as soon as you wake up. You may want a dream journal separate from your Book of Shadows.

Life is simpler when it's just consensual reality—"What you see is what you get." It's simpler when "the authorities"—scientists, radio talk-show hosts, government PR flacks, mainstream preachers—just tell you what to believe and experience, and what it means. But it means giving up your own beliefs, experiences, and meanings. Giving up your trust in yourself. Giving up your independence.

Witches won't do that. Our universe may be weird to some, but it's huge and endlessly fascinating, filled with wonder and magick.

If you want to develop your psychic gifts, it begins very simply with paying attention, listening, watching, and feeling the worlds around and within you.

The harder part is learning to trust yourself. When you intuit, sense, or feel something, it's real—and yet it's not necessarily what our culture says it is or what your mind thinks it is. We have to get past the prejudices of our culture ("There are no such things as ghosts!") and also resist the rationalizations of our own minds ("That noise…? Aw, just my imagination—nothing really there.").

The danger at the other end of the spectrum is believing too much, too easily, contrary to common sense and the evidence. Not everything glimpsed from the corner of your eye is a ghost, or a flying saucer, or Bigfoot. When something goes wrong in your life, it's not usually a demon, a curse, or a psychic attack. The challenge is to find a balance of open mind, reason, observation, and trust in your own senses—including your psychic senses.

This means looking thoughtfully at evidence on both sides of any issue, including psychic phenomena. Often it means withholding judgment or belief. Sometimes the only appropriate response is "I don't know." Is telekinesis possible? I tend to think so, but I don't know. Are there plesiosaurs swimming around in Loch Ness? Maybe, but I don't know. Is that an astral entity hovering outside my ritual circle? Seems to be, but I don't know.

On the other hand, if your own senses and experiences confirm the reality of telepathy or past lives, trust yourself and include those things in your reality. Maybe you're just crazy, but unless there is real evidence for that from people you trust, you can generally discount that possibility.

Once your mind and senses are open, and you're willing to explore and experiment with psychic skills, you can search for your own special gift. Many Witches have keen and accurate intuition. Azrael is very strong in past-life recall. Amber is a "finder" who can locate just about anything. Some Witches are naturals at energy healing. Clairvoyance, shielding, telempathy—what's your talent?

Deepening Your Practice
Exercises for Exploring the Worlds Beyond

Witches' Universe

- Draw your own model or diagram of the universe; it can be an existing model or totally original.

- Pretend you are a frog in a country pond. In your Book of Shadows, explore: How many "worlds" do you know well? What environments are you only vaguely aware of? How many are completely outside your experience (for example, a mountain peak)? Is this a good analogy for humanity and our awareness of other planes of existence?

Other Inhabitants

- Plant devas: Go to a park, garden, or wild area in nature. Shed preconceived ideas. Touch a plant; open your mind. What impressions do you get? Is there communication?

- Mindshifting: Imagine being a tree. Now ask a real tree if you may share its mind; if you get a positive response, send your mind into it and just experience its life from the inside. You may have to slow your thinking in order to match its experience. Thank it when you come back out.

- Ancestral spirits: Learn about some of your ancestors by asking your parents or elderly relatives for stories. Make a shrine to commemorate one who especially interests you. Meditate on that person. Ground, center, and send out an invitation to communicate; see what you receive back.

- Discarnate humans: Have you had any contact with "ghosts"? Write the story in your Book of Shadows. Have any of your family or friends had similar experiences?

- Faery folk: Research theories about them on the Internet or at a library. Think about them, discuss them with open-minded friends, and decide what you believe.

Astrology

- Find out where and at what time you were born. Find a local astrologer who will draw up your natal horoscope (birth chart) or use the Internet to create your own. What can you learn about you?

- Get an astrological calendar or almanac. Study the symbols until you begin to understand them. Now look up today's date, and find out what is happening astrologically right now. How could that affect what you were planning to do today?

Divination

- Buy or make a pendulum. Learn its yes and no responses. Ask questions where you know the answers to verify that they are consistently accurate. Now ask an important question for which you *don't* know the answer.

- Choose another divination method that interests you: tarot, runes, scrying, whatever. Make or get the basic tools you need; if you buy them, read the literature that comes with the set/deck/tool. Then just experiment, with a friend if possible. Write your experiences in your Book of Shadows.

Psychic Skills

- Sensitivity: Go to different places and just sense the energies. Describe them in your mind. Become used to being aware, simply noticing. What does it look, sound, and feel like?

- Intuition: Pick up a book at random in the library without even looking at the title, subject, or author's name. Does it "feel" bright, dull, light, heavy, or what? Write down the impressions you get. Now read it, or at least read enough to know whether your impressions were accurate.

- Shielding: Practice putting your shields up, using the breathing technique described on page 193. Do it several times in one day. Then go somewhere that usually makes you feel tense or frazzled. Put up your shields and note how your feelings change.

- Auras: Find a willing person, animal, or motionless object. Look for its aura. If necessary, unfocus your eyes a little or use your peripheral vision. If you can get close, hold out your palms and feel it. Then try the mental humming technique from chapter 5; see if the sound changes as you focus on different places in its energy field.

- Psychometry: Get an old object, perhaps an antique you don't know much about. Hold it and relax. Record any sensory impressions you receive, then research the item's history and see if it matches anything you felt.

- Dreamwork: Program yourself to remember a dream, and have paper by your bed so you can write it down the moment you wake up. Record your interpretation of its meaning. Try this for problem solving: focus on a problem or question just before you fall asleep, then let it go, and in the morning see if your dream has provided an answer.

- Past lives: Have you experienced déjà vu, the sensation that something is very familiar, even though it should be completely new to you? Or have you had a recurring dream about a place you have never visited in this life? Write about these experiences in your Book of Shadows.

CHAPTER 11
Circle Near the Old Oak Tree
Solitary, or Three or More

Dance the round with Pagan folk,
Touching magick, wielding power,
'Neath the stars, beside the oak,
I am a Witch at every hour.

"Ye may not be a Witch alone" is an old Craft saying. This is not to say that you cannot practice as a solitary, but almost everyone sooner or later hungers for like-minded friends and teachers— community. But if everyone around you follows a mainstream faith or none at all, how do you connect?

MAKING CONNECTIONS ONLINE

A relatively safe way to begin is with the Internet. This is not to say that everyone you meet online is sincere and trustworthy; there are scammers and predators who pretend to be High Priest Muckety-Muck of the Temple of Eternal Whatever, looking for careless young women or anyone with a credit card.

But fortunately these are fairly rare. It's not an easy scam to run; it does require some knowledge to look convincing, and there are risks involved for the scammer when real Witches discover him or her.

The great majority of those online are probably honest about who they are and what they can offer, whether it's an introduction to a local coven or information about community events. Observe normal precautions (don't give out your credit card number or detailed personal information, meet only in a public place at first), and you should avoid problems.

Far and away the best resource for contacting Witches in the United States (and Canada, Australia, and many locations around the world—including Antarctica!) is Witchvox.com, which has from a few to hundreds of listings for each area. An excellent resource for European Witches and Pagans is the Pagan Federation's website: paganfed.org. If you don't find what you need on these websites, do a search for "Wicca" and the name of your country, region, or state.

You can find classes online as well; a few are free, and others charge moderate fees but allow you to converse with real people instead of simply downloading assignments and reading lists. As with brick-and-mortar schools in the real world, the quality varies. Anyone with computer skills can set up a class online and present themselves as an expert in the Craft. Before you pay for an online class, check the teacher's experience and qualifications.

WHERE TO MEET WITCHES LOCALLY

Go to your nearest metaphysical or New Age shop—once called "occult bookstores"—and look at the bulletin board or chat with the staff. Besides selling books on everything spiritual or magickal, they are important information centers for the Pagan community. Besides, you'll have fun browsing among the crystals and incense and colorful tarot decks.

While in the shop, look for copies of a local newsletter that you can subscribe to. Some national Pagan magazines have classified ads to connect you with others in your area; contact information for *Witches & Pagans*, *Circle Magazine*, and other important periodicals is listed in appendix C.

If you live in or near a big city, there will be open events you can attend: public sabbat celebrations up to eight times a year, workshops (often held right in the bookshops), drumming circles, and concerts with Pagan musicians. Such events will be posted at the bookstores and listed in local newsletters or possibly online at Witchvox.

A few Wiccan/Pagan schools and retreat centers exist on the physical planes besides the ones that exist only in cyberspace, and the number is growing. You may be fortunate enough to live in New Mexico, near Ardantane Pagan Learning Center; or in Wisconsin, not far from Circle Sanctuary; or in Missouri, a short drive from Diana's Grove. There are others as well, listed in appendix C. Good advice: make an appointment before visiting, or better yet, register for a scheduled event. This will ensure that you don't appear at an inopportune time.

Pagan Pride Day events are popping up around the country like mushrooms, and these are a great place to meet people and learn about local groups. Typically they are held in August or September, in local parks of medium to large cities. They are very public events, so you can hear about them through radio and newspapers, or you can try an Internet search for "Pagan Pride Day" and your nearest city.

A well-organized PPD will have information tables for local groups, people selling ritual costumes or artwork or crafts, a food booth, mini workshops, games, and live music and dancing. Not so long ago, something this public would have been unthinkable, especially for Witches. It is still not possible everywhere.

At the bookstores, online, or at events like Pagan Pride Day, you can get information on meetings of Pagan organizations: in the United States, local councils of the Covenant of the Goddess, and in Europe, groups affiliated with the Pagan Federation, and many local networking groups. Advertised meetings are usually open to visitors. You can observe the meeting, then talk to people during the social period afterwards. Most Witches and other Pagans will be very friendly if you show a sincere interest.

FESTIVALS

Imagine that you are in a wooded campground; the red bark of ponderosa pines glows in afternoon sunlight, and you glimpse a blue lake through the trees. Canvas pavilions form rows along the dirt road; one merchant sells drums in many sizes, and a small child in blue coveralls bangs enthusiastically on a djembe drum as large as he is. A slender young woman in a beaded vest and a bearded Druid in white robes walk past you, talking together. She is wearing a tail, perhaps coyote or wolf.

At a jewelry booth glittering with silver and colored gemstones, a motherly looking woman in a tie-dyed caftan peers at an amulet; she has a handmade broom over her shoulder and wears a pointed hat edged with feathers. At the booth next door, a muscular young man, kilted, goat-horned, and bare-chested, swings a two-handed broadsword, getting a feel for the balance. Across the road, a black woman with beaded cornrow hair and a stack of books tries to explain a magickal operation to a wiry, lean man who looks like Wyatt Earp but is wearing a T-shirt proclaiming "Do not meddle in the affairs of dragons, for you are crunchy and good with ketchup." At another booth, no one is present, but a sign says, "Take what you want, leave the money in the cashbox."

You are at Merchant's Row at Dragonfest, one of the largest Pagan festivals in America. It looks and feels a little like Harry Potter's Diagon Alley transplanted to the Rocky Mountains, with a medieval undercurrent of the Society for Creative Anachronism and a strong dash of Sierra Club.

In every season of the year, in every part of the country, in countries throughout Western Europe and North America and Australia, Pagans gather in force: they gather to camp in the out-of-doors, to meet like-minded people, to perform ritual and celebrate together, to attend workshops on magick or healing or anything Pagan, and to shop among merchants and artisans.

Once, Witches and Pagans were so deeply closeted that they held no festivals. If you were fortunate enough to be in a coven, your coven brothers and sisters were the only Witches that you knew. Your religious community was very small, very tight, and limited to the knowledge and perspectives of a handful of people.

Then the festival phenomenon began. On private land in the country, at remote spots in the national forest, or in out-of-the-way state parks or retreat centers, Pagans gathered for the first time to meet others not of their immediate group.

Today, there are dozens, if not hundreds, of Pagan festivals. Most are still outdoor camping events held on long weekends. A few are held at hotels—perhaps the largest being PantheaCon, held each February in San Jose, California. Here, three thousand Pagans gather to enjoy more than 150 workshops, rituals, and concerts. Other large festivals in America have been going for decades: Pagan Spirit Gathering recently moved from Ohio to Missouri, EarthSpirit Rites of Spring in Massachusetts, the United Earth Assembly in Oklahoma or Texas, and Spring Mysteries Festival in

Washington State are some examples. However, there are also many smaller gatherings; every year, a few new ones are organized, and a few disappear.

Local Councils of the Covenant of the Goddess frequently hold festivals, such as Magickal Mountain Mabon in New Mexico. These smaller, more localized events are a good way to meet Witches living near you.

The Pagan Federation International (PFI) hosts conferences, "pubmoots," and other events in the British Isles, Europe, Canada, and Australia. National and regional associations sponsor gatherings in their own countries as well, and you can get information on these if you are connected with PFI.

The first things you will notice at a Pagan festival are the diversity and the friendliness of the people. You will meet Witches, Druids, Asatru, Dianic feminists, eclectic Pagans, and a sprinkling of Buddhists, Jews, liberal Christians, and people whose spiritual paths defy description. Ages range from babes in arms to graybeards and crones. People dress in jeans and T-shirts, or elaborate ceremonial robes, or nothing at all.

The one thing that all these people have in common is that they are friendly—to each other, and to new visitors—and tolerant of different lifestyles, beliefs, and religious practices.

Courtesy and respect are the watchwords. Rudeness, intolerance, discrimination, or sexual harassment will usually be handled quickly and effectively by volunteer staff—or, in extreme cases, a council of elders will be called to deal with the situation.

You are responsible for your own meals and lodging at most festivals. "Lodging" may be a pup tent, a hammock slung between two trees, or a fancy hotel suite.

The structure of the program is similar at most festivals. Workshops will be offered during the day by volunteer teachers, occasionally by nationally known Pagan authors and leaders, and cover a great variety of topics, from arts and crafts to ritual to magick to healing arts to various exotic religious paths. Each lasts an hour or two and is likely to be a wonderful introduction to some unusual subject.

Various rituals will be presented: an opening ritual to welcome people and establish camp rules, rites of passage from child blessings to handfastings to cronings, a main ritual that reflects the theme of the festival, special rituals for Witches or Druids or whomever, silly rituals just for fun, and a closing ritual. For entertainment, there will be bonfires with drumming and dancing, concerts by fine musicians and singers, or open bardic circles around a fire, where everyone takes turns leading a song or telling a story. Between scheduled programs, people cook meals, socialize, or shop at merchant booths. Attendance at anything is strictly voluntary; although some festivals prefer that you sign up for the workshops you plan to attend, most do not.

What to Expect at a Pagan Festival

Almost anything one can say about Pagan gatherings will have exceptions somewhere. However, the following are true of most Wiccan or Pagan festivals:

- Festivals often require that you preregister and pay in advance. Many events are limited in size by the park, retreat center, or hotel they are using.

- There will be a fee for attending, but it is usually modest.

- You will supply your own shelter and food at most festivals, but not all. It will cost more if it's in a hotel or if the cost of housing and meals is included.

- There will be a registration table where you check in and get a printed program. Here you will probably be asked to sign up for a work shift to help with routine tasks that enable the festival to happen.

- There will be merchants and craftspeople selling their wares; bring money (preferably cash; some accept checks or plastic).

- Festivals are a great place to meet renowned Pagan authors, musicians, leaders, and teachers.

- There will be first-aid personnel and a medical tent in case of illness or injury.

- The festival organizers will generally do their best to make facilities handicapped-accessible.

- Helpfulness, honesty, courtesy, and respect will be expected from every participant.

- There will be a few rules of expected conduct sent to you before the festival. You may be asked not to bring animal companions. You will be told not to bring guns or illegal drugs.

- Usually you wear whatever you like or whatever's comfortable, although nudity may be restricted in some times and places.

- Private sexual activity between consenting adults is accepted; sexual harassment is not.

- Normally, you may bring alcoholic beverages, although drunkenness and especially obnoxious drunken behavior may get you escorted off-site.

- Most festivals are very child- and family-friendly, and some provide children's activities onsite. Be aware that your child may see casual nudity.

- You will be welcomed if you follow the rules, which are a million times less restrictive than out in the muggle world; you will be expelled from the event if you do not.

This may seem more restrictive than you would imagine for a Pagan gathering. But we do give up a few possibilities (like illegal drugs) in order to gain the greater freedoms that come with this magickal village environment. Festivals must operate so that the authorities have no reason to step in and shut them down. Just as important, they must be friendly and safe for families with children and for people who cannot enjoy themselves in an atmosphere of drunkenness and total chaos. Being a Witch is often about sensuality and pleasure in the physical world, but it is also about self-discipline and respect for others, so we seek the balance.

Where to find information about festivals in your area? Head for your nearest metaphysical shop and check out the bulletin board or ask the staff about gatherings. There may be posters for local festivals or a newsletter with announcements of forthcoming events.

You can also gather information online. If you know the name of a particular festival, see if they have a website; otherwise see what is listed on Witchvox.com.

A Pagan festival is an instant village or community where it is safe to be yourself. Many Witches don't realize how stressful it is to live in a muggle world, where everyone around you is on a different spiritual wavelength (or no spiritual wavelength at all), until they escape into the woods for a festival. Then it sinks in: you're free here. You can be yourself. If you walk skyclad down the middle of the road, no one will make rude remarks, much less molest you. You can talk about spells and faery folk, and everyone will listen with respect. You can dance a wild and sensual dance around a blazing fire, and laugh your head off, and paint ancient designs all over your body with mud, and it's okay.

Small wonder that most people don't want to leave when the festival winds down. Something inside you opens up, and the wild-child, tree-sprite, primal woman or man has tasted freedom. It's hard to shut that down and return to the outside world.

FROM LARGE GROUP TO SMALL

You don't have to go to festivals or join anything to be a Witch, and many Witches are by nature independent beings who chafe at the thought of rules and membership fees. But people are social animals, and it is difficult to thrive for long without some kind of human contact. Another way to not be alone is to form a study group.

Putting together a study group is easier than creating a coven and can eventually evolve into one. Find a public meeting place, like a library or community center (many people will be more comfortable there than in a private home). Decide whether you want to make the program broadly focused ("The Nature Religions of Old Europe") or more specific ("Wicca: A New Religious Movement with Ancient Roots").

Limit the initial lifespan of the group, in case it doesn't go well and you want to let go of it. Eight weeks is a good length, with one meeting per week. You can always decide mutually that you want to continue for another eight weeks, or indefinitely.

Put together a program of readings, movies, and discussion. For the videos, you can show a mix of Discovery Channel–type documentaries and fictional movies with Pagan or witchy themes. You do not have to know everything about Wicca or Paganism; you only have to come up with some resources and then lead discussions. If you wish, you can lead a field trip to an open sabbat celebration or the nearest metaphysical bookstore. You might lead a few exercises, like designing and doing a simple ritual together.

For a Craft-oriented program, your eight topics could be:

- What Is a Witch? Terms and Definitions from Many Sources
- Witchcraft in the Middle Ages: The Burning Times
- Wise Women and Cunning Men: Witches as Healers and Midwives
- The Wheel of the Year and the Lunar Cycle
- Witchcraft and Magick, Spells, and Rituals
- Gerald Gardner and the Birth of Modern Wicca
- Mapping the Universe: The Worldview of Wicca
- Wicca in the Twenty-First Century: Feminism, the Environment, and Quantum Mechanics

For a more general Pagan-oriented program, your eight topics might be:

- Religion in the Paleolithic: An Overview
- Shamanism Around the World
- The Great Religions of the Pre-Christian World
- Gods and Goddesses in the Ancient World
- Nature as Sacred
- Living Indigenous Religions and Revivals of Classic Religions
- Neopaganism: The Rise of Wicca, Druidry, Asatru, and Goddess Spirituality
- Compare and Contrast: Neopaganism and the Mainstream Faiths

Keep each program manageable (two hours maximum), offer yummy refreshments, and charge little or nothing to participate; however, a cauldron for donations toward expenses is acceptable. If it's fun and you're learning a lot, keep it going and see where it leads.

Now let's talk about two other options: you can practice solitary or you can join or form a coven with other like-minded people.

What "coven" really means

Coven is based on the Latin root word convenire, meaning "to come together" or "to gather"; it's the root of the English word convene. The first recorded use of coven applied to Witches was in the 1662 Witch trial of Isobel Gowdie, which describes a coven of thirteen members. So it may not have been used by Witches at all before we had to form small underground groups for survival. But today almost every group of Witches uses "coven" or "circle" in its name: Coven of the Mystic Flame, Circle of the Moonlit Path, etc.

COVEN VS. SOLITARY

Wolves hunt in packs, mustangs run in herds, Witches make magick in covens...or not. Will you practice as a Solitary Witch, or seek a coven, or even create one? You have few choices at first; you may live in an isolated area, where coyotes outnumber Witches, or in a small town. Or you might be a city dweller with a dozen covens nearby but none that feel like a potential spiritual home.

So your choices are: (a) practice as a solitary for now; (b) practice with your family, if you have one and they are interested; (c) make do with a broader Pagan group until something more witchy turns up; (d) make long commutes to a great coven in another city; or (e) build your own coven (even if you call it a "study group" at first). We'll explore all these choices. First, here's an exercise for your Book of Shadows.

Am I Better Suited to Coven Work or Solitary Craft?

- Do I prefer to be around other people, or do I really enjoy solitary activities more?

- Do I want to share my spirituality with others, or is my spirituality very personal to me, and nobody else's business?

- How does my partner or family feel about my joining a coven?

- Could coven membership affect my job or my position in the community?

- What role do I usually wind up playing within a group? Active participant? Team player? Leader? Specialist? Aloof observer? Critic?

- Do I have the time and energy to take on what is virtually a new family and the responsibilities associated with that?

- If I have done ritual with others, did I generally enjoy it? Can I enjoy someone else's style of ritual?

- Do I usually accomplish more in a group or working alone?

- Do I learn new things more easily working face to face with other people or studying and practicing on my own?

- Can I chip in my share of money (modest dues), skills, and energy? Or is my life too demanding for me to be a reliable and contributing member?

WHY SOLITARY PRACTICE CAN BE GOOD

Most Witches start as solitaries, because even if you want to join a coven, it takes time to find one and get involved. Fortunately, there are positive aspects to practicing as a solitary!

First, you have the freedom to create your own practice, to do it your way. There is no one to tell you how you should do things. Occasionally you will make mistakes or try something that fizzles, but you learn from those experiences too. You will be creating your own unique spiritual path within the general framework of the Craft, using all the pieces and techniques that resonate best with you. And shouldn't spirituality be unique and personalized?

You can celebrate on your own schedule. That's no small thing in this busy, crowded culture of ours. No coordinating your efforts with seven or twelve other people; do the magick when the need arises, perform the ritual when you have the time and space.

Yes, we are social animals and often enjoy being with others of our species, but it's often messy. For a Solitary Witch, there are no relationship issues: no emotional entanglements, group politics, or personal disagreements. Of course, you won't be improving your social skills as a solitary, but you will be able to focus on other aspects of your growth without the group maintenance and relationship issues that require time and energy in any coven.

As a solitary, you learn what you want to learn at your own pace, through books and nature and solitary experimentation and practice. If you want to spend a month learning to cast the perfect circle, or exploring Bronze Age Goddess cultures, or wandering through field and forest identifying healing herbs, you can. And you don't have to squeeze it between lessons in the official coven training program.

Your solitary magick can be focused on exactly what you need. Your rituals may not have the *oomph* of a coven working, but they can be very, very focused on your particular goals, and focus is more important than sheer power.

Often in coven rituals, either the same favorite aspects are invoked over and over, or just the deities appropriate to the season are invited. But as a solitary, you are always free to call your patron deities, or spirit guides, or animal allies—whoever best suits your purpose.

If your religious choices need to stay private because of the town you live in or the job you hold, you can maintain privacy much more easily as a solitary. While coven-mates are oathbound never to "out" you, some neighbor might see you going into a certain house and hear faint chanting coming from behind closed drapes…and the rumors start. So there is less risk of exposure for a single Witch if that is a concern for you.

Being a solitary can be lonely, but it doesn't mean you have to be a hermit in a cave. If you need multi-Witch energy, drop in on the public sabbats, festivals, week-end classes, or meet-and-greet gatherings at pubs or restaurants that are popping up all over.

THE DOWNSIDE OF SOLO WITCHCRAFT

Much depends on your need for companionship. If you get lonely doing ritual by yourself, if you miss the pleasure of singing and dancing and raising power as a team, if you're very much a social animal—being solitary is not for you. Yes, you can go to public sabbat celebrations or interesting workshops, but those are momentary con-tacts, not warm and deep relationships. You can have Craft acquaintances, maybe friends if you're lucky, but it's not the same as having coven sisters and brothers who will always be there for you.

There's also the question of motivation. Practicing the Craft takes work, and you have to be a self-starter to celebrate the esbats and sabbats, and design and work the magick when you're the only one involved. It's easy to find excuses to slack off: "I know I should do a full moon ritual/study that book on tarot/try that visualization exercise for my shadow work, but it was a rough day…maybe tomorrow."

If that sounds familiar, maybe you need the structure and program of a coven to motivate you. It's not easy to put things off when there are other people waiting for you at the covenstead—and once you get there, you'll be glad you made the effort.

Also, many things are easier to learn in a group. You can cram your head with facts from all the books, but information does not equate to experience and skill. In a coven, you can read the tarot for others, watch someone make an herbal infusion, do energy work on your chakras under the guidance of an elder, and discuss what connection with Deity means with people who have experienced it in many different ways. Shared learning with others is both practical and enriching.

And when magick is needed for healing or spiritual transformation or making a better world, the power of a coven, joined in like mind and united will in a sacred circle, just cannot be matched by a Solitary Witch.

WHY COVEN MEMBERSHIP CAN BE GOOD

A coven is a spiritual and religious support group of like-minded people. You help one another make sense of life and get through it with wisdom, strength, and compassion. Your covenmates encourage you to be the best person you can, using the tools and understandings of the Craft. And for those who are not terribly self-disciplined, coven membership makes sure that you do not ignore your spiritual life because of a busy schedule.

The coven is a tool for learning. Many covens provide a structure for learning through the degree system. There will be classes on the goddesses and gods, the nature of reality, and the skills of magick and ritual. You may learn about your spiritual and cultural roots, and how our ancestors lived and worshiped. The coven elders have a lot to share, and every member will have skills and resources for you. If your coven rotates ritual leadership and encourages creativity, you will be able to experience different styles of ritual and choose the best parts for your personal work.

If you plan to use magick to improve yourself, or your life, or the world, it is incredibly useful to focus goals and brainstorm methods with a knowledgeable group of fellow magick workers. Also, the power of magick intensifies as more trained people lend their energies; in fact, it seems to increase exponentially.

The coven provides a social group you can travel with to festivals and other Pagan events. You might hesitate to attend a conference, festival, or class by yourself, but having covenmates along makes it a wonderful adventure.

The emotional benefits cannot be measured. Most covens are more than a religious support group; they are a "family of choice." Your covenmates become your sisters and brothers. If you do not have a close relationship with your family of birth, a coven may provide the unconditional love, companionship, and loyalty that are missing in your life. And even if your birth family is great, a few more close friendships can hardly hurt! Of course, no legitimate coven (or other religious group) will try to isolate you from your original family.

$\mathscr{D}$IANIC FEMINISTS AND RADICAL FAERIES

Most covens are mixed gender (although most have more women than men). However, many covens are designed as single-sex groups. Many of the all-women's groups are Dianic Feminist covens, focused on the sisterhood and empowerment of women, and celebrating the Goddess aspects of divinity. Many of the all-male groups are Radical Faery covens, composed of gay men celebrating the "Queer God" in his many forms. Within the mixed-sex covens, usually, straight, gay, bisexual, and transgender folks work together as sisters and brothers. There is plenty of room for diverse orientations and lifestyles in the Craft, as long as everyone follows the Rede.

THE DOWNSIDE OF COVEN MEMBERSHIP

So being part of a coven is like romping in a sunlit meadow, surrounded by bunnies, flowers, and butterflies—well, no. Membership in any group brings challenges. We are social animals, but none of us are flawlessly adept at it. We need companionship, but we sometimes get moody, stressed, angry, afraid, careless, irrational … rather—human.

In a coven, you take on responsibilities in order to get the rewards. You clear your calendar for coven events, and you show up unless you're sick or out of town or there's a family emergency. You do your share of planning, organizing, setting up, cleaning up, and ordinary chores that keep the coven running. Doing your share is a matter of honor. You may be asked to pay minimal dues to keep the covenstead in candles.

People have disagreements—even mature, intelligent people. If relatives annoy us, we might ignore them, especially if they live at a distance. If a coven member annoys you, you can't ignore them without leaving the coven. You have to work it out, even if it means asking another covener to mediate an honest discussion about your differences. There is no time or space to let problems fester—they can wreck the whole coven in a matter of days, and you have no right to let that happen.

So when there's conflict in the coven, you have to be an adult. That's hard and demanding…but if you don't run away, you'll become a deeper, stronger, more responsible person.

There's another challenge. Working solitary, no one ever has to know that you are Craft—assuming you don't do loud witchy chanting with the windows open or wear big pentagrams to the supermarket.

Once you join a coven, you are formally associated with Witchcraft. Your coven-mates will guard your privacy, and hopefully you'll never wind up in some "official Witch" database, but no security is perfect. If someone sees you with a known Witch or walking into a certain house, they may guess your path. If that matters to you—if your children or job may be at risk if you get "whispered out of the broom closet"—then think twice about joining any coven.

Not every single coven is led by wise and benevolent people. Most covens are filled with honest people doing their best to follow a good spiritual path. But some have members or even leaders who are not very wise, who make hurtful mistakes due to ignorance or ego. And a few "covens" are nasty scams where criminals use the charm and mystery of the Craft to draw victims for money, sex, and power.

How can you avoid these rare fake "covens" run by con artists? Read the questions on the next section; these reveal the danger signals that should warn you away from the imitations. Also check out a tool by respected Druid Isaac Bonewits, called "The Advanced Bonewits' Cult Danger Evaluation Frame," on the Internet.[14] Of course, calling something a cult doesn't make it so; one definition of a cult is "a disparaging term that big cults have for little cults." What is important is not who is name-calling at whom but the behavior of the group in question and whether it is respectful and empowering to its members or harmful. These are typical questions similar to those in the ABCDEF:

Signals That a Coven May Not Be Good for You

- Does this group pretend to have the one-true-right-and-only way of doing Witchcraft? Are they critical of other groups or traditions?

---

14 http://www.neopagan.net/ABCDEF.html

- Are students discouraged from mingling with other groups or taking classes elsewhere? Do leaders insist that they can teach everything you need to know?

- When you ask tough questions, are leaders secretive or evasive?

- Are large amounts of money demanded from members? (Modest dues are understandable.)

- Has anyone made unwanted sexual advances or implied that sexual activity is expected?

- Do leaders require you to perform personal services apart from helping to maintain the temple or ritual area?

- Do they promise advancement through the degrees of initiation in return for sexual favors, monetary contributions, or personal services?

- Is there discussion and acceptance of negative magick, magickal battles, revenge, counterspells, or the destruction of enemies?

- Are the decor, symbols, and altar on the creepy side, with a focus on darkness and death? (Other than at Samhain, when death and darkness are appropriate!)

- Are the leaders not to be questioned? Do they act as though their word is law?

- Do you get warning signals from your inner bell, intuition, or gut feelings?

Trust your instincts. If it feels bad, walk away.

FINDING A COVEN THAT FITS

Let's suppose that you want to join a coven and are starting the search. The perfect coven may not exist, but it's helpful to list everything you want in a coven, just to clarify your thinking. Ask yourself lots of questions and write the answers in your Book of Shadows.

Do you want a mixed-gender coven or single-sex? Highly organized or loose? Lots of activities or only a meeting or two each month? Heavy on training and education or on celebration and fun? Associated with a particular tradition or culture (Celtic, Egyptian, Norse, etc.) or totally eclectic in their gods and styles? Consensus decision making, voting, or "the word of the high priestess is the law"? Adult-oriented or kid-friendly? Into environmental activism or meditation?

You may not have much choice in coven size, but the traditional range is small anyway. Christians can join the "little church on the corner" with seventy-two adults or the Sacred Surroundsound Multiscreen Megachurch with ten thousand believers. Covens are almost always between three and thirteen members. Five is kind of the practical minimum, and the average coven size in the United States is seven adults. When a coven gets to thirteen members or more, they traditionally "hive," or split into two independent covens.

There are many denominations, or traditions, of Witchcraft in the world, but most of them won't be represented in any single area, so you won't always have a choice of traditions. In a large city there may be several. In a rural area, you may be lucky to find one coven and have to drive two hours to reach it. It is always worthwhile to ask what tradition a coven follows and how many other covens follow it. Ask how the coven's tradition is different from other traditions. This will start to give you a feel for the coveners' beliefs and style.

Covens can be found in a number of ways. You can try contacting covens online through Witchvox, the Covenant of the Goddess, Earth Spirit Alliance, Circle Sanctuary, Aquarian Tabernacle Church, the Pagan Federation, or other networking websites. You can hang out at your nearest metaphysical bookstore (which could be down the street or three counties away); talk to the staff, read the bulletin board, and look like an adorable puppy waiting to be adopted. You can go to festivals, public sabbat celebrations, and other Pagan events as discovered online or at the bookstore. Once there, attend lots of rituals and workshops, schmooze with merchants, and chat up folks at the fire circles until you get some leads on good covens.

Once you find a coven that looks good, you can't just wander into an esbat and sign the membership book. Some covens will be closed to new members at the moment and may tell you to check back in six months. Others follow the traditional rule of "ask me three times," so you have to prove that you are persistent and really want a chance. Some are just not very well organized and will lose your phone number.

Remember, covens don't get points with God for scooping up converts, nor do they worry that you might go to some mythical hell if you don't find The One True Faith. They want you in their coven only if it looks like everybody will benefit, and you are an unknown quantity until they get acquainted. So you may have to gently but repeatedly connect with coven members at several events, until they decide that you may be someone they would want as a covenmate.

CREATING YOUR OWN COVEN

The traditional way to create a coven is to study with an existing one for several years, then hive—that is, start a new coven based on the same tradition, taking with you however many of the original coven's members who want to come along.

In covens with the three-degree system of initiation, you would either hive when you are a second degree and lead the new coven under the guidance of your original high priest and high priestess until you are initiated to the third degree, or you would wait to hive until after you have received your third degree.

It's a fine system, when it works. But what if you can't find a local and compatible coven to teach you? Or what if you join a coven, and several years later the leaders are still saying, "No, I don't think you're quite ready yet…" It has been known to happen: sometimes the leaders are right, but sometimes they just can't bring themselves to let a fledgling fly from the nest. Witchcraft teachers should be working to empower you and help you operate ethically, responsibly, and independently—but not all of them remember this.

If all else fails, you can begin your own coven without the years of experience and training that you ideally should have, and even without the encouragement of your teachers. But make the transition as smooth, courteous, and respectful as you possibly can, and maintain the best relationships possible with your former covenmates.

You can begin by reading some books on this specific subject:

- *Coven Craft: Witchcraft for Three or More* by Amber K (Llewellyn, 1998)
- *Wicca Covens: How to Start and Organize Your Own* by Judy Harrow (Citadel, 2000)
- *Inside a Witches' Coven* by Edain McCoy (Llewellyn, 1997)

All three are written by experienced Craft leaders, yet they have very different perspectives. Comparing and contrasting their approaches will be extremely valuable when you create your own coven.

You should invest time thinking about the kind of coven you would like to have, as far as the cultural context and pantheon, program focus, degree system, decision-making process, and all the things you would consider if you were shopping for a coven to join. Start a journal and write it all down, then organize it as you would a charter or bylaws.

Please don't make the mistake of simply gathering a bunch of people who have an interest in Witchcraft, then opening the floor to everyone's wants, needs, and fantasies. If you reach agreement at all, you will end up with a hodge-podge compromise that doesn't serve anyone well. Remember, if *you* are the organizer and first leader, you have a right to create the coven according to your dream, then seek like-minded people who share that dream. In that way, the coven will be more clear and focused from the beginning.

There is often wisdom in beginning with a study group or Covenant of Unitarian Universalist Pagans (CUUPS) chapter, as described later, and getting to know several Paganfolk in that setting before you attempt a coven. When the time is right, you can contact selected people with whom you felt a connection and explain the kind of coven you have in mind. Some people whom you like and respect won't share your particular dream or want to join a coven at all. That's all right; it has to be all right. They can still be your friends. If you can find three or more people you would want for coven sisters and brothers, and who are interested in your coven project, invite them to a quiet meeting for further discussion.

At the meeting, explain again what you have in mind. Share the core concepts in your written vision, charter, or bylaws. Be clear on what parts are negotiable and which parts are not. Invite their input on the pieces where you are flexible. The point is to get everyone participating as full-fledged members of the team from day one, while you still hold the core principles intact.

It may help you to have a list, with issues that are "carved in stone" and issues that are "sketched in pencil." Here's a fictional example; yours may be very different:

Coven Firefox Issues and Decisions

Name: It has a name that's meaningful to us, for reasons I'll be happy to explain. When you hive off and start your own coven, you can pick the name.

Tradition: Eclectic, no particular brand. Negotiable as long as coven independence is preserved and the tradition is not too rigid.

Membership: Adults aged eighteen and over; both women and men are welcome. Not negotiable, due to legal issues with minors. Also, Rolf and I (Miriam) want to join together, so it will be a mixed coven. If we have public or family celebrations of sabbats, they can be open to pretty much anyone.

Cultural Context: Eclectic or Celtic emphasis. Celtic fine if we can include other cultures and pantheons occasionally. Negotiable to a point, except that we don't want to imitate Native American religions, and we don't want to always be confined to one pantheon.

Program Focus: Celebration, mutual support in spiritual growth, teaching and learning magick, community service. The mix is negotiable. Things we won't support: party paganism (indiscriminate sex, heavy drinking, illegal drugs), rivalry with other covens.

Ethics: The Wiccan Rede, the Law of Return, and the New Wiccan Book of the Law will guide our actions. The last is pretty extensive, and we are open to discussing it and creating our own version, as long as it's based on the Rede.

Leadership and Decision Making: For the first year and a day, my partner Rolf and I will be acting high priest and high priestess, then the coven will have an election. In any case, major decisions will be made by the whole membership. Minor decisions will be made by whoever holds the relevant office for the coven.

Degree System: We need some kind of structured program for learning and recognition. It could be a three-degree system, a five-degree (elemental) system, or something else. I think working that out together would be fun.

Legal Status: Right now we see no need for incorporation or tax-exempt status, but it's negotiable.

Meeting Schedule: Must include eight major sabbats and full moon esbats. Apart from that, negotiable; probably averaging one meeting each week would be good.

Meeting Place: We prefer to have the covenstead at our home, unless someone has a better space. Having a regular covenstead for most meetings is essential. We are okay with rotating occasionally to members' homes and outdoor sites.

Money: Maybe have modest dues, occasional fundraising projects, or in-kind donations of candles and supplies. Negotiable as long as we don't get hung up on money or make it hard for people to afford membership.

As the coven launches, it will encounter the normal bumps, tangles, and confusions of any new organization. If you put in the effort and are fair-minded and persistent, it will succeed…though usually not with exactly the same people you started with. There will be gains and losses in the first couple of years as the right mix of personalities come together.

Read the books mentioned above; you can really benefit from the experiences of others. Then find sources of ongoing counsel and support. Network with other leaders in your area, especially trusted elders and experienced Craft leaders in the Pagan community. Join local and regional networks, and national/international organizations such as Covenant of the Goddess, Circle, and the Pagan Federation. There is no excuse to be isolated unless you are one of those so-called leaders who fears having your power diminished if your coveners are exposed to different ideas.

LIFE IN A COVEN

Relationships in a coven can be confusing; it is like no other organization you have ever belonged to. It is a little like a family but without the baggage, good and bad, that comes from growing up together. It is somewhat like a church or temple but much smaller than mainstream religious institutions. Thus there is more intimacy— no meaningless "How ya doin'?" to a stranger in the next pew. There is also more responsibility; a large church has workers and floaters, those who make it happen and the others who are along for the ride. In a coven, everyone must pull their own weight: there is no room for observers or inactive members.

Many covens are hidden from the outside world, so they can feel like a secret society or underground movement. Within the coven, there is freedom to be yourself and to express sides of yourself that you could never reveal in the muggle world; at the same time, you are never anonymous, never in the background; every member is very visible to every other one at every meeting.

It takes courage to be part of something like that.

When you first join, chances are you will be called a "dedicant," "student," "seeker," or some such title. Most covens have a traditional period of "a year and a day," during which new people can explore the Craft and that particular coven. At any point, you can say goodbye and disappear into the sunset—"no harm, no foul," have a good life. Or the group could decide that it's not a good match and gently suggest that you explore some other path or coven.

If everyone is happy and harmonious after the year and a day, you might ask to be initiated as a full member of the Craft and the coven. Initiation is serious stuff, and if the others think you need more time, they will tell you. But if an initiation ritual is held, then you're officially a priestess or priest of the Old Religion, a Witch, and a full coven sister or brother.

What happens if you decide a year (or ten years) later that you don't want to be part of the coven? Then you resign and go do whatever you need to do. The coven will simply label you "alumnus" or "alumna" and wish you well…or, if it's not a happy parting, they may do ritual to cut all spiritual and emotional ties with you. Either way, you're free to go. Forget the B-movie blood oaths: "Once you have passed these doors, you are forever bound to this path…" Witches are committed to freedom and will respect yours.

Taking Your Measure

One of the old customs was to measure each candidate for initiation with a cord, marked to show the person's head, heart, and height. This cord was kept in a safe place by the leaders, and if the new member ever betrayed the coven, the cord could be used as a magickal link to punish the individual. Many covens have abandoned this practice, since we live in somewhat less dangerous times, so perhaps we can afford to be more trusting. Most covens today give the cord to the initiate to wear at all rituals.

ALTERNATIVES TO COVENS

We have mentioned starting a study group. You can also practice as a family. If you have children, you will not be training them to become priests and priestesses unless they are of age and want you to. But you can certainly celebrate the sabbats with them, and teach them about nature, and share little magickal techniques that will boost their confidence and help them be happy. Some useful books for Wiccan families are:

- *Ancient Ways: Reclaiming Pagan Traditions* by Pauline Campanelli (Llewellyn, 1991)

- *Wheel of the Year: Living the Magical Life* by Pauline Campanelli (Llewellyn, 1989)

- *Pagan Homeschooling* by Kristin Madden (Spilled Candy, 2002)—Useful even if you are not homeschooling!

- *Family Wicca: Revised and Expanded Edition* by Ashleen O'Gaea (Career Press, 2008)

- *Circle Round: Raising Children in Goddess Traditions* by Starhawk, et al. (Bantam, 2000)

You can do witchy outings together as a family to festivals and public sabbats. When the kids are asleep or at a friend's, you and your spouse or partner can do more serious magickal workings together.

Another option is starting or joining a CUUPS chapter. The Covenant of Unitarian Universalist Pagans is affiliated with the UU churches but caters specifically to Pagan or nature-oriented Unitarians. Anyone can form a CUUPS chapter in association with a local UU church or fellowship. Then you have church facilities to meet in and the sheltering presence of an established church. CUUPS chapters cannot be as exclusive in their membership as a coven, and CUUPS programs tend to be broadly Pagan rather than specifically Craft-oriented, but CUUPS makes sense for many Witches who would otherwise be alone. (For more information on CUUPS, check their website at www.cuups.org or e-mail info@cuups.org.)

Even if you don't choose to join any group, you may feel the need to join Craft sisters and brothers around a fire and lift a glass of mead, feel the bone-deep pulsation of a really hot drumming circle, pick up some tips on spellcasting at a festival workshop, or howl at a huge orange harvest moon with a few hundred other Witches on a crisp fall evening to remind yourself that you are not alone.

If you do decide to join or create a coven, remember that no choice is final. You may make different choices in one year or ten years down the road. If you join a coven, you can take a sabbatical or resign or hive if the coven no longer meets your needs. You can just leave.

If you practice as a solitary for now, either by choice or because you can't find a compatible coven, that can change at any time. It may take a year or more to find the right coven—or create it—but if that's what you need, you will do it.

If your family practices together, that's wonderful—and at some point you may all choose to affiliate with a coven, or attend festivals and open sabbats together, or even join an open-minded church or temple of some kind to enrich your spiritual community. (We know a Wiccan high priest and an Asatru elder who enjoy Buddhist meditation each morning, many Witches who also attend Unitarian churches, and a Wiccan/Christian mystic who sees Jesus as another avatar of the dying and resurrected grain god. Amber is very drawn to Taoism, and Azrael studies early Christianity. It's called "freedom of religion," or freedom to create your own unique spiritual path.)

Coven member or solitary, family Witch or religious blend; make a choice and give it your energy, your curiosity, and your commitment. Then review your spiritual health frequently, and adjust your practice as you need to.

CHAPTER 12

Sacred Priestess, Sacred Priest
Serving the Lady and the Lord

I am Goddess, neverborn,
Touching magick, wielding power,
I wear the crescent, wear the horn,
I am a Witch at every hour.

Long ago, before Azrael had ever heard of Wicca, she attended a seminar on expanding one's consciousness and role in the world. One of the first exercises was to write one's ideal vocation on a nametag. Although she had no trouble coming up with her preferred vocation, Azrael had a great deal of trouble with the idea of being called "Sacred Priestess" during the workshop—because she didn't feel she deserved it. In her mind, priestesses required years of training and initiation, and all she had was the desire. Well, she was eventually persuaded to write "Sacred Priestess" on the badge, and afterwards it stayed stuck to the dashboard of her car as a reminder of her goal until she was initiated as a first-degree Witch, a priestess to herself; then it became an affirmation of her accomplishment and path in life.

Almost every Witch is a priestess or priest of the Old Religion. We serve the Lady and the Lord and those in our communities who come to us for help. Some of us call ourselves "Wiccan clergy" to emphasize to the outside world that we share the legal rights and responsibilities held by clergy of other faiths. (The legal responsibilities are different in each state and nation. Some governments maintain a list of registered clergy and expect you to prove that you are qualified before you officiate at a wedding, for example. Most require you to notify authorities if you learn of child abuse or another crime while acting in your ministerial role. You will need to research local laws if you intend to act as clergy in a public role.)

Card-Carrying Witches

Some Witches would like to function as clergy in the wider society and know that they will sometimes need credentials to be recognized—say, if they want to perform a marriage, act as a hospital chaplain, or attend an interfaith conference. Organizations such as the Covenant of the Goddess and Aquarian Tabernacle Church are registered as churches and tax-exempt organizations with the U.S. federal government and do issue clergy credentials to members. Efforts are under way in Canada and some European countries to get similar recognition for Pagan clergy.

This doesn't mean that a priestess of the Craft has the same religious role as a Lutheran pastor or Roman Catholic priest or Jewish rabbi or Muslim imam. We might teach—as a rabbi does. We may offer comfort and spiritual support to a covener—as a pastor does with his or her "flock." We often officiate at rites of passage, though we call them handfastings and child blessings rather than weddings and baptisms. But we don't hear confessions, offer absolution for sins, interpret holy scripture, or stand as official channels between humanity and the gods.

Craft clergy are different in another way: we openly use magick in different forms for many positive purposes. Now, Christians and others perform magick in very restricted ways, but usually only an ordained clergyperson is allowed to. They call it transubstantiation (turning wine into the blood of Jesus), or faith healing, or other things. But the list of approved magickal practices, and the occasions where they can be performed, is very short—and they won't call it magick. And almost none of them will do divination.

Another difference is that the ministerial roles of the mainstream faiths are few in number and carefully limited. When Amber long ago considered studying toward ordination in the Unitarian Church, she had the choice of two seminary programs: congregational leadership or religious education. Today, specialties like youth ministry or military chaplaincy are better supported, but the roles are still pretty limited.

Contrast the many possible roles of a Witch—from bard to deathwalker to sacred clown—and it becomes clear that we have many different ways of serving the Goddess and the Old Gods, expressing the sacred in the world—being priestesses and priests!

WHAT GOD(S) DO WE SERVE?

Most Witches serve both the feminine and masculine faces of Deity. (Some focus exclusively on the Goddess; very few focus only on the God.) We personify them and call them Goddess and God, or Lady and Lord. Frequently we refine these great polarities further to more specific aspects like the Moon Goddess and the Hornéd God. We can get more specific still and speak of individual, named deities like the moon goddess Selene or the hornéd god Cernunnos. And even a named, individual goddess or god may have more than one aspect; we can see the Celtic goddess Brigit in her role as Healer, or Poet, or Smith.

THE GREEN MAN

One of the favorite God-forms in the Craft is the Green Man. He is masculine divine energy as expressed in the plant kingdom, especially the sprouting, growing, blossoming energy of the wilderness. He is often represented as a semihuman face, with leaves forming his hair and beard and even sprouting from his mouth. Many medieval cathedrals have the Green Man carved into the stone and wooden decorations. One theory is that Pagan artisans built and decorated these churches, and because they didn't know or care about Christian symbolism, they used the images of the Old Gods of nature.

Now, many Witches are perfectly happy working with, say, the Lady and the Lord, period. Usually they don't feel a need to get any more specific. Others might base their rituals on the Moon Goddess and the Sun God. And many others work with an entire pantheon from a specific culture, such as the Celtic deities Arianrhod, Brigit, Ceridwen, Dagda, Lugh, Manannan, the Morrigan, Rhiannon, and so on.

Though the old pantheons of northern and western Europe are popular among Witches generally, there is nothing to prevent one from working with any pantheon in a Wiccan context. That is, you can be a Witch and work with the deities and mythology of ancient Egypt or classical Greece or early China or anywhere else. You may feel strongly drawn to a particular culture and era—perhaps through a past-life connection—and feel both fascination and strange familiarity with the religion of that time and place. Follow your heart.

The Wild Hunt

On stormy nights, the spirits of the dead ride in the Wild Hunt. You may hear the thunder of their black horses, and the lightning struck by their hooves reveals their huge, dark forms in the clouds. If they catch you at some lonely crossroads, you may join them and ride the night forever. The huntsmen may be Faery folk or werewolves. Their leader may be Woden, Herne, Charlemagne, the Teutonic goddesses Holda or Berchta, or the Welsh god Gwynn ap Nudd. Our deities include the dark, mysterious, and dangerous, perhaps because we have no devil as a catch-all for anything difficult.

Many Witches work with a small number of deities special to them and develop a "divine circle" of guides and role models. For example, Azrael enjoys working with Brigit, Amaterasu, and Ganesh, whereas Amber has bonds with Brigit, Hecate, and Coyote. Divine relationships evolve and change, too. Once Azrael worked a great deal with Persephone, and Amber was deeply involved with Bast, but life changes, and those particular needs are no longer so great.

Still other Witches are deeply devoted to one particular goddess or god and work almost exclusively with that divine aspect. It could be Isis, Odin, Habondia, Pan, or any other. But in such cases the Witch may explain that she was chosen by the deity, rather than the other way around. The Witch is called to service and has no desire to seek elsewhere.

Many Dianic feminist Witches focus only on the Goddess. Their need and their joy is to explore the feminine side of the Divine that has been neglected and devalued for so long in Western patriarchal society. For some, the Goddess is simply their source of strength, pleasure, and inspiration, and there is no wish to divide their attention and explore male deities. For others, our civilization seems horribly out of balance in its focus on patriarchal gods and values, and Goddess awareness is essential to restore balance and harmony to the world.

Many of us explore God aspects that have been neglected by the mainstream faiths: God as Warrior, Lover, Brother, Sage, and Trickster, among others.

We all explore and honor the faces of Deity that seem right to us, and in the Craft we are free to do so.

Training, Initiation, and Degrees

Wicca has long been a religion of initiates. That is changing as more people want to be Witches but don't feel the need for an initiation. Others don't want to practice with others, except perhaps to attend a public ritual—for which you don't need initiation; you just have to show up. For many, the practice of Witchcraft is a private thing, and solitaries answer to no one but the Goddess and the Old Gods about their initiations or degrees.

However, a foundation of formal training is ideal, and now there are many choices of where to get that training. The traditional way, of course, is to join a training coven, committed to passing on Craft knowledge so their students can grow as Witches and eventually form their own covens, if they choose.

A second option is to take online courses. These can provide good information but cannot replace experience-based participation in a group for learning things like raising and grounding power.

A third alternative is to attend live workshops like those sponsored by metaphysical shops, at festivals, or at Ardantane. Here the teaching is face to face, and students gain the experience of practicing in a group. Of course, classes at bookstores and festivals are on whatever subject the teacher wants to teach, not necessarily what the student needs at the moment.

So what constitutes basic training for a Witch? Here is a list of skills and subjects that one coven covers in the first year of training:

Training for a First-Year Craft Dedicant

1. Achieving Balance

- Energy management: Controlling your own energy; sensing others' energy; balancing your chakras; daily exercises.
- Thou art God/dess: Taking care of your body, mind, soul, and emotions; a mixture of self-care, nutrition, breathing exercises, etc. Also recognizing the divinity in others.
- The Witches' Pyramid and the pentagram; self-assessment in terms of air/fire/water/earth/spirit balance.

2. Ritual Format

- Circlecasting, calling quarters, invoking Deity, and techniques for raising power and grounding.
- Ritual design (identifying ritual themes and purposes, selecting deities to work with, choosing activities).

3. Meditation/Trance

- Grounding and centering; solitary meditation.

4. The Deities of the Old Religion

- The Goddess: Maiden, Mother, Crone, and other feminine faces of the Divine.
- The God: the Hornéd God, Green Man, and other masculine faces of the Divine.
- Goddess and God are One; the many-facets model.

5. History and Tradition

- Terminology, symbols, myths, legends, and traditions of Witchcraft.
- The history of ancient religions, evolution of the Craft, and modern Wicca.

6. Ethics

- The Rede, the Law of Return, the Ordains, and informed consent.

7. Spellcasting

- Defining your goals; tools, design, and Words of Power; amulets and talismans.

8. Psychic Skills

- Exploring intuition, clairvoyance, psychometry, telepathy, etc.

9. Divination

- Ethics, issues, and methods (tarot, astrology, runes, etc.).

10. Ritual Tools

- The functions of the basic four, designing or choosing them, and hands-on fabrication.

11. Wicca in the Modern World

- Overview of modern Paganism; Wicca's relation to ecology, feminism, civil rights, peace, religious freedom, and interfaith efforts.

12. Wheel of the Year and Esbats

- The eight sabbats, solar and lunar cycles, rites of passage.

This list of subjects is only a sample—each coven will teach in the order it feels is appropriate, and some material may be expanded or deleted. You may use this as a checklist at the end of your year and a day—have you covered all of these subjects, or are there some that require more in-depth exploration before you call yourself a Witch?

Many traditions of Witchcraft recognize one's progress by conferring initiatory degrees on their students. These degrees can be structured in many ways. In the most traditional way, you begin by dedicating yourself to the study of the Craft for a year and a day and become known as a dedicant, candidate, seeker, or simply a first-year student.

After the year and a day, if you have finished all the classes and readings and have shown that you are ready, you may be initiated into the first degree, and you can call yourself a Witch. At this stage, you are considered a priest or priestess to yourself—you know the ethics of Witchcraft and some religious history, you are familiar with the Goddess and the Old Gods, you know basic spellcraft and ritual and are co-leading rituals, you understand the elements and basic correspondences, and you have a connection to nature, the greatest teacher of all.

There is one more requirement, and only the dedicant can know if he or she has achieved it—he or she must have undergone a spiritual initiation, had an up-close-and-personal experience of the Goddess or the God, and have formed a personal relationship with Divinity. The requirements listed here are derived from the Coven of Our Lady of the Woods but represent one way a person might be prepared to assume the title of priestess (or priest) and Witch.

Sample Requirements for First-Degree Initiation

As a minimum, candidates:

1. Must have experienced initiation on a spiritual level.

2. Must find the common beliefs, traditions, practices, and ethics of the Craft compatible with theirs.

3. Must have freely chosen Wicca as their spiritual path.

4. Must have been actively exploring the Craft for at least a year and a day.

5. Must have basic magickal skills and knowledge of Craft terms.

6. Must have read the required books and several of the recommended ones.

7. Must be willing to live by the Wiccan Rede; take an oath to honor and act in accord with the Goddess and God within, in daily life as well as in ritual; keep certain information confidential; and to aid and defend their sisters and brothers of the Craft.

8. Must devise a personal oath, declaring their present spiritual and magickal goals.

9. If in a coven, must be working to develop and maintain strong, wise, and caring relationships with each coven sister and brother, and communicate their needs, expectations, and resources to other coveners.

10. If in a coven, must actively participate in most coven activities and take a fair share of responsibility for planning, organization, and leadership.

11. If in a coven, must support the needs of the coven by exchange of energy through teaching or mentoring and by giving money, supplies, and/or time and energy to help with coven projects or fundraising.

12. Must create or obtain the basic garb and tools of the Craft and coven: a robe, athame, chalice, wand, and pentacle.

13. May choose a Craft name to mark a new stage of spiritual growth, and explain to the coven where and when it may be used.

After another year and a day of learning and practice, getting to know the Old Gods better, and doing shadow work, the Witch may be granted the second degree—sometimes considered a priest or priestess to others. At this stage, they can help newer students, lead rituals, teach some subjects, and assist with coven leadership—perhaps as maiden or summoner (who are often the high-priestess-in-training and the high-priest-in-training, respectively). The titles and duties will vary from one Witchcraft tradition to another.

The box below contains the most commonly used symbols in modern Craft traditions with three degrees. However, many who consider themselves Wiccan, or who are self-initiated, wear jewelry with the second-degree pentagram (point up) to show their spiritual inclination. It has effectively become the symbol of Wicca.

SYMBOLS OF THE DEGREES		
First Degree (Priest or Priestess)	Second Degree	Third Degree (High Priestess or High Priest)
Water triangle, an equilateral triangle with one point down	Pentagram, point up; some European traditions have the single point down, showing the Hornéd God's face (muzzle, ears, and horns)	Pentagram with point up, and above it, a fire triangle (triangle with one point up)
▽	☆	⛤

During the third year, Witches will work on the *hieros gamos*, or sacred marriage within—the balancing of male and female energies—so they become fully actualized people, free of limiting stereotypes. They continue to lead rituals and perform magick, and if planning to create a new coven, they learn about group dynamics, teaching techniques, and pastoral counseling.

When all this is completed and they are considered ready for leadership, they are granted the third degree—often considered priests or priestesses to the community. They will often take on a leadership role in their community, perhaps in a local council of the Covenant of the Goddess or the group that runs the local festival and public sabbats. They may assume leadership of their coven as high priests or high priestesses, or hive off from the coven and start their own.

Some traditions have a five-degree system, in which the entry level focuses on earth issues like prosperity and health, before students attain the earth degree. The next degree involves water issues like compassion, intuition, and silence. It's followed by the fire degree, where they work on issues of power, purpose, and will; then they hone skills of intellect and imagination before being granted the air degree. Finally, they work on connection to Deity to attain the spirit degree.

Some traditions have only two categories of membership: non-initiates—Witches in training—and initiates. All learning beyond the initiate level is considered a deepening of one's practice but is not recognized by any formal degree.

THE COLORS OF THE CORD

It is common for Witches to wear cords of different colors to mark their degree of initiation; different covens and traditions have different color schemes. Our own tradition has white cords for dedicants, green for first-degree initiates, red for second degree, and either silver (female) or gold (male) for third-degree initiates. Another tradition adds another color for each step up, not necessarily for degrees but for achievements, and their cords are eventually a multicolored wonder. But when you meet someone in the Craft for the first time, you may have to ask what their cord color signifies.

Beyond their highest degree, most traditions encourage further training and deeper focus in a specialty or vocation within Witchcraft. No further degrees are granted within the coven, but Witches might earn academic degrees or certificates at an institution like Ardantane or Cherry Hill, or a secular educational program, or they might apprentice with a master in a particular skill. Some examples of Witch specialties or spiritual callings follow—or you may invent your own!

SPIRITUAL VOCATIONS WITHIN WITCHCRAFT

Activist: Some Witches are called to work for causes in harmony with the Craft: environmental issues, social justice, feminist legislation, the peace and anti-nuclear movements, and many more. Starhawk is the founder of the Reclaiming Tradition, known for its political activism with a spiritual, nonviolent slant. Activism can also occur in the context of the judicial system, as in the coalition that won Wiccan military personnel the right to have a pentagram on their headstones in the national cemeteries.

Animal Advocate: One whose energy is directed toward helping animals: as a worker at the local animal shelter, an animal communicator, an animal-rescue specialist, an animal rights activist, a veterinarian, a habitat restoration specialist, an educator, and more.

Artist/Artisan: The arts can celebrate and express the God and Goddess, and thank them for their gifts. The Craft includes visual artists, costume designers, ritual toolmakers, stained glass craftspeople, dancers, choreographers, and many other kinds of artists.

Bard: While the Craft does not have a formal designation for bards, as the Druids do, we do have many musicians, singers, storytellers, and other performing artists among our number. Some Witch musicians earn their living with concerts and CD sales, while others simply use their talents in ritual and celebration whenever called upon by the Pagan community.

Chaplain: A chaplain is a spiritual counselor in an institutional setting, like a hospital, military unit, retirement home, youth program, or prison. (The military currently has no Wiccan chaplain. However, perhaps the time has come, and you may be the first officially recognized Wiccan chaplain!) This requires a degree in counseling or theology and credentials such as those available through the Covenant of the Goddess. Some chaplains work with prison inmates, teaching them about Wicca, leading rituals or classes, and counseling on spiritual matters.

Communicator: Many Witches work to keep information flowing in the Craft community as newsletter or magazine editors, Internet forum hosts, website designers, bloggers, or radio hosts. Communication makes us a worldwide Craft community rather than a collection of isolated, vulnerable groups.

Community Leader: Coven leaders are usually known as high priestesses and high priests, though some egalitarian covens do not use the old titles. Some are spiritual guides to individual students or visionary leaders of the wider community. Many Witches serve as officers of regional and national organizations, and others teach and serve on a local council of elders when needed. Some act as meeting facilitators or conflict mediators to form a stronger, more interconnected community.

Deathwalker: These priestesses and priests serve as hospice chaplains, grief counselors, or psychopomps (who communicate with the departed and help them on their way to the next life). This requires specialized training, such as that available in the School of Shamanic Studies at Ardantane. This calling is not to be entered into lightly.

Diviner: These specialists use divination tools such as tarot cards, astrology, rune stones, palmistry, casting the bones, or other methods to help people find clarity when they are confused, learn more about themselves and their paths, see trends into the future, and explore their potential choices.

Earthwalker: These Witches live in a way that embodies the key values of the Craft in their family relationships, career, and community service. In a sense, they are working to live as Goddess and/or God incarnate on earth. Their skills in "the art of living on the material plane" provide inspiring role models to others.

Event Organizer: This is a specialization within the vocation of community leadership; organizers plan and operate local, regional, and national Pagan festivals, Pagan Pride Day celebrations, open sabbat celebrations, and more.

Their efforts bring us together to build community, learn from one another, celebrate our heritage, and revitalize the Craft.

Guardian: This is a broad term for those who protect the community from harm. They are also called watchers, sentinels, safety personnel, security teams, Amazons, or peaceful warriors. Many train in the martial arts and serve at Pagan gatherings. Some are professional law enforcement officers. The Order of Scáthach is an international organization for those called to this role. Though parts of the world may be safer than they were, Witches (and those accused of Witchcraft) are oppressed and even in danger of their lives at certain times and places.

Healer: A high proportion of Witches are healers: either doctors, nurses, physician's assistants, or others in allopathic medicine; or doctors of Oriental medicine, naturopaths, chiropractors, herbalists, reiki practitioners, massage therapists, and so on. Since healing is viewed holistically by most Witches, we include spiritual and emotional healers, such as counselors.

Herbalist: Though herbalists are often healers, they also include makers of essential oils, incenses, herbal gifts, etc., and anyone whose life revolves around the magick of herbs.

Host/ess: They are essential to the Craft community, though often not recognized and honored as they should be. Some open their homes as covensteads, providing hospitality for coven meetings and a second home for coveners. They may also host local events like business meetings, drum circles, or small concerts. They often provide lodging for traveling Craft folk. Some go professional and become Pagan-friendly innkeepers or create and manage retreat centers. Though we all love the outdoors, most of us really appreciate a cozy shelter from time to time.

Interfaith Representative: These Witches interact with clergy and laity of other religions, to educate them about Witchcraft and work for the common good. They often design interfaith gatherings or rituals, celebrating the commonalities we all share. Most interfaith work is done locally, but some organizations, like the Covenant of the Goddess, have members who work on the international stage, attending the Parliament of the World's Religions and other gatherings of world religious leaders. Go to www.cog.org to learn more.

Magician: All Witches practice magick, but some make the Arts Magickal the focus of their lives. They become proficient in thaumaturgy and theurgy, ritual of all kinds, and spellcrafting, and teach others how to perform magick ethically and effectively.

Merchant: This is a very earthy way of serving the Craft community. The staff of metaphysical shops provide useful and inspirational goods for Witches, as well as community centers where people can make contacts or take classes. Others create or distribute goods that Pagans want or need, and are generous in sharing the wealth with the community. Online merchants provide a service for those who cannot shop in person.

Oracle or Channel: Some Witches develop skill in the high art of aspecting, also known as "Drawing Down the Moon" or "assuming the God-form." They can establish a direct connection with Deity and embody that divine personality. The incarnate god or goddess may speak through their lips. This is traditionally done by a priestess who aspects the lunar goddess—hence "Drawing Down the Moon"—but in recent years, many have practiced "Drawing Down the Sun." It is best to have training and support from an experienced Witch before you attempt this.

Ritualist/Ritual Leader: Any Witch is a ritualist, since even solitaries perform personal rituals, but this vocation particularly refers to those who lead community rituals. Ritual leaders must be comfortable with large groups, adept at guiding participants to a common purpose, and skilled at sensing and manipulating energy. They should have a touch of the entertainer but also be able to involve participants emotionally and spiritually. They must also be able to mobilize and coordinate the talents of others, so the ritual never becomes an exercise in personal ego.

Sacred Architect or Landscaper: Anyone who creates ritual circles, labyrinths, sacred gardens, stone circles, shrines, temples, or medicine wheels is included. In ancient times, such people designed projects that involved moving hundreds of tons of earth and stone over several years—such as Silbury Hill or Stonehenge in Britain, or the temples of Malta. Such projects required a deep knowledge of astronomy and sacred geometry. Though few of us build modern Stonehenges today, many create shrines, gardens, and outdoor ritual circles.

Sacred Fool: This calling, also called "sacred clown," is honored in many Native American religions and has become important in Pagan circles. These Witches embody the divine Trickster at rituals and festivals by clowning, telling stories, or mimicking those who deserve a little mockery. This is not an excuse to be naughty, nor is it simple entertainment. The Fool, or Trickster, is a teacher and a guardian of the community's spirit. By acting out behavior that disrupts the values of the community and showing us the results, the Clown teaches us what to avoid. He or she may also teach through storytelling and circus-style clowning, or through pranks that make us look at ourselves with new eyes.

Scholar: Every religion has researchers, scholars, historians, and archivists. The Craft presents an unusual challenge for such folks. The prehistoric roots of our spiritual path were never recorded in writing, and much of our early history was destroyed by missionaries eager to burn manuscripts, deface statues, and tear down ritual sites. We have few material resources to work with, yet many of us hunger to know more about our spiritual heritage and life when the whole world was Pagan. Scholars who can illumine any part of this provide a gift to us all.

Teacher: Obviously, anyone who teaches Witchcraft or its associated skills is a teacher. This includes teaching within the Craft community or to youth only, or public education about the Craft. Closely aligned are those who create and administer schools and seminaries. By tradition, teaching that leads to initiation as a Witch is free. Craft teachers of collateral subjects, those not directly aimed toward initiation, may charge reasonable fees.

One or more of these may call to you—there is no rule that you must only do or be one thing. Because everything is connected, all of these overlap. In your Book of Shadows, write about the one or more vocations that call to you. What will you need to learn in order to do this? Could you make a career of it, or would it have to remain an avocation? Find one that especially calls to you, write that title on a name badge, and place it on your car's dashboard to remind yourself what you are aiming toward. It may sound nuts—but it works!

Practitioners of the Sacred

You might be intrigued by this priest/priestess aspect of the Craft but worry whether you are "holy" or "pure" enough. You do not have to be perfect to have a sacred calling. You do have to be committed, self-aware, and willing to work continuously on yourself—to learn and grow and transform so that you are a credit to the Goddess and the God.

This chapter may be surprising if you have thought of Witches as magick makers and rebels rather than clergy, of all things. And there are Witches who do not want to do the priest or priestess thing, not in any way that remotely relates to mainstream clergy roles.

The point is that we Witches are not mainstream clergy but are deeply involved in the sacred, in our own unique ways. If you feel a special thrill under the full moon or deep in a forest and can only call it spiritual; if you sense a living presence all around you in stars and stones and soil; if you sense mysterious realms beyond the world of material form; if you feel a relationship with the spirits of animals and plants and ancient deities, and they speak to you, then you have what is necessary to be a priestess or priest—to yourself, and perhaps to many others.

CHAPTER 13

The Witch in the World
and In or Out of the Broom Closet

We may forgive, but we can't forget,
Touching magick, wielding power,
We'll claim our place in sunlight yet,
I am a Witch at every hour.

James lives in San Francisco, and he's a Witch. Not only that, he teaches the Craft—both in his coven and through classes at the Ancient Wisdom bookstore. James has a way about him; he radiates confidence, strength, and good will. On the few occasions when someone has questioned his spiritual path, he responds with such courtesy, respect, and openness that his detractors are disarmed. He's usually smiling, and his joy in life seems to be contagious. He has friends everywhere, including conservative Christians who wonder how they can like him so much—a Witch, and unrepentant at that!

That's one story. Here's a very different one. Sarah lived outside Charleston, South Carolina, for years, and was happily married—for about six months. Gradually it became clear that her husband had some character traits he hadn't shown during the courtship. He was aggressive but insecure, not very successful in business, and took out his frustrations on Sarah. His anger really exploded when he caught her reading a book about Wicca, because he was sure that "the taint of Witchcraft" would ruin his already shaky business. Sarah tried to accommodate his wishes after their daughter was born, but he grew worse; at wit's end, she ran away with her young child. There was an ugly divorce, and the ex-husband was awarded full custody of their child. The community chose sides, and Sarah the reputed Witch had to move out of state to escape harassment.

An Early Witch Trial

In 1324, Dame Alice Kyteler of Kilkenny, Ireland, was arrested and charged with Witchcraft, the first major recorded Witch trial in Ireland. Her group of thirteen practiced magick at night, at a crossroads, and were clearly not of the Christian persuasion. (The added accusation of poisoning her husband may have been fabricated to bolster the case against her.) She fled to England with one covener; others also escaped, one recanted, and one woman died at the stake, still refusing to embrace Christianity. The bishop who charged them was persecuted and driven from Ireland—it seems Dame Alice had powerful friends.

All of us face challenges, great times, and heartbreak; some do it with grace and serenity, others trip over their own feet at every turn. However well you dance the dance, becoming a Witch will change your style. You may find that you now have more challenges to face and more resources to face them with. You may find yourself living with a depth and intensity you've never experienced before. You will have days when you wish you could just go to work, come home, and kick back with a beer and TV every night. But once you know you're a Witch, everything changes—including most of your relationships.

This chapter's subtitle was going to be "Personal and Community Relations." That's what it's really all about—how do you interact with other people differently now that you are a Witch? In your Book of Shadows, start a page entitled "How I Treated People Before Becoming a Witch." Write down, honestly, how you perceived people and how you treated them. If it's easier by lumping people in categories, do that: how you saw and related to your parents, siblings, friends, teachers, acquaintances, store clerks, people you disagreed with, etc. Then list what you've gotten out of acting that way, both your internal feelings (it felt good to put them down because you felt superior to them) and external reactions (your little brother started crying and Mom lectured you).

Then think about the basic tenets of Witchcraft and how they apply to your interactions with people. For instance, how would you treat each of those people differently if you truly believed:

- All people have a spark of the Divine within them.

- Thou art Goddess, thou art God—and "thou" includes everyone (including you).

- There is no One True Way; Wicca or Witchcraft is only one valid path among many.

- Words have power, and your magickal self hears every word you say.

- You are how you behave and what you think.

- It's impossible to be a victim and a Witch at the same time.

- The Goddess knew what she was doing when she created each and every thing and person.

- Witches are responsible for every thought they have and action they take.

- Life is a spiral; you may find yourself in a similar situation, but you are not the same person now.

- We are all connected, and what you do to or for someone else will come back to you threefold.

Now write down how you *want* to behave toward each of those people you listed before. Will you start thanking the cashier at the supermarket? Will you listen to your little brother instead of shrugging him off? Will you respect your parents' religious views and not flaunt your Witchcraft in their faces? What will you gain by changing your behavior, and what will it cost you? Is it worth it?

Let's turn to how you feel about yourself. If you are comfortable in your own skin, you will be confident and centered with other people. This applies not only to your feelings about being a Witch but to how you feel about being (choose any that apply): female, male; tall, short, or medium; straight, gay, bisexual, or transgendered; skinny, average, or chubby; white, black, Asian, mixed race, or other; very educated or not much; a dog person or a cat person; a sci-fi or romance fan—in short, how do you feel about who you are?

The Goddess and the Old Gods like you just fine—and expect you to be constantly improving yourself. If you want to change, you have found the right path, because the Goddess changes everything she touches, just like the chant says. If you have achieved perfection and don't want to change or grow in any way, you may need to find another path.

Get out your Book of Shadows again, and write about how you feel inside your own skin, then what you would like to change. Then ask yourself, and write down, "What would that do for me?" and answer it. This will help you get to the roots of what motivates you toward change. Now for the tricky part. Do it six more times, up to a total of seven (magick number there)—answer "What would that do for me?" Each time you answer, you come to a deeper level of what is important to you. When you can go no deeper, you have found your true motivation, what's really at the core of why you want to change. It may be as simple and profound as "Then I would like myself" or "Then I would be okay." So, to bring this around full circle, if you *did* make that change, and you *are* okay, how would you be in the world differently than you are now? Write it down.

Example: What you would like to change. **I want to get more exercise.**

And what would that do for me?

- I wouldn't huff and puff up the stairs.
- I wouldn't be embarrassed when walking in a group.
- I would be able to hold my head up high.
- I would feel proud of myself.
- I would be self-confident.
- I would be self-confident. (Same answer twice in a row, end exercise)

So what I really want is to be self-confident, and exercise is one way I can improve my self-confidence. What are other ways?

Then start acting as if you have made that change. Your actions define you. Some people call this strategy "fake it 'til you make it," but if you are changing, it's not fake—it's as real as it gets. Once you start acting and speaking from the new you, the real you, taking responsibility and speaking with honesty, the world will begin to treat you differently. Of course, you can't expect everyone to come along for the ride without questions—most people don't like change; it upsets them when people change too fast. Be gentle with them.

One of the biggest changes you are making is that you are becoming a Witch. Depending on where you live and with whom, and your job and social circle, you may not want to leap out of the broom closet (come out as a Witch) right away. Let's look at that decision.

THE BROOM CLOSET
In or Out

Once you have become a Witch, you may feel like spreading the word about this cool path you've found! We would urge caution and careful thought. The average person still thinks green skin, warty noses, and evil spells when they hear the word *Witch*. Even the word *Wiccan* is misunderstood—not everyone has read the chapter on ethics, and some even equate Wicca with devil worship. Seriously. Life can get very complicated if you are not careful, so consider carefully before telling the world that you are a Witch. Here's our first piece of advice: choose whether to be in the broom closet or out of it—you can't easily straddle the threshold. To rephrase: half-way out rarely works.

You can be in the broom closet (except with immediate family and covenmates) or completely out. Being in the broom closet is a lot of hard work, and you need to come up with creative answers to some inevitable questions. Let's take a look at some of those questions.

If you practice at home and maybe travel to Pagan festivals, and someone asks what you're planning to do for the weekend, you can always say you're going "camping with friends." True as far as it goes, and avoids the whole clichéd "Pagans dancing naked around the bonfire" image.

Likewise, when someone asks, "What church do you go to?" you can't tell an outright lie—bad for your karma and your magick (words have power, and your magickal self hears every word you say). You need a response ready that's true as far as it goes but won't get you in trouble. For example, "My spirituality has always been a very personal and private thing."

If the question is broader, your answer can be as well. To "What is your religion?" you can say: "I've found that most religions have something valuable to teach, so I study several different ones." Which is probably true, since much of Wicca is based on so very many sources. If they really get in your face, answer: "I've found that discussing religion or politics can lead to arguments, so I avoid those topics of conversation." And then you change the subject: "So how are your kids doing?" or "Some weather for August, isn't it?"

An even broader question is "What do you believe?" And a great answer that is absolutely true and rarely offends is "I believe that all people have a spark of the Divine in them, and I try to honor that in my daily life."

What is being halfway out of the broom closet, and why doesn't it work? Halfway out means your family knows (or sometimes not, and that gets really sticky); some of your more liberal friends know, but other friends are seriously into their own religions and wouldn't understand; your neighbors don't know, and your grandmother can't know, but your cousin is also a Witch...are you confused about who you can talk to? And it never gets easier, especially when a close friends asks, "How was the ritual Friday night?" while your grandmother is standing next to you. Halfway doesn't work, no matter how many answers you have prepared—sooner or later, the word gets to the wrong ears, and they wonder why you didn't share the truth with them.

Even if you are out of the broom closet, having answers at the tip of your tongue is a good idea, for those situations in which it's really none of their business and you don't have time to educate them on the finer points of Wiccan theology and ethics.

So, what's it like being out of the broom closet? It doesn't mean you introduce yourself as a Witch to everyone you meet (any more than most people mention their religion up front), but you don't hide it from anyone either. If people ask, you answer honestly, no matter who they are or what reason they may have for asking. This is the "we are everywhere" campaign in action. The more of us who are open and educating those we meet, the safer all of us are. If you decide to be totally out, have some short, quick answers ready for the inevitable questions that are sure to follow your declaration that "I'm a Witch" or "I'm Wiccan." Later in this chapter we will share some of those sound bites. But first, let's discuss whether and how to tell family and friends.

When Invisibility Is in order
Staying in the Broom Closet

This may be the most serious section in this book, because it concerns your physical safety, your relationship with your children, and your job. Not every place is Pagan-friendly, much less Witch-friendly. Where do you live? San Francisco? Minneapolis? The Bible Belt? You probably have a good idea of which parts of the country require good thick walls around your broom closet. Fortunately, we are making inroads in public understanding and acceptance, as a quick glance at www.witchvox.com will show.

However, progress is slow in some regions. Many Witches move to friendlier places rather than stay in the broom closet. No one can blame you for wanting to keep yourself and your family safe. Children have been taken away, jobs have been lost, and people have been physically attacked because they emerged from the broom closet, voluntarily or involuntarily. (Involuntary outing is often accidental and the result of trying to be halfway in and halfway out—someone who knows forgets and blabs to the wrong person.) Fighting for custody of the kids or fighting a discrimination suit at work because you are a Witch is not anyone's idea of a good hobby.

If you must live in an intolerant place, go deep. If you must, for your sanity, be a public Witch, move to a more hospitable environment. There are lots of them.

A side note for those of you who are already out of the broom closet: Please respect the decisions made by those who are not ready to come out yet. They have valid reasons for staying quiet about their path—it is never up to you to "out" them before they are ready. One of the worst things a Witch can do is to betray another Witch's privacy.

Telling Family and Friends

Telling your family and others close to you can be traumatic. This section addresses questions you should consider before deciding whether and how to tell your mother and father, your children and spouse, your coworkers, your best friend (if they are not right by your side on the Wiccan path), and the poker club.

The first question is, "Do they have a need to know?" If they don't, and you don't know their religious preferences, then you probably don't have to tell them, either in words or by the jewelry you wear.

The second is, "What legal or other power do they have over you?" Are you a minor? If so, your parents have legal authority over you until you are eighteen. Whether you tell them depends on your relationship with them and what their beliefs are. Only you can answer the question, "Is it safe to tell my parents, or should I hold out until I'm eighteen?" If it is simply not safe physically, emotionally, financially, or otherwise, don't push it. That's hard to hear, but it may be the only wise choice. Keep reading and practicing in private, and wait.

On the other hand, if your parents are pretty open-minded, there are good ways and bad ways to tell them you're a Witch. Blurting "Mom, Dad, I'm a Witch" at the dinner table is probably not the best approach. Take a more circuitous route: talk about your belief in the sacredness of the earth, the importance of living an ethical life, or your view that the Creator has had many names and faces throughout human history.

A third question, if you are a parent: could coming out put your children in jeopardy? If your spouse doesn't know of your spiritual inclinations and wouldn't be supportive, then your marriage may have deeper problems than whether you are a Witch. On the other hand, if the marriage has already fallen apart and there is a question of custody, you will have to weigh the possible cost of telling your ex. Staying in the closet may be the best and only answer. Another factor is the ages of your children. Family conflict or separation can be more traumatic for little ones than for almost-grown teenagers.

EDUCATING THE PUBLIC

Suppose you've decided that for you, being out of the broom closet is the right choice. Because Witches are still relatively rare, you have just become the only expert on Witchcraft that most of your acquaintances will ever know. If you are planning to wear a pentagram in public or otherwise declare to the world that you are a Witch, be prepared for questions and have the answers ready. This is part of being confident in your own skin, knowing what you're talking about, and showing the world that Wicca is something to be proud of.

Most people can straightforwardly tell you the basic tenets of their religion in a few sentences, with no fumbling. You should be able to do the same. Below, we've listed some of the questions you can expect and short answers that are likely to be well received. Take these, put them in your own words, and you can confidently wear your pentagram in public.

Q. Is that a Star of David? I didn't know you were Jewish.

A. No, it's not, and I'm not. It's a pentagram, an ancient symbol of protection and balance.

Q. I thought a pentagram was a symbol of devil worship.

A. The upside-down pentagram has been used that way, like an upside-down crucifix, but this one is right-side-up. For me, it's a symbol of Wicca.

Q. So what is Wicca?

A. Wicca is based on the ancient religions of Europe, mostly. It's a religion that honors the earth as sacred, and we celebrate nature and the seasons of the year.

Q. So, Wicca is actually a religion?

A. Yes, it's a real religion, recognized by the federal government and everything.

Q. Do you believe in God?

A. I do believe in God, but also in the equal feminine energy in the universe that we call the Goddess.

Q. But there's just one God.

A. Maybe so, but the Divine has both masculine and feminine sides, and we often think of them as two divine persons, God and Goddess.

Q. So you don't believe in Jesus Christ?

A. I believe he was a very loving and wise teacher, but I don't worship him.

Q. Well, do you believe in evil? Or the devil?

A. I believe that people can do evil things, but I don't believe in any all-evil entity, so I don't believe in the devil.

Q. So, don't you follow the Ten Commandments?

A. In general, I have no problem with the Ten Commandments, but I follow something called the Wiccan Rede. Part of it is that I should harm no one and do good to others, because whatever I put out into the world comes back to me.

Q. What do you mean, comes back to you?

A. You know, "What goes around, comes around." Or "What you sow, so shall you reap." If you do something good for someone, then you will receive more good things back. Likewise, if you do harm to someone, bad stuff will happen to you. So I try not to harm other people.

Q. Do you go to church services like we do?

A. We celebrate at seasonal holy days and the phases of the moon.

Q. The phases of the moon—that sounds like Witchcraft.

A. That's another name for it, though it's nothing like movie witchcraft or fantasy books.

Q. So do you do magic, like put spells on people and stuff?

A. No. As I said, I expect everything I do to come back to me, so why would I put a spell on anyone? Besides, that would be interfering with their free will, and that's not right.

Q. Could you show me some magic right now? Just one trick?

A. Our magic isn't like stage tricks. It's serious stuff, more like prayer. And we don't perform magick on demand. But if you want to learn about it, I can recommend a good book.

If you get into a religious discussion and someone starts quoting the Bible (or any holy book), you have three choices. You can decide that nothing productive is going to come of the discussion, and walk away. Of course, your "opponent" will figure that you gave up because you couldn't argue with the "word of God," but that's not your problem.

Or, you can be very straightforward and say something like, "I know the Bible is important to you, but I'm not a Christian, so arguments based on the Bible don't have any meaning for me."

If you want to hold a discussion on their theological turf, debating as though the Bible had any weight for you, then really get to know the Bible well. You will need to have a response for every Bible quotation that gets thrown at you, and your lines must come from the Bible, too.

Of course, even if you memorize the whole book and become a world-famous Bible expert, they can always reject anything you say with the line, "The devil quotes Scripture for his own ends." In other words, they are saying, "When I quote the Bible, I am sharing God's word; when you do the same thing, you are being manipulated by Satan." Go figure.

Our recommendation: don't let yourself get caught in the whole "But the Bible says..." discussion (or the Koran, Torah, etc.). You can always say simply, "I am not Christian (or whatever), but if you are, and it works for you, I honor that. I hope you can respect my right to my own beliefs as well."

Stick to what you are and what works for you, and you will come across as confident in your own spiritual path; there's really no arguing against you when you are coming from a place of strength. The strength of Witchcraft is in what it is, not how it compares to other religions—so don't bash other faiths; stick to the positives of Witchcraft (and there are lots of them).

WHEN TO STAND ON YOUR RIGHTS

Usually there is no need at all to discuss the Craft, or religion of any kind, with people outside the Craft. You may choose to do so if you are already out of the broom closet and someone seems open-minded and really curious. Just don't get all evangelical and try to persuade them that they should be a Witch too. We have a long tradition in the Craft of *not* witnessing or proselytizing, much less recruiting muggles door-to-door. We do not have a monopoly on truth, every spiritual path is right for someone, and it is arrogant and disrespectful to try to change someone's religious convictions—unless those convictions including burning heretics, of course.

Yet the time may come when someone with different ideas is pushing you hard, and you or those you love are at risk. What do you do?

First, stop and think. No blurting or yelling. Ground and center, and just watch your opponent while you pull your thoughts together. Then act with strength and certainty.

Example One

County clerk: "This is a registry for regular clergy members, ministers in recognized churches. I'm sorry, but that Wicca thing is just Witchcraft, a cult."

You: "I am a member of the clergy, and I have shown you my credentials from (COG, ATC, whatever). Wicca is recognized as a religion by the United States government, including the Departments of Defense and the Treasury. Now please put me in that registry, or I can speak to your supervisor and my attorney about your violation of the laws regarding equal protection for all faiths."

Example Two

Judge of family court: "We have to do what's best for the child, and I'm not persuaded that being exposed to Witchcraft is in the child's best interests. Why should I not grant custody to the ex-husband?"

Your lawyer: "With respect, Your Honor, Mr. X's attorney is attempting to push your buttons with the word *Witchcraft*, which frightens many people. Please forget the B-movie depictions of spooky rituals and such, and consider the real practices of Wicca we have documented. Loving nature and celebrating seasonal festivals is not going to damage my client's daughter—it certainly hasn't so far. Besides, the other attorney is asking you to do something that the law forbids: he is asking you in effect to declare that one specific religion is bad for children, whereas others are not. How does that square with equal protection?"

Example Three

School principal: "Your son was suspended because he wore a pentagram pendant to school, and the dress code specifically says that students may not wear gang-related or occult items here."

You: "Fine, except that the pentagram is not gang-related or occult—*occult* simply means 'hidden.' It's a religious medallion and is a protected symbol just like a Catholic crucifix or a Star of David. If you were to ban all religious jewelry, at least you would be consistent. But you may not pick out our religious symbol to ban, or I guarantee you and the school board will face some very expensive litigation. Now will you allow the pentagram, or do you plan to disallow all religious jewelry?"

Example Four

Huge, scruffy drunk in bar: "I heard you was a Witch, and we don't like no f----g Satan worshipers comin' around here. I'm gonna punch out your lights!"

You: "Who told you I was a Witch? Was it Sam? Was it? I'm gonna find him and punch out *his* lights!" (Never mind that you don't know any "Sam." Leave the bar, go directly home, and avoid that bar in the future.)

A wise general always picks his or her battles; never fight except at a time and place of your choosing. According to the laws of the United States and most Western nations, you may not be harassed or persecuted because of your religion. But that is no help in an emergency where there is no police officer around, local officials are ignorant and prejudiced, or some thug with a broken bottle is glaring at you.

In cases like these, do what it takes now to keep yourself and your family safe, then discuss the situation with friends, elders, and legal counsel before you choose your next step. Use your divination and your magick. Do not take on a whole town, school system, or mob unless wisdom and honor demand it. If there is no other choice and you must confront injustice, then do it intelligently and find all the allies you can. The Craft has had enough martyrs.

Becoming a Witch isn't a game. It's about your whole life and how you will live for all the years ahead. It's about your heart and mind and spirit, and even about your safety and survival. But it's not just about you. It's about the well-being of the people you love, and the community where you live, and the ancestors who lived and died so that you could be here and make these choices.

Choose wisely. In fact, we would ask a favor of you. If you decide you are a Witch and that you will be open about it, don't tell the world for a year and a day. Learn everything you can about the Craft so that you may speak from knowledge. Cultivate your serenity and inner strength. Judge your words and actions before you speak or act, and then act and speak from love and kindness. Learn to see the magick all around you, so that curiosity and wonder are alive within you. Remember that you are holy and all people around you are sacred, and light the world with the radiance of the Goddess and God within you.

After that, if it seems wise, let the world know that you are a Witch. Then you will do honor to the Craft, the ancestors, and yourself.

CONCLUSION

The Path from This Place
Ever Learning, Ever Changing

Many seek, a few may find,
Touching magick, wielding power,
That Witchcraft feeds the heart and mind,
I am a Witch at every hour.

Witchcraft: not what the movies and fantasy novels told us. Obviously no green skin, pointy hats, or soaring across the full moon on your broomstick. No miraculous magickal powers, no constant drama, certainly no evil-sorceress stuff and neither the shriveled, cackling hag nor the voluptuous, eternally sexy dark queen.

Just a lot of real people, walking a different path to Spirit that involves a lot of hard work. It's not the One True Path, a title which has been claimed by a hundred other religions around the world. There is no one-size-fits-all spiritual truth, not for us little folks circling an average star in a corner of one ordinary galaxy out of millions. How arrogant to believe that our little minds could encompass the whole truth, God-Reality-the-Universe-and-Everything, when most of us can't even do algebra.

There is no One True Path for all humanity. But there is one that is right for you, that fits your needs and understanding at this time in your life. It might be Witchcraft; it might not. Nobody can decide for you.

You probably do need something, you know. Some kind of religious or philosophical framework that gets you through life, some clear set of beliefs that enables you to play well with others and to like what you see in the mirror. All religions are attempts to provide that and also to give you a chance at reconnecting with what is real and true and good at the heart of things. Don't we all have a sense of longing, a sense that somewhere everything is the way it should be? That there's a haven, a sanctuary, in your mother's lap or your lover's arms, in heaven or paradise or Summerland, on a distant star or in a dream? And isn't religion, each religion, just a knapsack of ideas and supplies to help you in your search for that place? And don't we each travel a different road and need different things on that journey?

Choosing your path is a big deal. Choose wrong, and you'll spin your wheels in theological mud, get lost on some dead end of conflict and confusion, or mistake the road for the destination.

If you choose Witchcraft, you are choosing a lifestyle, a fluid and evolving set of beliefs and a certain way of understanding and experiencing life. You are also choosing to ally yourself with a community of seekers, all gathered under one banner but each one unique. Some Witches are the finest, truest, best friends and sisters and brothers you could ever hope to walk with—and some are selfish, shallow, irritating creeps that take all the "fun" out of dysfunctional. In other words, they're human. Just as human as anyone of any faith you might meet anywhere. But most of us, most of the time, are trying our best to become *better* people.

What is it about Witchcraft that calls to you? Is there something that whispers in your blood, some past-life heritage or ancestral voice that calls you back to the old ways when we were one with earth, blood kin to every creature that runs or flies or swims?

Is it the Goddess and knowing that a woman is so much more than a virgin, a sex kitten, or a bitch? A mighty affirmation that female *is* sacred, that the mysteries and body-knowing and birthing, creating, nurturing, sustaining, protecting ways of women are the prime and essential core of life. That you, girl, are *good*?

Is it the deep certainty that God, the male part of the Divine, is much, much more than either a nice man in a white robe or an evil-tempered tyrant in the sky? That God is and must be the quickening, bright, joyful dancer at the gates of dawn, the loving father and bold explorer and wise healer and a thousand other ways for men to be?

Is it simply this, that sacredness and the heart of creation are in the forests and seas and mountains, that nature is holy everywhere and always, and the books and temples and rules of men are a pale shadow of the power and grace of the earth?

Or is it still deeper and subtler, a sense that the world we see is only a fragment of All That Is, that there are realms and realities beyond this one—in the world of spirit, on the astral planes, in dimensions half-seen by mystics and magicians—that you must explore?

You can still walk away from Witchcraft. There are many excellent spiritual paths and ways of life that can help you grow, enjoy life, and progress toward your destiny. You might be very happy giving your heart to one of the mainstream faiths…or casting aside religion and turning to rational, humanist values…or seeking contentment in your family and career, looking no further than the good things immediately in front of you.

If not—if the moonlight calls you, and you can hear the panpipes and see the flames of the sabbat bonfire dancing—we'll be waiting in the forest, in a circle near the old oak tree.

APPENDIX A

Recommended Reading

We have designated the following books as "classics" because of their effect on the Wicca/Witchcraft movement in the past several decades.

THIRTEEN CLASSICS OF WITCHCRAFT AND WICCA

Aradia, or, The Gospel of the Witches by Charles G. Leland (New Page Books, 2003)

Buckland's Complete Book of Witchcraft by Raymond Buckland (Llewellyn, 1986)

Diary of a Witch by Sybil Leek (Prentice-Hall, 1968)

Drawing Down the Moon: Witches, Druids, Goddess-Worshippers, and Other Pagans in America by Margot Adler (revised and updated; Penguin, 2006)

The God of the Witches by Margaret Murray (NuVision, 2009)

Grimoire of Lady Sheba by Lady Sheba (Llewellyn, 2001)

The Holy Book of Women's Mysteries by Zsuzsanna Emese Budapest (Susan B. Anthony Coven No. 1, 1979)

The Meaning of Witchcraft by Gerald Gardner (Weiser, 2004)

A New Wiccan Book of the Law by Lady Galadriel (Moonstone Publications, 1992)

The Spiral Dance: A Rebirth of the Ancient Religion of the Great Goddess by Starhawk (20th anniversary edition; HarperOne, 1999)

Witchcraft for Tomorrow by Doreen Valiente (Robert Hale, 1993)

Witchcraft Today by Gerald Gardner (Citadel, 2004)

The Witches' Way by Janet Farrar and Stewart Farrar (Phoenix Publishing, 1984)

Nine Witchcraft and Wicca Books for Beginners

Complete Idiot's Guide to Wicca and Witchcraft by Denise Zimmerman and Katherine Gleason (Alpha, 2006)

Exploring Wicca by Lady Sabrina (New Page, 2006)

The Mystic Foundation: Understanding and Exploring the Magical Universe by Christopher Penczak (Llewellyn, 2006; not specifically Wiccan but the foundations of our magick)

Positive Magick: Ancient Metaphysical Techniques for Modern Lives by Marion Weinstein (revised edition; Career Press, 2008)

True Magick: A Beginner's Guide by Amber K (fifteenth anniversary edition; Llewellyn, 2006)

The Truth About Witchcraft Today by Scott Cunningham (Llewellyn, 2002)

21st Century Wicca: A Young Witch's Guide to Living the Magical Life by Jennifer Hunter (Citadel, 2000)

Wicca and Witchcraft for Dummies by Diane Smith (For Dummies, 2005)

Wicca for Beginners: Fundamentals of Philosophy & Practice by Thea Sabin (Llewellyn, 2006)

Seven Books for Solitary Witches

Living Wicca: A Further Guide for the Solitary Practitioner by Scott Cunningham (Llewellyn, 2002)

Solitary Wicca for Life: A Complete Guide to Mastering the Craft on Your Own by Arin Murphy-Hiscock (Provenance, 2005)

Solitary Witch: The Ultimate Book of Shadows for the New Generation by Silver RavenWolf (Llewellyn, 2003)

Wicca: A Guide for the Solitary Practitioner by Scott Cunningham (Llewellyn, 1989)

The Wiccan Path: A Guide for the Solitary Practitioner by Rae Beth (Crossing Press, 1995)

The Wiccan Way: Magical Spirituality for the Solitary Pagan by Rae Beth (Phoenix, 2002)

A Witch Alone: Thirteen Moons to Master Natural Magic (new edition) by Marian Green (Thorsons, 2002)

MORE WORTHWHILE BOOKS ON WICCA AND WITCHCRAFT

Cabot, Laurie, and Tom Cowan

Power of the Witch: The Earth, the Moon, and the Magical Path to Enlightenment (Delta, 1990)

Campanelli, Pauline, and Dan Campanelli

Ancient Ways: Reclaiming Pagan Traditions (Llewellyn, 1991)

Circles, Groves & Sanctuaries (Llewellyn, 1992)

Wheel of the Year: Living the Magical Life (Llewellyn, 1989)

Crowley, Vivianne

Wicca: A Comprehensive Guide to the Old Religion in the Modern World, new edition (Element Books Ltd., 2003)

Cummer, Veronica

Sorgitzak: Old Forest Craft (Pendraig, 2008)

Cunningham, Scott

Earth, Air, Fire, and Water: More Techniques of Natural Magic (Llewellyn, 2002)

Earth Power: Techniques of Natural Magic (Llewellyn, 2002)

Curott, Phyllis

Book of Shadows: A Modern Woman's Journey into the Wisdom of Witchcraft and the Magic of the Goddess (Broadway, 1999)

Witch Crafting: A Spiritual Guide to Making Magic (Thorsons, 2002)

Farrar, Janet, and Stewart Farrar

Eight Sabbats for Witches (Phoenix, 1983)

A Witches' Bible: The Complete Witches' Handbook (Phoenix Publishing, 1992)

The Witches' God: Lord of the Dance (Phoenix, 1989)

The Witches' Goddess: The Feminine Principle of Divinity (Phoenix, 1987)

Farrar, Stewart

What Witches Do (Robert Hale, 2010)

Fitch, Ed

A Grimoire of Shadows: Witchcraft, Paganism, and Magick (Llewellyn, 1996)

Magical Rites from the Crystal Well (Llewellyn, 1984)

Galenorn, Yasmine

Embracing the Moon: A Witch's Guide to Rituals, Spellcraft and Shadow Work
(Llewellyn, 2002)

Green, Marian

The Elements of Natural Magic (Element Books, 1997)

The Gentle Arts of Natural Magic (Thoth, 1998)

Natural Witchcraft: The Timeless Arts and Crafts of the Country Witch (Thorsons,
2002)

Practical Techniques of Modern Magic (Thoth, 1993)

White Magic (Southwater, 2005)

Wild Witchcraft: A Guide to Natural, Herbal and Earth Magic (Thorsons, 2003)

Grey Cat

Deepening Witchcraft: Advancing Skills & Knowledge (Ecw Press, 2002)

Grimassi, Raven

Encyclopedia of Wicca & Witchcraft (Llewellyn, 2000)

Spirit of the Witch: Religion & Spirituality in Contemporary Witchcraft (Llewellyn,
2003)

Wiccan Magick: Inner Teachings of the Craft (Llewellyn, 2002)

The Wiccan Mysteries: Ancient Origins & Teachings (Llewellyn, 2002)

The Witches' Craft: The Roots of Witchcraft & Magical Transformation (Llewellyn, 2002)

Guiley, Rosemary Ellen

The Encyclopedia of Witches, Witchcraft, and Wicca (Checkmark, 2008)

Harrow, Judy

Devoted To You: Honoring Deity in Wiccan Practice (Citadel, 2003)

Wicca Covens: How to Start and Organize Your Own (Citadel, 2000)

Holland, Eileen

The Wicca Handbook (Weiser, 2008)

Hutton, Ronald

The Triumph of the Moon: A History of Modern Pagan Witchcraft (Oxford University Press, 2001)

Illes, Judika

The Element Encyclopedia of Witchcraft: The Complete A–Z for the Entire Magical World (Thorsons Element, 2005)

Jade

To Know: A Guide to Women's Magic and Spirituality (Delphi, 1991)

K, Amber

Coven Craft: Witchcraft for Three or More (Llewellyn, 2002)

Moonrise: Welcome to Dianic Wicca (Re-formed Congregation of the Goddess, 1992)

K, Azrael Arynn, and Amber K

RitualCraft: Creating Rites for Transformation and Celebration (Llewellyn, 2006)

Klein, Kenny

The Flowering Rod: Men and Their Role in Paganism (Megalithica, 2009)

Leek, Sybil

The Complete Art of Witchcraft: Penetrating the Secrets of White Magic (Signet, 1973)

McColman, Carl

When Someone You Love Is Wiccan: A Guide to Witchcraft and Paganism for Concerned Friends, Nervous Parents, and Curious Coworkers (Career Press, 2008)

Morrison, Dorothy

The Craft: A Witch's Book of Shadows (Llewellyn, 2001)

Moura, Ann

Green Magic: The Sacred Connection to Nature (Llewellyn, 2002)

Green Witchcraft: Folk Magic, Fairy Lore and Herb Craft (Llewellyn, 2002)

Grimoire for the Green Witch: A Complete Book of Shadows (Llewellyn, 2003)

Murray, Margaret

The Witch-cult in Western Europe (Book Jungle, 2010)

Penczak, Christopher

The Inner Temple of Witchcraft: Magick, Meditation and Psychic Development (Llewellyn, 2002)

The Living Temple of Witchcraft Volume One: The Descent of the Goddess (Llewellyn, 2008)

The Living Temple of Witchcraft Volume Two: The Journey of the God (Llewellyn, 2009)

The Outer Temple of Witchcraft: Circles, Spells and Rituals (Llewellyn, 2004)

The Temple of High Witchcraft: Ceremonies, Spheres and the Witches' Qabalah (Llewellyn, 2007)

The Temple of Shamanic Witchcraft: Shadows, Spirits, and the Healing Journey (Llewellyn, 2005)

Polson, Willow, and M. Macha Nightmare

The Veil's Edge: Exploring the Boundaries of Magic (Citadel Press, 2003)

Rabinovitch, Shelley

with Meredith Macdonald: *An Ye Harm None: Magical Morality and Modern Ethics* (Citadel, 2004)

with James Lewis: *The Encyclopedia of Modern Witchcraft and Neopaganism* (Citadel, 2004)

Sheba, Lady

The Grimoire of Lady Sheba (Llewellyn, 2001)

Sylvan, Dianne

The Circle Within: Creating a Wiccan Spiritual Tradition (Llewellyn, 2003)

Telesco, Patricia

Which Witch Is Which? A Concise Guide to Wiccan and Neo-Pagan Paths and Traditions (New Page Books, 2004)

Your Book of Shadows: How to Write Your Own Magical Spells (Citadel, 2000)

Valiente, Doreen

An ABC of Witchcraft Past and Present (Phoenix, 1988)

Natural Magic (Robert Hale, 1999)

The Rebirth of Witchcraft (Robert Hale, 2008)

Witchcraft for Tomorrow (Robert Hale, 1988)

Weinstein, Marion

Earth Magic: A Book of Shadows for Positive Witches (revised edition; Career Press, 2008)

Positive Magick: Ancient Metaphysical Techniques for Modern Lives (revised edition; Career Press, 2008)

Wood, Robin

When, Why, If...An Ethics Workbook (Robin Wood Enterprises, 1997)

...and the Sabbat series from Llewellyn Publications

Yule: A Celebration of Light and Warmth by Dorothy Morrison (2000)

Candlemas: Feast of Flames by Amber K and Azrael Arynn K (2001)

Ostara: Customs, Spells & Rituals for the Rites of Spring by Edain McCoy (2002)

Beltane: Springtime Rituals, Lore & Celebration by Raven Grimassi (2001)

Midsummer: Magical Celebrations of the Summer Solstice by Anna Franklin (2002)

Lammas: Celebrating the Fruits of the First Harvest by Anna Franklin and Paul Mason (2001)

Autumn Equinox: The Enchantment of Mabon by Ellen Dugan (2005)

Halloween: Customs, Recipes & Spells by Silver Ravenwolf (1999)

APPENDIX B
Glossary

Affirmation: A statement designed as a message to younger self, which, repeated at frequent intervals, aids in self-transformation.

Air: One of the classic four elements; represents the mind, intellect, or imagination; it frequently corresponds to the east and the colors light blue and yellow.

Amulet: A small item of natural material, such as wood, stone, or shell, charged for a magickal purpose, such as protection, and either carried or worn as a pendant.

Animals: Present in magick as familiars (companions and helpers), power animals (animal spirits that guide, protect, and empower individuals), and totem animals (those spirits that guide, protect, and empower clans or tribes).

Aspect: Usually, to invoke an aspect of Deity into yourself; to invite a god or goddess to become incarnate in your body. Also known as "assuming the god-form," or "Drawing Down the Moon" in the case of a lunar deity. One can also aspect an animal, tree, or other entity.

Aspects: Forms, facets, or personas of Deity, deities: for example, Artemis, Persephone, and Kore are deities, aspects of the Maiden, and the Maiden is an aspect of the Goddess. Helios, Ra, and Apollo are all solar aspects of the God. "All goddesses are one Goddess, all gods are one God; God and Goddess are One."

Asperge: To cleanse and purify the ritual space prior to ritual. Often done with saltwater, incense, or a besom.

Astrology: The study of the relationships and movements of the planets as they relate to human qualities and events.

Athame: (*a-thay'-me* or *AH-tha-may*) A ritual tool with a double-edged blade and usually a black handle, used for casting the circle and other magickal operations.

Attunement: An activity that brings the minds, emotions, and psyches of a group into harmony prior to ritual; chanting, singing, guided meditation, and breathing exercises are common ways to attune.

Aura: The energy field of the human body, especially that radiant portion visible to the third eye, or psychic vision, which can reveal information about an individual's health and emotional state.

Banishing: Causing to depart; used by some traditions as the procedure for releasing the elemental spirits of the quarters at the end of a ritual.

Beltane: A sabbat celebrating the burgeoning of spring; also called May Eve or May Day.

BNP: "Big Name Pagan," slang term for a Pagan celebrity, usually an author or leader.

Bolline: A white-handled knife used by Witches for cutting, carving, or inscribing things in the course of a ritual—candles, talismans, cords, etc. It is usually single-edged and sometimes has a sickle-shaped blade.

Book of Shadows: A magickal journal kept by each Wiccan dedicant and initiate, in which spells, invocations, ritual notes, herbal recipes, dreams, divination results, and material from the coven book can be recorded. Some people write it in Theban Script or in other alphabets for privacy.

Broom (also called a Besom): Sometimes used to ritually cleanse an area.

Burning Times: The era in European and American history when accused Witches, heretics, gay people, and others were oppressed and often tortured and killed for their supposed beliefs. Roughly 1400 to 1700 CE.

Cakes and Wine (or "Cakes and Ale"): After the magickal work and before the circle is opened, Wiccans and some other groups share food and drink. This custom is a sacrament of thanks for the gifts of Mother Earth, and a way of earthing excess psychic energy.

Calling the Quarters: Invitation for the spirits of air, fire, water, and earth (from the east, south, west, and north, respectively) to attend a ritual and lend their powers to its success. It is a means of fully engaging the mind, will, emotions, and body in the magickal working.

Candlemas: See *Imbolc*.

Casting: In divination, tossing the stones, runes, or sticks on the ground or on a special board or cloth, and gaining insights from their patterns and relationships.

Casting the Circle: The psychic creation of a sphere of energy around the area where ritual is to be performed, both to concentrate and focus the power raised and to keep out unwanted influences and distractions. The space enclosed exists outside ordinary space and time.

Cauldron: In ritual, a symbol of rebirth from Celtic mythology; sometimes used to heat herbal healing preparations or cook food for a sabbat feast.

Centering: The process of moving one's consciousness to one's spiritual or psychic center, leading to a feeling of great peace, calmness, strength, clarity, and stability.

Chalice: A goblet or cup, usually holding wine, which is shared around the circle in Wiccan ritual. It is both a female and a water symbol, and it can also be used for scrying or crystal gazing.

Charge: To intentionally imbue with energy, as "to charge a talisman with healing energy."

Charge of the Goddess: The primary sacred text of the Craft. The original version was recorded by Charles Leland in *Aradia*; Doreen Valiente, Starhawk, and others have rewritten popular versions.

Circle: An ongoing group of Pagans, such as a Druid grove or Witches' coven. Also the space created for ritual. See also *Casting the Circle*.

Cone of Power: The energy raised during magick is imaged as a cone, which at its peak of power is released toward a specific goal.

Congregation: Until rather recently, Witches were either solitary or gathered in covens of priestesses and priests. Now, some covens have organized congregations, or groves, of Wiccan/Pagan laity, loose-knit spiritual communities who meet to celebrate the sabbats.

Consecration: To solemnly dedicate or devote someone or something to a sacred purpose and/or to the service of a deity; for example, to consecrate a ritual tool to the purpose of protection, or to consecrate a priestess to the service of Artemis.

Cord: Either a heavy string used in binding and releasing magick or the piece of apparel circling the magician's waist (also called a "girdle"). In many covens and magickal lodges, the color of the cord indicates the wearer's degree of attainment or initiation.

Correspondences: The magickal energies associated with symbols, herbs, colors, elements, etc. The symbolic language of magick.

Coven: A group of Witches who gather regularly to celebrate their faith and work magick. Most covens limit their size to thirteen or fewer. Covens are self-governing and vary in their styles and interests. Some are affiliated with a particular tradition of the Craft, while others are eclectic.

Cowan: A person who is not a Witch. See also *Muggle*.

Craft, the: See *Wicca* and *Witchcraft*.

Crescent: A lunar symbol popular with many Wiccans and other magicians. In many traditions of Witchcraft, the high priestess wears a silver crescent on her tiara or headband as a recognition that the Moon Goddess rules magick and the moon symbolizes the powers of women.

Crone: A woman often but not always beyond childbearing age, recognized by her peers as being a leader or resource in the community. Also the elder aspect of a female deity; part of the tripartite Goddess with Maiden and Mother; that part that represents age and wisdom.

Croning Ritual: A rite of passage that marks a woman's transition to crone status. It may occur at menopause, at age fifty-six (second Saturn Return), or whenever a woman and her peers feel it is appropriate.

Cunning Man: The male equivalent of the wise woman; knowledgeable in the ways of nature and the hunt. Frequently an expert in the use of spells, herbs, and charms. A Witch.

Dark of the Moon: Popularly, the part of the cycle during which the moon is not visible from the earth. It lasts from one and a half to three and a half days, depending on the orientation of the moon and sun. This is traditionally the best time to do divination (scrying, tarot, reading the runes, etc.).

Degree: Many, but not all, covens have a training system of three degrees of learning and skill. In general, a first-degree initiate has the essential skills of a Witch; a second-degree initiate is more advanced and is sometimes considered an elder; and a third-degree initiate is qualified to lead a coven and pass on their tradition of the Craft.

Deity: God or Goddess, or both; the unifying creative principle in the universe.

Deosil: (*jesh'-ul*) Clockwise or "sunwise." This is the direction the priestess or priest moves when casting the circle and calling the quarters; it is the direction of attraction, creation, and growth. See *widdershins* for the opposite.

Dismissing the Quarters: Releasing or saying farewell to the spirits of the elements.

Divination: The art or practice of foreseeing future trends or discovering hidden knowledge using such tools as the tarot, the I Ching, runes, casting stones, or a showstone. Useful prior to ritual magick.

Drawing Down the Moon: A ritual in which a priestess aspects the moon goddess. See *aspect*.

Earth: The element corresponding to north, the body, the material world, health, strength, abundance, prosperity, the foundation of all things material and solid, and the colors black, brown, olive green, and yellow. Also the planet, our Mother Earth, and an aspect of Deity.

Earthing: Sending excess energy into the earth; done in ritual after power has been raised and sent to its goal.

East: One of the directions of the elements, usually corresponding to air.

Elements: In classical magick, earth, air, fire, or water, each of which represents a class of energies within the universe, and all of which together (along with spirit) make up the reality we know. See listings in this section for each element.

Esbat: A gathering of Witches to celebrate a certain phase of the moon (usually the full moon), work magick, and socialize; from a French word meaning "to frolic."

Familiar: An animal companion trained to assist in magickal workings.

Famtrad: A Witch who received early training through their family, sometimes passed down through generations.

Farewell to the Quarters: At the end of a ritual, thanking the quarters for their attendance at the ritual and sending them on their way.

Fire: The element corresponding to south, energy, will, passion, determination, ambition, and the colors red, red orange, and gold.

Fluffy Bunny: Slang; contemptuous term for Witches or other Pagans who are completely focused on the positive side of life—springtime, rainbows, bunnies, and white light—and pay little attention to the dark side or their shadow issues.

Full Moon: That phase in the lunar cycle when the moon is at her brightest and appears perfectly round; a high point of lunar power when Witches traditionally gather to work magick for healing and abundance and to celebrate the Goddess; the esbat celebrating the full moon.

God: God (capitalized), half of the ultimate creative force of the universe; god (lowercased), a personification or an aspect of God.

Goddess: Goddess (capitalized), half of the ultimate creative force of the universe; goddess (lowercased), a personification or an aspect of Goddess.

Great Rite: The union of Lord and Lady during a ritual, usually symbolic, celebrating the ultimate creative act.

Grimoire: A book of magickal spells and techniques. Although some of the medieval grimoires seem very mysterious and romantic, often they are merely collections of magickal "recipes" that are ineffective in the hands of anyone but a trained magician.

Grounding: Psychically reinforcing one's connections with the earth by reopening an energy channel between your aura and the earth, often visualized as a golden cord or tree roots.

Handfasting: A celebration of commitment between two or more people, sometimes a marriage.

Herbcraft: Herbs may be used for healing in a very direct and mundane way using teas, poultices, and tinctures, or in a magickal ritual through their correspondences.

High Magick: See *Theurgy.*

High Priest: Often the male leader of a coven. His duties include protecting the coven from outside harm and often the initiation of female Witches.

High Priestess: Often the female leader of a coven. Her duties include the spiritual welfare of the members of the coven and often the initiation of male Witches.

Imbolc, Imbolg, or Candlemas: One of the eight sabbats; celebrates the return of the sun's strength and the beginning of spring. Held on or about February 2.

Initiation: A profound spiritual experience in which one's unity with Deity and the universe is realized; also, the ritual by which such an experience is celebrated, and/or one is welcomed as a full member of a particular religious tradition or magickal group.

Invocation: Calling on a "higher spirit," Deity, or divine aspect to manifest; also an invocatory prayer or incantation.

Lady: A title of respect for the Great Goddess, the overarching divine female power; sometimes used for female leaders or elders in the Craft.

Lammas: See *Lughnassad.*

Lamps of Art: These are the two candles on the altar that provide illumination and may represent Goddess and God (Spirit). Choose white, or gold and silver for God and Goddess, or use colors based on the season or on the nature of the magick being done.

Law of Return: Whatever energy is sent out is returned to the sender multiplied (some traditions say it is multiplied by three and therefore call this principle the Threefold Law).

Litha or Midsummer: One of the eight sabbats; celebrates the Summer Solstice and the power of the sun. Usually celebrated on the solstice, June 21–23.

Lord: A title of respect for the Great God, the overarching divine male power; sometimes used for male leaders or elders in the Craft.

Low Magick: See *Thaumaturgy.*

Lughnassad or Lammas: One of the eight sabbats. Celebrates the first (grain) harvest and is held on or around August 1.

Lunar Cycle: The roughly twenty-nine-day cycle during which the moon waxes from dark to full and wanes to dark again; much magickal work is geared to the energies of the different phases of the moon.

Mabon: One of the eight sabbats. Celebrates the second (fruit) harvest and the Wild Hunt, as well as the autumnal equinox. It is usually celebrated near the equinox, September 21–23.

Magick: The use of focused will and energy to accomplish a goal; also the art of changing consciousness at will.

Magickal Name: A new name chosen by an individual or conferred by a teacher, either when someone becomes Pagan or is initiated. Such names are often drawn from nature or mythology.

Maiden: (1) Part of the tripartite Goddess with Mother and Crone, that aspect of deity representing youth, vigor, and potential; (2) An office in a coven; assistant (sometimes apprentice) to the high priestess, often in charge of preparing the ritual space.

Merry Meet, Merry Part, and Merry Meet Again: The traditional closing blessing of a Wiccan circle, a reminder that we have all met before, will part, and will meet again in this or another life.

Moon: Symbol of the triple Goddess (Maiden, Mother, and Crone) in the Wiccan faith, and of feminine powers of intuition and magick, and of female physiological cycles which are attuned to her. However, in some religions, the moon is personified as a god (Sin for the Babylonians, Khonsu for the Egyptians).

Moon Rituals: Rituals timed to coincide with a particular phase of the moon, to use that particular lunar energy in magickal work. See also *Esbat*.

Mother: Part of the tripartite Goddess with Maiden and Crone; the part representing maturity, fertility, and nurturing.

Muggle: A term adopted from the Harry Potter books by J. K. Rowling meaning a non-magickal person. See also *Cowan*.

Neopagans: Modern Pagans; those who have revived or reconstructed the ancient pre-Christian religions of Europe.

New Moon: The moment when moon and sun are in conjunction. Magickally, a time to initiate new projects. Originally, however, the time when the new crescent first became visible.

North: One of the directions corresponding to the elements, usually earth.

Offering: A gift to Deity or a particular divine aspect given in gratitude for blessings received or expected. In Neopagan religions today, this might include the burning of incense, a libation of wine, work toward a worthy cause, or food for wildlife—but never blood sacrifices.

Opening the Circle: Sometimes called banishing the circle; gathering in the sphere of energy that was cast at the beginning of the ritual; returning the space to its mundane state.

Ordains: A set of traditional laws from an unknown source that guide the conduct of many Witches and covens. Modernized versions have been published, such as *A New Wiccan Book of the Law* by the late Lady Galadriel.

Ostara: One of the eight sabbats. Celebrates spring, fertility (rabbits and eggs), and the vernal equinox; usually celebrated around March 21.

Outer Court: A group of Pagans affiliated with a coven, who gather regularly to celebrate the sabbats and hold educational and social events. Members of the outer court are not initiates (priestesses or priests) but are more similar to a congregation.

Pentacle: This is a disc of metal, ceramic, or wood with a pentagram and/or other symbols inscribed on it. It is a symbol of the earth element; sometimes salt or cakes are placed upon it, though it can also be used in rituals of protection as a magickal shield.

Pentagram: A starlike five-pointed figure of very ancient origin, used magickally for blessing, protection, and balance. The five points stand for the four elements plus spirit. Witches often wear a silver pentagram encircled, with one point up to symbolize spirit guiding and balancing the elements.

Priest: An initiated male Wiccan spiritual leader.

Priestess: An initiated female Wiccan spiritual leader.

Purification: An action that cleanses a person, space, or thing of negative energy, thoughts, or emotions.

Quarter Calls: The portion of a ritual when the elemental powers are invited to be present and lend their energies to the magickal working.

Quarters: A shorthand term for the four elemental powers and the directions they correspond to; the portions of the magickal circle influenced by the elements—each quarter is centered on its direction (e.g., the north quarter of the circle is actually from northwest to northeast, centered on north). Sometimes erroneously called the "corners"—but circles don't have corners!

Raising Power: Drawing ambient energy (or specific energies such as solar or lunar) into the circle and the aura, using techniques such as drumming or chanting, preparatory to sending the energy to a specific goal.

Rite of Passage: A ritual that marks the transition of an individual from one stage of life into the next, usually witnessed by their community. Birthing ceremonies, coming-of-age rites, handfastings, and memorial services are examples.

Ritual: A planned series of events leading to the accomplishment of a goal through magickal means; also a rite of passage or a celebration of the seasons.

Ritual Tools: Any tools, such as an altar, an athame, a chalice, salt and water bowls, lamps of art, or a pentacle, used in ritual to aid younger self in becoming engaged.

Sabbat: One of the eight great holy days of Wicca and many other Neopagan religions, celebrating themes (such as birth, fertility, or death) related to the turning of the seasons of the year. They have more than one name each, but one set of names is Yule, Imbolc, Ostara, Beltane, Litha, Lughnassad, Mabon, and Samhain. Not all traditions celebrate all eight.

Sacred Space: Of course all space is sacred, but the term usually refers to the area enclosed when the circle is cast. See also *Casting the Circle.*

Samhain: (*sow'-wen* or *so-veen'*) A sabbat usually celebrated October 31; traditionally the night the veils between this world and the next are thinnest. Witches often contact the spirits of the ancestors and/or their beloved dead at Samhain.

Scrying: The art of divination by gazing into a reflective surface such as a showstone; the images seen with the third eye, or psychic vision, can illuminate events or trends in your life.

Shadow Work: The emotional journey a Witch undertakes in order to confront and come to terms with "dark" issues such as pain, fear, illness, death, and grief. Such work is an ongoing part of a Witch's spiritual growth.

Skyclad: Naked; clad only by the sky. Some Witches go skyclad at their rituals.

Smudging: Using incense, traditionally sage, to cleanse an area and people before a ritual.

So Mote It Be: Traditional words used at the end of a spell in order to seal and finalize it, to make it happen.

South: One of the directions corresponding to the elements, usually corresponding to fire.

Spell: A pattern or series of words and/or actions performed with magickal intent, or sometimes simply a spoken incantation or chant.

Spirit: The nonphysical, immortal component of an entity; the soul. With earth, air, fire, and water, one of the five basic components of All That Is; represented by the top point of the pentagram.

Summerland: The traditional destination for a Witch after death. It is said to be a state of being where one can rest and absorb the lessons of one's most recent life before moving on to another incarnation.

Sun: Not simply the star that warms and lights our world, but also a symbol of success, expansiveness, spiritual illumination, and healing, as well as a powerful energy source for magick. In some religions, the sun is personified as a goddess (Amaterasu Omikami, Arinna, Bast, etc.) and in some as a god (Apollo, Ra, Helios, etc.).

Talisman: A drawn symbol or constructed item that is charged with a very specific energy and carried, worn as jewelry, or put in a special place. If carried on one's person, its energy exerts a continual subtle influence on one; if placed somewhere, the emanation of its energy influences the immediate environment.

Tarot: A divination tool consisting of a deck of cards (in classic decks, seventy-eight) with powerful scenes or images representing various energies, processes, or spiritual conditions. They are divided into four suits (wands or rods, pentacles or disks, cups, and swords, usually) that make up the Minor Arcana, and twenty-two other cards that make up the Major Arcana.

Temple: An area reserved and sometimes decorated and equipped specifically for religious or magickal activities; also any area consecrated as sacred space, whether or not it is normally considered so.

Thaumaturgy: "Low magick" used to influence things and events in everyday life: to protect your house, get a job, heal your cold, travel safely, etc.

Theurgy: "High magick" employed to connect with Deity and foster spiritual growth.

Threefold Law: The idea that whatever you send out (energy, words, ideas, actions, either good or bad) will come back to you threefold. Also called the Law of Return.

Tradition: A branch or denomination of Wicca. There are dozens of traditions; most share common values but vary in their ritual practices and program emphases.

Wand: A stick traditionally about eighteen inches long, or "from elbow to fingertips," often carved from one of the traditional sacred woods and used to channel power (attract or repel) and represent air or fire, according to various traditions.

Waning Moon: The period during which the visible part of the moon shrinks from full to dark; an appropriate time for spells of banishing, release, or cleansing.

Warlock: An oath-breaker or traitor. Mistakenly used by some cowans to mean a male Witch.

Water: Mixed with salt, may be used to purify; the bowl (or large shell) containing it is kept on the altar. Also the element that corresponds to the west, emotions, love, and intuition, and the colors light green, blue, and silver.

Waxing Moon: The period during which the visible part of the moon grows from dark to full; an appropriate time for spells for growth or increase.

West: One of the directions corresponding to the elements, usually water.

Wheel of the Year: The solar year and the sabbats that mark the turning of the seasons.

Wicca: A beneficent and magickal earth religion that celebrates immanent Deity, often in the forms of the Triple Goddess of the Moon and the Hornéd God of Nature; also called the Old Religion, the Craft, or Witchcraft.

Wiccan: A practitioner of Wicca, and the adjective form of Wicca, e.g., the Wiccan Rede.

Wiccan Rede: The ethics of the Craft are summed up in the Rede's eight words: "An ye harm none, do as ye will," meaning "As long as you do not harm anyone (including yourself), follow your inner guidance, your true will."

Widdershins: Counterclockwise, the direction a magician moves around the circle when wishing to banish, remove, or release energy; the opposite of deosil.

Wise Woman: The female equivalent of cunning man, also often a midwife and healer; one who uses nature magick. Frequently an expert in the use of spells, herbs, and charms. A Witch.

Witch: A priestess or priest of the Old Religion, Wicca. Some Witches distinguish between themselves and Wiccans, but it is mostly semantics as long as the Witch adheres to a code of ethics along the lines of the Wiccan Rede or similar.

Witchcraft: The skills and arts of the Witch; also Wicca. Sometimes distinguished from Wicca as not necessarily including the religious foundation.

Witch Jewels: Special headgear, necklaces, rings, or bracelets worn by Craft priests and priestesses. A high priestess may wear a crescent-moon tiara, a necklace of amber and jet, and a silver cord; a high priest may wear an antler crown, a torc, and a gold cord.

Witches' Pyramid: A model of magick made up of four sides aligned with the elements, with a base of knowledge, filled with love, and crowned by spirit.

Witchy-in-the-Night: Slang term for Witches who are especially in love with all things dark, mysterious, and eerie. Some dress the part.

Wizard: A male magician.

Woo-Woo: Slang term for all the arcane, esoteric, and mystical parts of the Craft.

Yule: One of the eight sabbats. Celebrates the Winter Solstice, the return of the light in the midst of winter; usually celebrated on the Winter Solstice, December 21–23.

APPENDIX C

Contact Points

ORGANIZATIONS

Circle Network

From the website: "Founded in 1977 by Selena Fox, Circle Network is an international Nature Spirituality network of individuals and groups, centers, periodicals, gathering communities, and other organizations.

"Circle Network includes those who are involved in one or more paths of Wiccan spirituality, Druidism, Animism, Pantheism, Ecospirituality, Shamanism, Goddess spirituality, Egyptian mystery traditions, Heathenism, ancient and contemporary forms of Paganism, and related ways.

"The purpose of Circle Network is to help Pagans from many paths and places connect with each other and share information, ideas, and energy to mutually benefit each other, Pagan culture, and the greater web of Life on planet Earth and the universe. There is no fee to be affiliated with Circle Network."

Circle offers newsletters, festivals and other events, and opportunities to connect with other Pagans.

Address: Circle Sanctuary, P.O. Box 9, Barneveld, WI 53507 USA

Website: www.circlesanctuary.org/network/

Covenant of the Goddess

COG was organized in 1975, in order "to increase cooperation among Witches and to secure for Witches and covens the legal protection enjoyed by members of other religions." It is one of the largest and oldest Wiccan religious organizations and serves primarily the United States.

COG fosters cooperation and mutual support among Witches. The Covenant publishes a newsletter, issues ministerial credentials on request to qualified persons, sponsors a national festival each summer, and encourages networking nationally as well as regionally through local councils. The Covenant is non-hierarchical and governed by consensus.

The Covenant has taken part in spiritual and educational conferences, interfaith outreach, large public rituals, environmental activism, community projects and social action, as well as efforts to correct negative stereotypes and promote accurate media portrayals. Its clergy perform legal marriages (or handfastings), preside at funerals and other rituals of life transition, and provide counseling to Witches, including those in the military and in prisons.

COG offers membership to Goddess-supporting covens or solitaries who meet certain criteria. Potential members must:

- Generally focus theology and ritual, etc., around the worship of the Goddess and the Old Gods (or the Goddess alone; coven or solitary)
- Proclaim themselves Witches or Wiccans in their Statement of Practice (coven or solitary).
- Believe in and follow a code of ethics compatible with that of the Covenant (coven or solitary).
- Have been meeting monthly or more often for at least six months (coven).
- Have three or more members who have been formally accepted into the clergy (coven).
- Be a cohesive, self-perpetuating group (coven).

A Local Council is a branch of the Covenant, consisting of at least three member covens of at least two different traditions in reasonably close geographic proximity. They meet at least twice a year and usually more often. They may initiate independent projects, sponsor local festivals, and work together for common goals close to home.

Address: P. O. Box 1226, Berkeley, CA 94701 USA

Website: www.cog.org

The Pagan Federation

Founded in 1971 primarily for the United Kingdom, the Pagan Federation now has programs in many countries and thousands of members from many different traditions of Paganism. It was organized to "actively fight…ignorance and negative attitudes toward Paganism" and to "create a network of like-minded people who… work together for the benefit of Paganism."

The Pagan Federation offers Associate Memberships which, after one year, may become Full Memberships. Members can read the newsletter, receive invitations to events, and help with the work of the Federation. Members must subscribe to the following three principles:

"(1) Love for and Kinship with Nature. Reverence for the life force and its ever-renewing cycles of life and death; (2) A positive morality, in which the individual is responsible for the discovery and development of their true nature in harmony with the outer world and community. This is often expressed as "Do what you will, as long as it harms none"; and (3) Recognition of the Divine, which transcends gender, acknowledging both the female and male aspect of Deity."

Address: PFI International, P. O. Box 473, 3700 Al Zeist, The Netherlands

Website: www.paganfederation.org

WEBSITE

The Witches' Voice (Witchvox)

This is "a proactive educational network providing news, information services and resources for and about Pagans, Heathens, Witches and Wiccans." Witchvox provides thousands upon thousands of listings of Pagan groups, individuals, clergy, events, stores, and much more, listed by country, state, or province.

The "critical resource tools" they offer include articles that can be used for public education regarding Paganism. "We provide educational materials on the basic beliefs of the religion of Witchcraft/Wicca to dispel the stereotypical image perpetuated by the media and centuries of negative propaganda. We uphold the civil and religious freedom guaranteed to all citizens in the Constitution and Bill of Rights and will actively resist those who would seek to suppress or restrict these rights."

The website tries to maintain a neutral, even-handed policy toward all Pagan religions that follow a positive code of ethics.

Website: www.witchvox.com

MAGAZINES AND NEWSLETTERS

Circle Magazine

From the website: *"CIRCLE Magazine* is a 72-page magazine published quarterly, with each issue dedicated to a particular theme and filled with a variety of articles, rituals, meditations, illustrations, invocations, contacts, news, photos, herbal formulas, reviews, magical development exercises, chants, advertisements, and other material."

Address: Circle Magazine, P. O. Box 9, Barneveld, WI 53507 USA

Telephone: (608) 924-2216

E-mail: circle@circlesanctuary.org

Website: www.circlesanctuary.org

New Moon Rising Journal

From the website: *"New Moon Rising* is a magickal Pagan journal, begun in 1989 and committed to being a vital international stimulus in the continuing Pagan Renaissance as an intelligent forum on Magick, Pagan culture, history and practice. NMR aligns with no particular school or tradition…NMR explores such varied topics as: Chaos, magickal theory and practice, Northern and Western Mystery Traditions, Shamanism, Thelema, the Craft, herbal lore, Pagan pantheons, biographies, Neopaganism, Druidry, faery lore, folklore, Earth mysteries, Alchemy, rituals, spellwork, runes, poetry, fiction, pilgrimages, divination…." Issued eight times a year at the major festivals.

Address: New Moon Rising, P. O. Box 16273, Phoenix, AZ 85011 USA

Telephone: (440) 551-4781

E-mail: info@nmrising.com

Website: www.nmrjournal.com

Witches & Pagans

The new 96-page pan-Pagan magazine "combining the fire and passion of *new-Witch* with the gravitas and depth of *PanGaia*." Look for interviews with Pagan artists, thinkers, writers, musicians, and celebrities, plus practical magick, AstroSpell, Pagan muses and mentors, including R. J. Stewart, Isaac Bonewits, Galina Krasskova, Kenaz Filan, Judy Harrow, Good Witch/Bad Witch, and much, much more.

Address: Witches & Pagans Magazine, BBI Media, P. O. Box 687, Forest Grove, OR 97116 USA

Telephone: (888) 724-3966

Website: www.bbimedia.com

SageWoman

From the website: "At *SageWoman* magazine, we believe that you are the Goddess, and we're devoted to celebrating your journey. With every issue, you'll connect with Goddess-loving women from around the world, rejoicing in our gifts, sharing our wisdom, reaching out to our sisters. In our pages, you'll be supported, uplifted, and challenged to envision the Goddess in all women, especially, in yourself. We invite you to subscribe today and join our circle."

Address: SageWoman Magazine, P. O. Box 687, Forest Grove, OR 97116 USA

Telephone: (503) 430-8817

E-mail: editor2@bbimedia.com

Website: www.sagewoman.com

SCHOOLS AND EDUCATIONAL PROGRAMS

Ardantane

Teaching ancient wisdom, living magick.

Ardantane is a Pagan learning center and seminary, and an independent, registered 501c3 nonprofit corporation. It offers classes and certificate programs in the areas of Healing Arts, Magick and Witchcraft, Pagan Leadership, Pagan Spirituality, Sacred Living, and Shamanic Studies. Students who meet requirements may be granted a certificate in any of these areas or in more specialized areas of study. Most classes are weekend intensives; many are offered at the main campus in New Mexico, but also in various cities around the United States. Students may either simply attend individual classes or apply to a certificate program by e-mailing an application to the dean of the appropriate school, or by mailing it to Ardantane.

Address: Ardantane, P. O. Box 307, Jemez Springs, NM 87025 USA

Telephone: (505) 469-7777

E-mail: Ardantane-director@ardantane.org

Website: www.ardantane.org

Cherry Hill Seminary

From the website: Cherry Hill offers "Quality higher education and practical training in Pagan ministry…The first and only graduate-level education for Pagan ministry in the modern world…Online distance-learning classes, regional workshops and intensive retreats."

Address: CHS, P. O. Box 5405, Columbia, SC 29250-5405 USA

Telephone: (888) 503-4131

E-mail: CHS@cherryhillseminary.org

Website: www.cherryhillseminary.org

Women's Thealogical Institute

From the website: "WTI is a multidimensional school and seminary for women who wish to further their understanding of the Goddess, women's spirituality, and/or women's witchcraft. Being a part of WTI lets women learn, practice, and share their spiritual work with others on similar paths. There are three ways you can participate in WTI...through weekend classes, online programs, and online classes.... there are many ways to celebrate and serve the Goddess. Within the Cella Program there are six Paths or areas of specialization. They are: Creatrix, Earthwalker, Scholar/Teacher, Ritualist, Healer, and Organizer." WTI is part of the Re-formed Congregation of the Goddess, International.

Address: WTI, P. O. Box 6677, Madison, WI 53716 USA

Telephone: (608) 226-9998

E-mail: rcgiorg@aol.com

Website: www.rcgi.org/wti/wti.asp

ENVIRONMENTAL ORGANIZATIONS

There are many more organizations doing good work for the earth. For ratings on the effectiveness of environmental (and other) charities, see www.charitynavigator .org. All of the following have earned three or four stars from Charity Navigator.

Arbor Day Foundation

Inspiring people to plant, nurture, and celebrate trees.

Address: 100 Arbor Avenue, Nebraska City, NE 68410

Donations to: 211 North Twelfth St., Lincoln, NE 68508

Website: www.arborday.org

Telephone: (888) 448-7337

CN Rating: 3M, 50.37

The Conservation Fund

America's partner in conservation.

Address: 1655 North Fort Meyer Dr., Suite 1300, Arlington, VA 22209

Website: www.conservationfund.org

Telephone: (703) 525-6300

CN Rating: 4M, 67.15

Earth Island Institute

You are here.

Address: 2150 Allston Way, Suite 460, Berkeley, CA 94704-1375

Website: www.earthisland.org

Telephone: (510) 859-9100

CN Rating: 4M, 63.54

Earthjustice

Because the earth needs a good lawyer.

Address: 426 Seventeenth St., 6th Floor, Oakland, CA 94612

Website: www.earthjustice.org

Telephone: (800) 584-6460

CN Rating: 4M, 62.89

Environmental Defense Fund

Finding the ways that work.

Address: 257 Park Ave. South, New York, NY 10010

Donations to: 1875 Connecticut Ave. NW, Suite 600, Washington, DC 20009

Website: www.edf.org

Telephone: (800) 684-3322

CN Rating: 4M, 63.01

Greenpeace Fund

Promoting solutions that are essential to a green and peaceful future.

Address: 702 H St. NW, Suite 300, Washington, DC 20001

Website: www.greenpeace.org

Telephone: (800) 722-6995

CN Rating: 4M, 60.98

Nature Conservancy

Protecting nature. Preserving life.

Address: 4245 North Fairfax Dr., Suite 100, Arlington, VA 22203-1606

Website: www.nature.org

Telephone: (703) 841-5300

CN Rating: 4M, 65.45

Ocean Conservancy

Start a sea change.

Address: 1300 Nineteenth St. NW, 8th Floor, Washington, DC 20036

Website: www.oceanconservancy.org

Telephone: (800) 519-1541

CN Rating: 3M, 62.89

Pollinator Partnership

Your source for pollinator action and information.

Address: 423 Washington St., 5th Floor, San Francisco, CA 94111

Website: http://pollinator.org

Telephone: (415) 362-1137

CN Rating: 4M, 53.34

Sea Shepherd Conservation Society

Ending the destruction of habitat and slaughter of wildlife in the world's oceans.

Address: P. O. Box 2616, Friday Harbor, WA 98250

Website: www.seashepherd.org

Telephone: (360) 370-5650

CN Rating: 4M, 60.58

Sierra Club Foundation

Explore, enjoy, and protect the planet.

Address: 85 Second St., Suite 750, San Francisco, CA 94105

Website: www.sierraclub.org/foundation/

Telephone: (415) 995-1780

CN Rating: 3M, 56.46

World Wildlife Fund

Protecting the future of nature.

Address: 1250 24th St. NW, P. O. Box 97180, Washington, DC 20090

Website: www.worldwildlife.org

Telephone: (800) 960-0993

CN Rating: 4M, 65.64

APPENDIX D
Color and Metal Correspondences

The following correspondences will be familiar to many practitioners of magick, but you should feel free to choose the ones that seem meaningful and appropriate to you, even if they do not match those given here.

COLOR CORRESPONDENCES
For Clothing, Candles, Altar Cloths, Etc.

Once you have selected your color or colors for a particular working, you can obtain candles, robes, cords, wall hangings, or an altar cloth of the appropriate color. (*Note:* This list is an expanded version of appendix 3 from the fifteenth-anniversary edition of *True Magick*; as a rule, we try not to duplicate material from our other books, but this is one of those lists that is handy to have in more than one place.)

Abstinence, Sobriety, Temperance, or Moderation: Purple, black

Cheerfulness: Turquoise, bright yellow

Children: The primary colors: bright yellow, red, blue, and green

Confidence: Royal blue

Courage: Bright red

Energy: Orange

Fertility: Green, especially a light spring green

Friendship: Royal blue, gold, golden brown, or tan

Healing or Health: Medium green, rose

Home (new): Bright orange, sunlight yellow

Home (blessing): Rose, gold, light blue

Home (purification): White, light blue

Hope: Sky blue

Inner Peace: Light blue, lavender, white

Joy: Rainbow

Love: Rose

Money, Prosperity, or Wealth: Gold, emerald green

Protection (physical): Blue, black, turquoise

Protection (psychic): Silver

Purification: White

Spiritual Growth: Violet, purple, or lavender

Study or Learning: Orange

Success: Gold, royal blue

Sun Gods: Gold

Travel: Light blue

Unity (of polarities): Rainbow

Water Magick: Blue, green, aqua

CORRESPONDENCES FOR METALS
For Jewelry, Talismans, Ritual Tools, Etc.

Balance (polarities): Copper, bronze

Commerce: Mercury (**HAZARDOUS**)

Communication: Mercury (**HAZARDOUS**)

Courage: Gold

Divination: Silver

Dreamwork: Silver

Eloquence: Mercury (**HAZARDOUS**)

Emotions: Silver

Energy (directing): Copper

Fire Magick: Gold, brass

Good Fortune: Tin (hard to find, use pewter)

Grounding: Lead (**HAZARDOUS**)

Healing: Silver, copper, iron, brass

Intuition: Silver

Jupiter: Tin

Love: Copper

Luck: Copper

Mercury: Mercury (**HAZARDOUS**)

Moon Goddesses: Silver

Moon Magick: Silver

Negativity (deflects): Lead (**HAZARDOUS**)

Power: Gold

Prosperity: Gold, tin, brass

Protection: Gold, silver, copper, iron, lead (**HAZARDOUS**), brass

Psychic Energy (blocks): Iron

Psychic Work: Silver

Saturn: Lead (HAZARDOUS)

Scrying: Silver

Self-Confidence: Gold

Solar Magick: Gold, brass

Strength: Iron, gold

Success: Gold

Sun: Gold, brass

Sun Gods: Gold, brass, bronze

Travel: Mercury (HAZARDOUS)

Unity (of polarities): Electrum

Venus: Copper

Water Magick: Silver

Warnings

- Mercury is extremely poisonous! Do not touch, breathe, or ingest. Use sterling silver as a substitute.

- Lead is poisonous when absorbed by the body; use hematite or pewter as a substitute.

- Copper can turn your skin green when worn touching the skin for too long.

APPENDIX E
The Wiccan Rede

Being known as the counsel of the Wise Ones:

Bide the Wiccan Laws ye must
In Perfect Love and Perfect Trust.
Live an' let live
Fairly take an' fairly give.
Cast the Circle thrice about
To keep all evil spirits out.
To bind the spell every time
Let the spell be spake in rhyme.
Soft of eye an' light of touch
Speak little, listen much.

Deosil go by the waxing Moon
Sing and dance the Wiccan rune.
Widdershins go when the Moon doth wane,
An' the Werewolf howls by the dread Wolfsbane.
When the Lady's Moon is new,
Kiss thy hand to Her times two.
When the Moon rides at Her peak
Then your heart's desire seek.

Heed the Northwind's mighty gale,
Lock the door and drop the sail.
When the wind comes from the South,
Love will kiss thee on the mouth.
When the wind blows from the East,
Expect the new and set the feast.
When the West wind blows o'er thee,
Departed spirits restless be.

Nine woods in the Cauldron go,
Burn them quick an' burn them slow.
Elder be ye Lady's tree,
Burn it not or cursed ye'll be.
When the Wheel begins to turn,
Let the Beltane fires burn.
When the Wheel has turned a Yule,
Light the Log an' let Pan rule.

Heed ye flower bush an' tree,
By the Lady Blessèd Be.
Where the rippling waters go,
Cast a stone an' truth ye'll know.
When ye have need,
Hearken not to others' greed.
With the fool no season spend
Or be counted as his friend.

Merry meet an' merry part
Bright the cheeks an' warm the heart.
Mind the Threefold Law ye should
Three times bad an' three times good.

When misfortune is enow,
Wear the Blue Star on thy brow.
True in love ever be
Unless thy lover's false to thee.

Eight words ye Wiccan Rede fulfill
An it harm none, do what ye will.

From the website of the New England Covens of Traditionalist Witches:

"This version of the Rede has appeared in many publications, on various sites and in many stores. These printed versions come from *The Green Egg,* where it was first published by Lady Gwynne Thompson, primary teacher of N.E.C.T.W. (1928–1986). In *Green Egg* #69, she attributed our Tradition's version of the Rede to Adriana Porter, her paternal grandmother, 'who was well into her 90's when she crossed over into the Summerlands in 1946.'

"Lady Gwynne gave this Rede to the universe, and for this and everything else she gave us, we honor her and carry on her tradition."[15]

15 See http://www.nectw.org/ladygwynne.html.

APPENDIX F

Rite of Self-Dedication to the Craft of the Wise

We recommend that you write your own ritual so that it comes from the heart and your spirit is infused throughout it. However, if you are absolutely stuck as to what to do, this may give you a starting point. This self-dedication ritual is loosely based on the dedication rite from the Ladywood Tradition of Wicca. You can change it to fit your needs or the tradition that most interests you. As long as the basic steps are included, feel free to adapt and amend this as you will.

PRELIMINARIES

In this ritual, you will present yourself to the quarters (elements) and to the God and Goddess of nature. You will put on a white cord, the sign of a dedicant, and speak your new Craft name. After this, you may begin creating your own astral temple. You will then do a short divinatory reading that signifies your current path or work as a dedicant. There is a self-blessing, followed by cakes and wine and giving thanks. Try to do the ritual during the waxing or full moon, when you have plenty of time and will not be interrupted or disturbed.

In a quiet and private place, set up the altar. You will need the following items:

- An altar: a table or other flat surface inside or a flat stone, section of log, or grassy spot outdoors
- An altar cloth in colors that remind you of the Craft, new beginnings, or the season
- Two candles

- Statues or symbols of the Goddess and the God—either traditional forms such as the Moon Goddess and the Hornéd God, or your favorite aspects
- Symbols of the elements (such as a shell, red candle, stone, and feather)
- Small bowls of water and of salt
- Incense, holder, and matches
- A cup or chalice of water with a few drops of wine in it
- A small cake or piece of bread on a plate (or other nourishing food if you do not have cake or bread of any kind)
- A white cord, nine feet long; use drapery cord from a fabric store or weave it yourself
- A tarot deck, rune set, or other form of divination
- Your Book of Shadows and a pen
- The ritual, written in the book, in large-enough lettering to read in low light

Prepare yourself by fasting for a few hours before the ritual. Cleanse yourself thoroughly, perhaps in a candlelit bath, with music and fragrant oils. Then find a quiet place away from your altar, preferably a beautiful place outdoors in nature.

Take along your Book of Shadows and a pen.

Meditate on your impending dedication. Ask yourself questions, and answer honestly:

- Why do I choose to do this?
- How do I feel right now?
- What aspects of this are exciting? What aspects are frightening?
- How much time and energy am I willing to put into my spiritual path in the months ahead?
- What do I hope this ritual will do for me?
- Am I ready for change in myself and in my life?

Write your answers in your Book of Shadows.

If you have not done so already, choose the name by which you will be known to the Craft community and the spirit world.

The Ritual

1—Arrival: Proceed to the place where you have set up the altar. If it is dark, you will want a candle or lantern.

2—Centering: Chant quietly to yourself for a time (you may chant along with a recorded chant if you wish). Here is one you might use:

I am a circle within a circle
With no beginning and never ending

3—Purification: Cleanse and purify the area and yourself.

Hold your hand over the salt bowl, saying: "I conjure thee, O spirit of salt (charge with a glowing pentagram using your athame or finger), casting out all impurities that may lie within."

And over the water bowl: "Likewise do I conjure thee, O spirit of water (again charge with a glowing pentagram using your athame or finger), casting out all impurities that may lie within."

Mix three bits of salt into the water and stir. Now sprinkle the saltwater lightly around the altar and over yourself, saying: "By water and earth am I cleansed and purified."

Now hold your hand over a candle, saying: "I conjure thee, O spirit of fire (charge with a glowing pentagram using your athame or finger), casting out all impurities that may lie within."

And over the incense: "Likewise do I conjure thee, O spirit of air (again charge with a glowing pentagram using your athame or finger), casting out all impurities that may lie within."

Light the incense and waft its smoke around the altar and over yourself, saying: "By fire and air am I cleansed and purified."

4—Casting the Circle: With your athame or hand pointing to the ground before you, walk deosil (clockwise) around the altar area and say: "I conjure thee, O circle of power, that thou be a boundary between the world of humanity and the realms of the mighty ones, a guardian and protection to preserve and contain the power I shall raise within; wherefore do I bless and consecrate thee."

5—**Calling the Quarters:** Proceed in the following way:

Face the east, raise your hand or athame, and say: "Guardians of the watchtowers of the east, spirits of air, I call upon thee. Lend your presence and power to this circle as I dedicate myself to the study of the Craft of the Wise. Grant me a clear mind and a vivid imagination. Golden eagle of the eastern skies, I do summon, stir, and call thee up!" Visualize the element appearing just outside the circle as an animal spirit (or an elemental spirit or appropriate deity if you wish). Kiss your athame's blade (or your hand), and salute the elemental presence.

Face the south, raise your hand or athame, and say: "Guardians of the watchtowers of the south, spirits of fire, I call upon thee. Lend your presence and power to this circle as I dedicate myself to the study of the Craft of the Wise. Grant me a strong will and high energy. Red dragon of the southern desert, I do summon, stir, and call thee up!" Visualize the element appearing just outside the circle as an animal spirit (or an elemental spirit or appropriate deity if you wish). Kiss your athame's blade (or your hand), and salute the elemental presence.

Face the west, raise your hand or athame, and say: "Guardians of the watchtowers of the west, spirits of water, I call upon thee. Lend your presence and power to this circle as I dedicate myself to the study of the Craft of the Wise. Grant me a loving heart and deep feelings. Silver dolphin of the western seas, I do summon, stir, and call thee up!" Visualize the element appearing just outside the circle as an animal spirit (or an elemental spirit or appropriate deity if you wish). Kiss your athame's blade (or your hand), and salute the elemental presence.

Face the north, raise your hand or athame, and say: "Guardians of the watchtowers of the north, spirits of earth, I call upon thee. Lend your presence and power to this circle as I dedicate myself to the study of the Craft of the Wise. Grant me a healthy body and a prosperous life. Black bull of the northern forest, I do summon, stir, and call thee up!" Visualize the element appearing just outside the circle as an animal spirit (or an elemental spirit or appropriate deity if you wish). Kiss your athame's blade (or your hand), and salute the elemental presence.

6—**Invoking Deity:** Do this in the form that feels most powerful or appropriate to you. Some options:

- "I call upon the Hornéd God of wild things, the Lord of Death and Rebirth, to be present and witness this rite."

  "I call upon the Triple Goddess of the Moon—Maiden, Mother, and Crone—to be present and witness this rite."

- "Come to me, Great God, thou who art Sun Lord, Harvest King, Hornéd God of the wilderness, Divine Male Principle of many names and faces, Pan, Woden, Ra, Tammuz, Bel—join this rite."

  "Come to me, Great Goddess, thou who art Moon Lady, Earth Mother, Sovereign Queen, Divine Female Principle of many names and faces, Diana, Gaia, Freya, Brigit, Isis—join this rite."

- (Goddess only) "Lady of a Thousand Names, Maiden Huntress, Earth Mother, Lady of Forest and Field, Shining Moon, Sovereign of the Seas, Queen of the Dark Underworld, Starry Goddess of the Night, Mistress of Magick, come to me now and witness this, my rite of dedication."

7—**Pledges:** Make your pledges to the gods and the elemental powers:

"I have come to this circle to dedicate myself to the study of the Craft of the Wise."

"From this moment forward, among the Craft community and the world of spirit, I shall be known as _____. I have chosen this name because _____."

"I know that the hand of the Goddess will be upon me, and that she changes everything she touches. And I am ready to begin the transformation."

"As I begin this journey, I do promise and swear to live my life by the Wiccan Rede, 'An ye harm none, do as ye will,' and to use the Craft only when it harms none."

"Further do I promise and swear to keep the secrets of the circle. Never shall I reveal or speak of any personal information about Craft sisters and brothers outside the circle without their express permission. And never shall I reveal or teach the secrets of the Craft except to those who have made these same promises."

"And more, I do commit myself to work diligently at the study of the Craft for as long as I choose to be a dedicant."

8—**Presentation to the Elemental Powers:** Present yourself to each quarter, saying at each:

"Spirits of air, guardians of the watchtowers of the east,

I, (name), have come to this circle to learn the Craft of the Wise.

I have promised to live by the Wiccan Rede and to keep the secrets.

May you recognize me within this circle and guard me well,

and may your intellect and imagination be mine."

"Spirits of fire, guardians of the watchtowers of the south,

I, (name), have come to this circle to learn the Craft of the Wise.

I have promised to live by the Wiccan Rede and to keep the secrets.

May you recognize me within this circle and guard me well,

and may your will and energy be mine."

"Spirits of water, guardians of the watchtowers of the west,

I, (name), have come to this circle to learn the Craft of the Wise.

I have promised to live by the Wiccan Rede and to keep the secrets.

May you recognize me within this circle and guard me well,

and may your depth of feeling and love be mine."

"Spirits of earth, guardians of the watchtowers of the north,

I, (name), have come to this circle to learn the Craft of the Wise.

I have promised to live by the Wiccan Rede and to keep the secrets.

May you recognize me within this circle and guard me well,

and may your strength and endurance be mine."

9—**Presentation to the God:** Stand before the altar and present yourself to the God in the person of his statue or symbol (unless the ritual is focused only on the Goddess), saying:

"My Lord, I, (name), have been presented to the spirits of the four directions. Now I present myself before you, all ye gods of nature! I have come to this circle to learn the Craft of the Wise. May you recognize me within this circle and guide me to share your wisdom, love, and power."

10—**Presentation to the Goddess:** Stand before the altar and present yourself to the Goddess in the person of her statue or symbol, saying:

"My Lady, I, (name), have been presented to the spirits of the four directions and all the gods of nature. Now I present myself before you, all ye goddesses of nature! I have come to this circle to learn the Craft of the Wise. May you recognize me within this circle and touch my life to change me according to your wisdom."

11—**Accepting the Cord:** Next you may take up the white cord. Place it around your waist and tie it, saying: "A white cord is the sign of a dedicant within many traditions. Whenever I wear this cord, I shall remember this night and the promises I have made."

12—**The First Lessons:** "I have dedicated myself to the study of the Craft. Let my study begin this evening with three pieces of wisdom:

The first is the Rede:

Bide the Wiccan Law ye must,

In perfect love, in perfect trust,

Eight words the Wiccan Rede fulfill:

An ye harm none, do as ye will.

And ever mind the Rule of Three:

What you send out returns to thee.

Follow this with mind and heart,

And merry ye meet, and merry ye part.

The second enjoins me to silence and discretion. Knowledge and magick and power may I learn within this circle, and all the skills of the Craft of the Wise. In like manner, when I have mastered the arts, shall I pass them on, and so our circle grows. But I must remember well that I may only teach those who have sworn to keep the secrets and to follow the Wiccan Rede.

The third explains the cycle of life, death, and rebirth. Within this circle, love is the law and love is the bond. To fulfill love, I must be reborn in the same time and place, and remember and find those I have loved before. To be reborn, I must first die. To die, I must first be born. To be born, there must be love. And that is all the magick."

13—**Divination:** Perform a short divination; for example, with one tarot card or rune. Ask the question, "What are the energies that should guide my studies for the coming months?" Meditate on the card or rune until your general direction or approach becomes clear.

14—**Self-Blessing:** Perform a self-blessing. Take a chalice of water mixed with a few drops of wine. Touch your feet with a dab of the liquid and say, "Blessed be my feet that have brought me to this path."

Touch your genitals and say, "Blessed be my loins, source of creation and of pleasure."

Touch your heart and say, "Blessed be my breast, formed in beauty and in strength."

Touch your lips and say, "Blessed be my lips that speak the names of the Lady and the Lord."

Touch your forehead and say, "Blessed be me, (magickal name), beloved child of the Goddess."

Stand a moment in silence, and just feel.

15—Cakes and Wine: Bless and taste the cakes and wine (food and beverage).

Lift the food before the altar, and say, "Thank you, Lady, for this nourishment, the bounty of the earth." Take a bit and savor it, then put the plate down.

Lift the cup or chalice before the altar, and say, "Thank you, Lord, for this drink, a gift from the earth quickened by your sunlight." Sip a little and savor it, then put the cup down.

16—Farewell to Goddess (and God, if invoked): Express your thanks in your own words, then add "Hail and farewell!"

17—Farewell to the Quarters: Begin in the north and proceed widdershins (counterclockwise):

"Guardians of the watchtowers of the north, powers of earth, I thank thee for attending. Stay if you will, go if ye must; and if you must go, I say 'Hail and farewell!'"

"Guardians of the watchtowers of the west, powers of water, I thank thee for attending. Stay if you will, go if ye must; and if you must go, I say 'Hail and farewell!'"

"Guardians of the watchtowers of the south, powers of fire, I thank thee for attending. Stay if you will, go if ye must; and if you must go, I say 'Hail and farewell!'"

"Guardians of the watchtowers of the east, powers of air, I thank thee for attending. Stay if you will, go if ye must; and if you must go, I say 'Hail and farewell!'"

18—Open the Circle: Face the east, and with your hand or athame stretched before you, turn widdershins and draw in the energy of the circle. Then face the altar and say, "The circle is open but never broken. Merry meet, merry part, and merry meet again! Blessed be."

When this is done, you may meditate, enjoy a quiet meal, or go to sleep.

INDEX

abortion, 110

abundance, 48, 50, 62–64, 82, 105, 109, 271, 272

abundance model of the universe, 105

acting in accord, 154

activist, 235

affirmations, 117–118, 149, 161

air, 50, 56–57, 95–97, 99, 132, 149, 168, 170, 174–175, 177, 181, 234

air (element), 29, 59–62, 64–65, 69, 71, 75, 77, 85, 87, 96, 118–119, 124, 125, 127, 153, 156, 163, 166–167, 172, 181, 187, 230, 267, 269, 271–272, 278–279, 301–302, 304, 307

Akashic Records, 186

alcohol, 110–111, 160

All Hallows Eve, 41, 52

All That Is, 179, 257, 278

allies, 2, 14, 29, 79, 121, 147, 160, 170, 182, 211, 253

altar, 13–14, 53, 67–70, 76–77, 79, 81–83, 115–117, 120, 128–129, 148, 151, 155–158, 216, 273, 277, 279, 291, 299–301, 305, 307–308

American Religious Identification Survey, 36

amulets, 96, 110, 148–149, 170, 231

An ye harm none, 77–78, 93, 128, 131, 134, 279–280, 303, 306

ancestors, 6, 10, 16, 18–19, 23, 36, 42, 51–53, 66, 81, 121, 127, 145, 181, 197, 213, 254, 277

ancestral spirits, 197

animal advocate, 235

animal allies, 2, 121, 147, 160, 170, 182, 211

animal companions, 10, 36, 103, 206, 267, 272

animals, 10, 16, 18, 29, 46, 51, 62, 77, 81–82, 84, 88, 89, 90, 93–94, 97, 103–104, 113, 132, 141, 170, 181–182, 188, 190, 208, 211, 214, 235, 240, 267

Aquarian Tabernacle Church, 217, 226

archangels, 17, 182

archetypes, 27

Ardantane, 2, 77, 177, 203, 229, 235–236, 286

Ardaynes, 134

artist, artisan, 4, 186, 204, 227, 235

As above, so below, 91, 172–173

Asatru, 6, 28, 205, 209, 224

aspect, 11, 16, 26–27, 54–55, 81, 100, 121, 146, 153, 188, 227, 229, 240, 267, 270–275, 283

astral plane, 29, 180–181

astrology, 171, 183, 185, 188, 197, 231, 236, 267

athame, 69, 77–78, 84, 86, 152, 154, 233, 268, 277, 301–303, 307

attunement, 152, 156, 268

aura, auras, 14, 99, 192, 198, 268, 273, 276

bard, 49, 227, 235

Beardman jugs, 150

bell, 7, 73, 75, 81, 87, 99, 128, 133, 191, 216

Bellarmine jars, 150

Beltane, 41–42, 46, 48, 156, 266, 268, 277, 296

besom, 88, 152, 267–268

bibliomancy, 190

birth chart, 183, 197

bisexual, 3, 102, 214, 243

blue beads, 97

bolline, 86, 268

Bonewits, Isaac, 215, 285

bonfire, 5, 10, 20, 48–49, 66, 85, 87, 205, 245, 257

Book of Shadows, 21–22, 58, 60–65, 67–68, 75–77, 80–84, 87, 113, 117–118, 128–129, 148, 155, 157, 163–164, 170, 176–177, 190–191, 195–199, 210, 216, 239, 241–242, 244, 259–261, 264–265, 268, 300

books for beginners, 259–260

books for families, 223

books for Solitary Witches, 259–260

breathing, breath, 14, 51, 62, 64–69, 91, 99–100, 116, 118–120, 123, 147, 149, 168, 170, 172, 193–194, 198, 230, 268, 294

broom, 21, 36, 73, 88, 107, 152, 203, 255, 268

wand, wands, 6, 14, 46, 60, 69, 73, 78–80, 84, 86, 88, 90, 112, 121, 149, 194, 233, 278–279

war and peace, 110

Warlock, 15, 279

Watchtowers, 17, 302, 304–305, 307

water, 19, 56–57, 69, 86, 91, 96, 106, 124, 132, 138–139, 152, 159, 164–167, 171, 174–175, 177, 189–191, 233, 267, 277–279, 292, 294, 300–302, 304, 306–307

water (element), 29, 59–62, 66–67, 71, 75, 80–81, 85, 96, 127, 153, 156, 167, 181, 187, 191, 230, 234, 269, 272, 279

wealth, 20, 48, 64, 105, 113, 149–150, 238, 292

Weinstein, Marion, 7, 191, 260, 265

west, 60, 69, 75, 80–81, 86, 123, 139, 153, 156, 191, 194, 269, 279, 296, 302, 304, 307

Wheel of the Year, 20, 35, 39–41, 43, 52–53, 57–58, 156, 208, 223, 231, 261, 279

Wicca, 1–2, 4–6, 8–11, 15–17, 23, 25–30, 36, 102–103, 111, 135, 181, 202, 208–209, 218, 223, 225, 229–233, 236, 241, 243, 245–246, 248–249, 252, 259–263, 270, 277, 279–280, 283, 299

Wiccan, 2, 4, 15, 17, 25, 27, 32–33, 59, 76, 78, 81, 91, 93, 101–102, 106, 112–113, 131, 134–135, 137, 140, 142–143, 153, 157, 180, 194, 203, 206, 220, 223–225, 228, 232–233, 235, 245–247, 250, 259–261, 263–265, 268–270, 274–276, 279–282, 295, 297, 303–306

Wiccan clergy, 225, 281–282

Wiccan Law, 134–135, 137, 220, 259, 275, 295, 305–306

Wiccan Rede, 78, 93, 101, 112, 131, 134, 137, 220, 232, 250, 279–280, 295, 297, 303–306

wicce, 15

widdershins, 153–154, 190, 271, 280, 295, 307

Wild Hunt, 18, 228, 274

wilderness, 4, 167, 177, 227, 303

will, see True Will

wisdom, 2, 28, 33–34, 56, 88, 100, 108, 112, 133, 136–137, 143, 154, 163, 182, 190, 213, 219, 241, 253, 261, 270, 285–286, 305

wisewoman, 25

Witch Balls, 158

Witch Jewels, 89–90, 280

Witch Trial, 208–209, 241–242

Witchcraft Act of 1735, 23

Witches' Alphabet, 75–76, 189

Witches' Pyramid, 73–75, 78, 80–83, 229–230, 280

Witches' voice, 80, 137, 190–191, 256, 283

Witchfinder General, 22

witching, 171, 189–190

Witchvox, 202, 207, 217, 247, 283–284

Women's Thealogical Institute, 287

words of power, 18, 30, 83, 86, 117–118, 131, 147, 152–153, 156, 169, 231, 254, 256, 278–279, 306

workplace, 104

wortcunning, 149

writing rituals, 155

year and a day, 35, 40, 42, 45, 57–58, 63, 101, 157–158, 202, 205, 220–222, 230–233, 254

Yggdrasil, 180

younger self, 5, 11, 88–89, 117, 267, 277

Yule, 35, 41–43, 47, 51, 266, 277, 280, 296

Zell, Oberon, 173

zodiac, 54–55, 85, 125, 171, 184

GET MORE AT LLEWELLYN.COM

Visit us online to browse hundreds of our books and decks, plus sign up to receive our e-newsletters and exclusive online offers.

- Free tarot readings • Spell-a-Day • Moon phases
- Recipes, spells, and tips • Blogs • Encyclopedia
- Author interviews, articles, and upcoming events

GET SOCIAL WITH LLEWELLYN

Find us on

www.Facebook.com/LlewellynBooks

Follow us on

www.Twitter.com/Llewellynbooks

GET BOOKS AT LLEWELLYN

LLEWELLYN ORDERING INFORMATION

 Order online: Visit our website at www.llewellyn.com to select your books and place an order on our secure server.

 Order by phone:
- Call toll free within the U.S. at 1-877-NEW-WRLD (1-877-639-9753)
- Call toll free within Canada at 1-866-NEW-WRLD (1-866-639-9753)
- We accept VISA, MasterCard, and American Express

 Order by mail:
Send the full price of your order (MN residents add 6.875% sales tax) in U.S. funds, plus postage and handling to: Llewellyn Worldwide, 2143 Wooddale Drive, Woodbury, MN 55125-2989

POSTAGE AND HANDLING

STANDARD (U.S. & Canada):
(Please allow 12 business days)
$25.00 and under, add $4.00.
$25.01 and over, FREE SHIPPING.

INTERNATIONAL ORDERS (airmail only):
$16.00 for one book, plus $3.00
for each additional book.

Visit us online for more shipping options.
Prices subject to change.

FREE CATALOG!

To order, call
1-877-
NEW-WRLD
ext. 8236
or visit our
website

OVER 200,000 SOLD

True
Magick

A Beginner's Guide

REVISED & EXPANDED
Amber K

True Magick
A Beginner's Guide
Amber K

For fifteen years, Amber K's "little green book" has guided thousands down the life-changing path of magick. Selling more than 200,000 copies, *True Magick* has truly struck a chord with Witches, Pagans, and magicians around the world.

Presented here for the first time is the revised and expanded anniversary edition of *True Magick*. It features the same delightful introduction to the history and lore of magick, in addition to several varieties of magick, ranging from shamanism and Norse Magick to Voudun and Qabala. Amber K explains the basics, such as how to find or create ritual tools, establish a temple, plan a ritual, and cast spells safely and ethically. New material includes six more chapters, recommending reading for each chapter, and more than 100 added exercises.

978-0-7387-0823-2

US $15.95 CAN $18.50

6 x 9

360 PP.

GLOSSARY, SUGGESTED READING, APPENDICES
